Natural Born Learners

Unschooling and Autonomy in Education

Beatrice Ekwa Ekoko and Carlo Ricci

DEDICATION

To Gina Luongo, Annabel Ricci, and Karina Ricci. My love keeps growing.
—Carlo Ricci

To Randy Kay, Evelyna Kay, Madeleine Kay and Bronwyn Kay.
"Not all those who wander are lost."
—J. R. R. Tolkien, *The Fellowship of the Ring*.
—Beatrice Ekwa Ekoko

Acknowledgments

We give heartfelt thanks to our marvellous volunteers for transcribing the interviews. Without their contribution this work would surely have languished in a folder for another decade. Thank you Sandhya Singh, Sarah Rainsberger, Theresa Vaz, Sherri Kirkpatrick, Cathy Morgan, Sara McGrath, Nicole Bradford, Stefanie Mohsennia, Elaine Neely, Lisa Winter-Card, Glen Prevost, Cory Spitzer, Lyndsay Kirkham, Karin Van Vlack, Denean Easton Sweet and Robin Bentley, Tom Raczka. Special thanks to Linda Clement, Amy Andrews, Nadine Bernacki and Bilal Buttar for their contribution as proof-readers, and to Miranda Kett for designing the book cover. Thanks to Isabelle de Faria for providing the photo of her son Maximus.

Contents

Foreword

This is a warning: there will be late nights, struggle, challenges missed and met. There will be satisfaction and joy, but no money for your efforts.

Creating a weekly half hour radio program on campus/community radio is like running down a train track with your pants around your ankles and a locomotive on your heels. It requires focus and energy and a dose of humility. It's like raising children, like most things important, actually.

I can't really complain, since I suggested combining our educational pursuits for our three daughters (born, 1995, 1997, 1998) who had never been to school with my love of campus radio: the adventure truly picked up steam the moment we were welcomed to the airwaves on 93.3fm at McMaster's CFMU, and for the next six years Radio Free School was our learning juggernaut.

We touched fossilized mammoth excrement in the office of a world-renowned geneticist researcher, hiked forest trails with loving ecologists, belly-danced, scuba dived, and searched the galaxies with a range of experts and doers who shared their knowledge and passion. Week after week, the shows we created were guided from the outset by our children's—and our own— interests. There were no boundaries about what we would study, the only constant was constant learning; that, and the weekly deadline to complete the show.

We would take our video camera everywhere, record

field interviews, then using the audio mixer we edited and added music at home to produce the show. The show included a heavy dose of children's voices, voices so rarely heard on radio. Our daughters voices were not just heard, but in control, both of content, and simultaneously, their own learning.

Using digital audio editing software meant we could prepare our half hour shows and then upload it from the comfort of our home. The show was uploaded to the very useful and alive radio4all.net where we were quickly picked up, to our astonishment, by an internet station in Japan; a pirate radio station in Santa Cruz California; then Fredericton, New Brunswick's campus station CHSR 97.9 FM; and several other stations around the world over the show's tenure from May 2002 until we folded shop in June 2008 with a last show on one of our favourite and oft repeated topics: Math!

We didn't really stop there though, but gone were the weekly midnight editing sessions the night before the show aired. We kept our web presence, and of course our interest and growing experience with alternatives to what has become the standardized education system. In the process we advanced our understanding and knowledge, and shared our progress weekly with our listeners and friends. We had, along the way, spoken to some of the best minds and commentators on the topic of learning outside of regular school.

Since we sidestepped schools for a different model of learning, we were conscious that we were not separate, not above, just different. We were trying our best to find out how to allow our children, and ourselves, to experience our own worlds, with our own unique minds and talents. It is in this spirit that we come to you now.

This collection of interviews transcribed (and some reworked) from Radio Free School continue the dialogue and the experience of the production of over 200 radio shows. I hope that this work will bring insight and inspiration as well as being the airwaves to your personal libraries.

Randy Kay,
December, 2013

Randy Kay is a full time volunteer with a part time job. His unpaid pursuits, where he derives much satisfaction as an active citizen, include advocacy for: local sustainable transportation, rehabilitating floodplains lost to parking lots at McMaster University, and improved air quality in neighbourhoods by planting street trees; as well he has logged several years as a radio host on CFMU 93.3 FM, most recently Radio Free School. He lives in Hamilton, Ontario during what we will look back on as the golden age of a re-emerging city, and battles petty tyrants wherever they are found. He works as Coordinator of Volunteers at OPIRG McMaster and is married to Beatrice Ekwa Ekoko with whom he has three resolute and multi-talented daughters.

Introduction

Most of the pieces in this book are derived from interviews aired on the Radio Free School program that ran from 2002 to 2008 on 93.3 fm CFMU. Once we decided that we would co-edit the book, we divided the book into three sections:

1. What is unschooling/natural learning/self-determined learning;
2. What does it look like in practice, and;
3. The stories of those who unschooled and are now adults.

Next, we contacted interviewees and asked if they would be willing to be a part of our book. We were fortunate that all those we contacted agreed to be a part of our project, and that they were supportive. The next step was to transcribe all of the audio interviews into written text. We quickly realized that this would be a very time-consuming process, and so we sent an email to various homeschooling groups that we belong to asking for volunteers to help us with the transcribing. In no time offers came in and with their help the interviews were transcribed in a very timely manner.

With the interviews transcribed, the interviewees were invited to review and polish up their transcripts to a form they were happy with. The next step was to create a draft where we put the pieces together in the appropriate sections, in the way that we envisioned the book to be divided. Once that was done, we each took turns reading and editing the book as we saw fit. Finally, chapters were sent back to each of the interviewees and they were asked to reread the edited version and make changes as they saw fit, and to approve the form that it was in.

Although most of the pieces are transcribed and edited versions of interviews that were conducted for Radio Free School, some are pieces that were written for the Radio Free School blogspot. A handful of pieces were ones we solicited later because we felt they provided a valuable addition to the book.

Although, we do not claim to agree with everything that is written in the book, our goal is to provide an overview of what unschoolers, and those sympathetic to unschooling and self-determined education, are thinking and doing; and then allow each reader to make use of the ideas presented as they see fit. We think you will find the pieces worthwhile and, in some cases, provocative.

We see unschooling as a learner-centered, democratic approach to education. We believe that it is through self-determination and autonomy that learning happens at its best. Furthermore, we believe that the unschooling worldview is about more than learning: it is about taking charge of one's own life.

In editing this book, we are hoping to help people to realize that unschooling is not something foreign, but that it is something that we all do, all of the time. And more than that, when we unschool our most powerful learning usually happens. We unschool when we self-determine our learning about most anything. It could be about cooking, bike repairs, home repairs, math, physics, reading, music and so on. The list is infinitely long. Since we all do it, and it works so well, the goal is to ensure that we become more mindful of what we do when we self-determine our learning, and that we extend this powerful way of learning to more areas of our lives.

As humans, we are curious, natural learners, and we know best how and what we want and need to learn about.

We believe that there is no critical period for learning for most things, and that the best time to learn something is when the need or desire arises. This is supported by contemporary research. For example, Worden, Hinton, & Fischer (2011, May) explain how, "While there is evidence for limited critical periods in brain development in limited domains (such as the strength of vision in the two eyes), no evidence supports a critical period for academic skills" (p. 11).

We would like to thank all of the authors and all of the volunteers for their time and willingness to share their insights with us. Without them, this book would not have been possible.

Beatrice Ekwa Ekoko and Carlo Ricci,
December, 2013.

References

Worden, J.M., Hinton, C., & Fischer, K.W. (2011, May). What does the brain have to do with learning. *Phi Delta Kappan, 92(8),* 8-13.

Beatrice Ekwa Ekoko is a free-lance writer and blogger. She blogs extensively at Natural Born Learners (radiofreeschool.blogspot.com) and has founded Personalized Education Hamilton to facilitate self-determined learning in her community. She works for a not-for-profit environmental organization as a project manager and coordinator. She lives in Hamilton, Ontario with her husband and three children.
Visit her website to see other writing at bekoko.ca.

Carlo Ricci is a professor of education and currently teaches in the Graduate Program at the Schulich School of Education, Nipissing University. He edits and founded the *Journal of Unschooling and Alternative Learning*. He has written and edited a number of books including *The Willed Curriculum, Unschooling, and Self-Direction: What Do Love, Trust, Respect, Care, and Compassion Have to Do With Learning*; and *Turning points: 35 Visionaries in Education Tell Their Own Stories (AERO, 2010)* with Jerry Mintz; and *The Legacy of John Holt: A Man Who Genuinely Understood, Trusted, and Respected Children* (HoltGWS, 2013) with Patrick Farenga. He has also written numerous articles on unschooling and self-determined learning. He lives in Toronto, Ontario with his wife and two children.

PART 1

WHAT IS SELF-DETERMINED

LEARNING AND UNSCHOOLING?

CHAPTER 1

SCHOOLING:

A HIGHLY QUESTIONABLE PRACTICE

JOHN TAYLOR GATTO

I was a New York City public school teacher of junior high school kids. I taught in the white aristocratic ghetto of the upper west side of Manhattan, the Spanish ghetto of Manhattan, and the black ghetto of Manhattan, for thirty years. During that time, I began to draw some conclusions about the institution of schooling, and about the nature of kids and their learning. When I left teaching in 1991, I published an editorial on the op-ed page of the *Wall Street Journal*, called "I May Be a Teacher, but I'm Not an Educator" (1991, July 25). I was going to become a garlic farmer in upstate New York. And, I do indeed own a farm there near Ithaca, New York, in the little village of Oxford.

But I got a phone call from the Librarian's Association in Colorado, and then I got another call a few days later from the Engineer's Colloquium at NASA Goddard space center. Then I got a call from the Vice President of the United States. All asked me to give a talk.

With those three appearances, I was off and running. Although I never advertised, as the calls came in I responded. When I go to Australia next week to do the keynote for Australia's Education Convention, it will mark the three millionth mile I've travelled in the last twelve years!

I had a tremendous anger back then, and the anger fuelled me into trying to disseminate a message that schooling itself is a highly questionable practice (that includes good schools as well as bad). It's possible to derive some value from it, but the damage is always, I think, much greater than any value that's possible. In many, many instances, there is no value offered. It's simply a confinement exercise.

When I started out, I probably would have fit the definition of a school reformer. But I researched, travelled, spoke, and re-evaluated my thirty classroom years—which was by school's lights quite successful: I was New York State Teacher of the Year, and the New York City Teacher of the Year three consecutive years, so by the system's evaluation I was doing great. As I looked back over my encounters with kids, parents, administrators, and myself, I came to see a set of much darker themes. I began to write books; I've written five to this moment, and I'm working on a sixth, which I pray will be the last. It is tentatively titled, *The Guerrilla Curriculum: How To Get An Education In Spite of School.*

I never want to hear the word school for the rest of my life. Or see a school building. I have taken a much darker tack—or should I say, it was a course that imposed itself on me. The more I understood the historical currents at work in this institution, the more I saw that it can't lead to the kind of world I personally want to live in. School definitely has a distinct purpose, unlike what most of us think. It's about social control, and that purpose has been successfully achieved. Our form of schooling has been spread worldwide; we now have a well-schooled planet. As I gaze out after seventy-five years of life, I am not at all pleased with the planet, let alone with the schooling that sustains it.

1. JOHN TAYLOR GATTO

What is the Purpose of Public Education?

Throughout western history, schooling has existed. It was always short term, and people never considered it very important. It might occupy six weeks or two months out of a year. Its stated purpose was to discover the will of God, so that good lives could be lead by harmonizing with that will. Call that the first purpose of schooling. Call it the religious purpose, the ancient and common purpose.

Around the time of the French Revolution, a second purpose emerged; not to say that it didn't always exist, but it emerged then as dominant. That was: to make good citizens. A citizen is not somebody who follows orders, it's someone who takes an active part in the public market place of ideas, and deals himself or herself a seat at the policy table whether the policy table wants him or not.

So, in order to have an opportunity to try and be a good citizen, you require a package of skills, two of which are quite possible to transmit through formal schooling. Those are to write well and convincingly in an organized fashion, and to speak well and convincingly in an organized fashion. Almost immediately, from the inception of forced schooling, schools abandoned those purposes with the explanation that there wasn't time to teach them, those which used to be known as the "active literacies."

The reason writing and speaking are so powerfully important to a citizen is that if you can read well and think well, you still are locked up in the prison of your own mind. You have to have rhetorical skill in order to express ideas, to create followers, to make allies.

So back to active literacies, because this idea is decisively important. I don't think I am exaggerating to say that this concept literally doesn't exist in the minds of most people. There may be some vague tropism toward it, but the idea of active literacies as the key to good citizenship, and to gain an effective set of powers just doesn't occur. Schools allow those powers to die on the vine.

It's perfectly possible to acquire these literacies outside of school if you know how important they are, and if you are willing to substitute television time or baseball time or whatever to get them. But, if you rely on school to make you adequate at these things, you are in for an unpleasant surprise. You will arrive at adult life always uncomfortable speaking before strangers, always unable to sustain an idea. Mostly what you will be able to do is to register opinions, sometimes emphatically.

In writing, the situation is probably worse, because to formally write in such a way that you engage your audience is a tricky thing to do. It's been studied for thousands of years. It's quite possible to learn and transmit, but someone first has to alert the audience that it's important, more important than adding and subtracting, for example.

You can see how far we have deviated from that, deviated deliberately, and I'll come to the purpose of that deviation up ahead. The first purpose of education was the religious purpose: to make good people. Let's call the second purpose, the public purpose: to make good citizens. Good citizens argue effectively, they do not simply follow orders—that's not the role of a citizen.

The third purpose comes about with the general expansion of wealth, prosperity, and easeful lives in Western society, as our military and trading policies begin to dominate the planet. Personal prosperity is the thing most parents think about as the purpose of schooling. They think about self-improvement as this third purpose—to make each individual his or her personal best. We can call that the private purpose.

So, now we have three traditional purposes for schooling:

to make good people (the religious purpose); to make good citizens (the public purpose), and; to make people their personal best (the private purpose).

Sometime around the middle of the 19th Century, a fourth purpose arose outside the consciousness of ordinary citizens. The fourth purpose coincides with the rise of fossil fuel-driven technologies. Prior to the 19th Century, for all practical purposes, the sources of energy other than human labour were wind, water, and wood, all very unreliable. They come and they go. When wood is burned, it doesn't grow back for a long time.

Most organized factory work was near some source of water or wind, or it relied exclusively on labour. None of the institutional production mechanisms were very effective. They didn't dominate the life of the community. With development of coal, and steam power (and then, about a half-century later, the development of oil), for the first time in human history, economic managers gained the power to predict the future. They could work around the clock; they could make pretty accurate guesses about how many units they could produce in that time. A need arose to concentrate people in urban centers: to make them the assistants of coal, steam, and oil. With that understanding on the part of society's managers, human beings ceased to be what they had been for all of human history: sovereign spirits, at least in embryo. Rather, human beings were now productive units.

The sentimentality that religion lends to the social order, that your terrestrial achievement is inferior to your salvation, for example, or that you are your brother's keeper, all those things could be set aside by equations that led to industrial efficiency.

We are now between 1830 and 1880, and we have intense drawing room conversation about how to make the most of this radical transformation in economic life. The guy in the street having a beer, he is aware of changes but he isn't aware these changes are going to lead to radical changes in his relationship to management.

The first serious attempts to manage people in this fashion in America are provoked by war. The American Civil War was partially an institutional war, the first war in history where every unit wore the same uniform. During the French Revolution, which wasn't very much earlier, every unit wore a uniform the wife of the commanding officer of the unit designed. The Napoleonic Wars did not look at all like artistic renderings of them; there was a crazy quilt aspect. So, too, the American Revolution. The Civil War was different. There are three million of you and you all wear the same hat, and the same jacket, the same pants, the same socks, the same shoes, with only minor variations. As soon as that happens, when you know that one order of hats can make you quite wealthy—just a single order—and that this order (as heads get blown off), will be repeated over and over again, you have a situation ripe for corruption.

Recall that the people being centrally-managed have come out of an American Libertarian tradition. Their ideal, their American dream, is to have independent livelihoods. But, that doesn't butter a steel manufacturer's bread at all. There was so much difficulty trying to bend the American population to this new corporate sell that the flood gates of emigration had to be opened. It isn't that people flocked to the United States for opportunity; they were brought to the United States and sold in wagonloads to brokers who then resold them to corporations. Sold sometimes a long, long way from where they landed.

Most respectable histories deal with this, but the irony is there isn't a school in the United States that actually uses a respectable history text. All those texts have been politically modified. There are plenty of first class commercial history books that haven't been modified, but most people don't really read. They certainly don't read long history books.

All this long-winded stuff is leading you to an understanding of the progressive insight. That insight was the devil with trying to convince older people to go along, to pass legislation forcing them to yield their children to confinement for long periods of time, confinement with total strangers who will condition them to comply.

Now, if that isn't the most radical idea in human history, I don't know what is. The very fact that we take these school places for granted is bizarre. If you reduce the scheme to simple statements like, "I want you to surrender your child for the next twelve years, for the principal part of every day, five days a week, to a set of total strangers about whom you will know nothing whatsoever." Can there be a more radical idea than that: giving your kids away to strangers? Would you give your television set to repair to somebody you couldn't check up on?

What are these institutional people supposed to do with your kids? One thing they inherited was earlier rhetorical models of school: to make good people, to make good citizens, and to make people their personal best. But that's not what schools were going to be about in the States or in Canada. In fact, the two national systems grew up intimately allied with one another.

Because the history of the Canadian state and its peoples was slightly different than that of the USA, there were cosmetic differences, but that's all. Egerton Ryerson was the big name in Canada; Horace Mann was the big U.S. name. They were in constant communication with one another; they were out for the same thing.

What was that thing? They were out to produce a labour force, which would not seek independent livelihood. Were the workers so foolish as to try, they wouldn't have the mental equipment, wouldn't know how to do the independent livelihood thing. They would have habits indoctrinated into their minds that would prevent all but a small fraction from finding a way out of the trap.

The idea was to create a population susceptible to management. If you think just for a minute, the principal heritage in Canada is Anglican, from particular parts of Britain (not the same parts as the mass settlement in the United States). The United States was settled by the dissenting population of Britain, Congregationalists and Presbyterians et al, but Anglicans are the state church of England, and that is the principal influence on the culture of Canada. There are huge differences between those theologies. Schools in the U.S.A. had to cancel out the dissenting minds coming from Britain. It had to cancel them out by training children in habits of obedience.

Not obedience to parents, not obedience to religion, not obedience to traditions, but obedience to strangers hired by the political state. Once again, we're talking about major league radicalism here. It really is scary, the ultimate purpose.

Once Darwin checked onto the British scene in the middle of the 19th Century, a key was in hand to justify what was under way. Prior to Darwin's *Origin of Species,* in 1859, and his *Descent of Man,* in 1871, you had to justify elites and social privileges by religion. The Anglican Church taught that God has ordained these different levels of society, that to want to get out of your particular position was sacrilegious. That's a pretty good straightjacket!

Social privilege was also protected by the police power of the state. Superior wealth hired police as insurance, to keep the classes subordinated. The USA didn't have that attitude (for a long time), except in the British-influenced coastal parts of the east. Prior to the telegraph and roads and cars and similar things, to actually reach out and fine-tune the life of communities was impossible, except near large population bases. Quite a libertarian population occurred in both North American countries. But gradually, with the rise

9

of technology, easy transport, etc., those libertarian elements were more and more marginalized.

Then along came Darwin. It's no accident Darwinism is the single, great, "scientific truth" taught by schools, taught in every school in Canada and the United States. It's part and parcel of the universal scheme of social control. I'm not arguing against theories of evolution here; I'm talking about the social ramifications of these theories.

You drill children in forms of separation. By competition, you teach them not to trust one another; you teach them that they are in deadly competition with one another for future prizes.

It's all horse manure, of course. But, it is true if you believe it is true. One out of every five wealthy people in Canada and the United States comes from the working class. They manage to preserve the insight that once you learn to do something that a lot of people want done, you can get just as rich as a surgeon or a stock broker. You won't hear that in any school in the United States or in Canada.

It's not exactly that schools are suppressing information, because they don't recognize it themselves. Examine the standardized test scores and grades of the principal politicians who set the agendas for our societies. You will discover the majority of them are quite mediocre, or worse. George Bush, President of the United States, had quite a mediocre academic career. It's on record if anyone cares to dig it out. Among candidates who opposed him, Al Gore flunked out of his first college and was a C and D student at his second college. Bush had, I think, a 550 on his verbal SAT exam. But his competition had worse. And the man held up as the intellectual in that election, Bill Bradley, got 480 on his verbal SAT. If tests and grades were really predicative, these people shouldn't be in those positions. But, of course, the tests are not predicative.

On March 9, 2003, the admissions officer at Harvard,

Marilyn McGrath, on the front page of the *New York Times*, told readers Harvard only accepts students who show evidence of distinction. Many people skipped that article because they assumed they already knew that high grades get you in. But McGrath said test scores and grades are not evidence of distinction—you can't get into Harvard that way!

I thought that was a stunning revelation. Not that I didn't know it, but to actually admit it on the front page of the *New York Times*. Wow!

I wrote her immediately and asked, "What would an evidence of distinction be?" although I already knew the answer. The Harvard lady quickly covered up: her reply was an exercise in dissimulation, backing off her *New York Times* statement.

By the time someone reaches eighteen, there are tens of thousands of such people—but not millions—tens of thousands who have records of distinction. They have sailed around the world alone; they have walked from the South Pole to the North Pole; they've started a charity; they've earned a million dollars—not because they are such superior geniuses, but because a number of families preserve traditions of effectiveness and ways to reach real goals. The methods aren't difficult and they aren't expensive.

If you read Ben Franklin's autobiography, you'll see they were used among many ordinary people in the 18th Century United States. Franklin was thrown out of two schools before he was 11-years-old. He started a business selling beer to printers, through which he amassed capital to buy into a printing company later on. He was 12-years-old.

Once I was on that trail I looked into intimate details of colonial life here in the Americas. The minute you do that, detailed evidence appears about the different ways young people were reared back then.

Take the American Revolution, for instance. Virtually

everybody who made the American Revolution was a teenager! Washington was the Grand Old Man. I think he was 42. But Jefferson and Hamilton and really the whole pack of them were 17, 18, 19, 20, 21. The myth that keeps us small and in our place blows away with that discovery. The US young people, with free minds, were able to overthrow the most powerful military nation on earth, Great Britain.

An audio version of this piece appears in podcast and can be found at:
Gatto, J.T. (2004, December 15). Interview by B. Ekwa Ekoko [Podcast]. Outing School with John Taylor Gatto Part 1, Radio Free School. Hamilton, Ontario.
    Retrieved from http://radio4all.net/index.php/program/10633
    http://radio4all.net/index.php/program/10633
Gatto, J.T. (2004, December 22). Interview by B. Ekwa Ekoko [Podcast]. Outing School with John Taylor Gatto Part 2, Radio Free School. Hamilton, Ontario.
    http://radio4all.net/index.php/program/10634

References

Calvin, J. (1578). *The institution of the Christian religion.* (T. Norton, Trans.). London: Thomas Vautrollier for William Norton. (Original work published in 1536)

Darwin, C. (1859). *On the origin of species.* London, U.K: John Murray.

Darwin, C. (1871). *The descent of man, and selection in relation to sex.* London: John Murray.

Gatto, J. T. (1991, July 25). I may be a teacher, but I'm not an educator. *The Wall Street Journal*, p. A8.

John Taylor Gatto (born December 15, 1935) is an American retired school teacher of 29 years and 8 months experience in the classroom and author of several books on education including *Dumbing us Down: The Hidden Curriculum of Compulsory Schooling* (2005); and *Weapons of Mass Instruction: A Schoolteacher's Journey Through The Dark World of Compulsory Schooling* (2009). He is an activist critical of compulsory schooling and of what he characterizes as the hegemonic nature of discourse on education and the education professions.

Gatto's office is in New York City, his home in Oxford, New York, where he is currently at work on a documentary film about the nature of modern schooling entitled *The Fourth Purpose,* with his friend and former student, Roland Legiardi-Laura. For more information about this film, visit *The Fourth Purpose*. Gatto has been married for forty years to the same woman, and has two grown children and a cat. He hopes to build a rural retreat and library for the use of families pondering local and personal issues of school reform.

(http://www.johntaylorgatto.com/index.htm).

CHAPTER 2

YOU DON'T HAVE TO GO TO GROW:

GROWING WITHOUT SCHOOLING

PAT FARENGA

This is based on an interview I did in 2003, with Radio Free School, the year my revised edition of *Teach Your Own* came out.

I'm the author of several books and articles about homeschooling, the most recent being *Teach Your Own: The John Holt Book of Homeschooling* (2003). I worked with the late John Holt from 1981 until his death, in 1985. John left Holt Associates Inc. to me, and a board of directors, to continue his work. I published the magazine *Growing Without Schooling* (in Press) (*GWS*) for 16 years after John died. *GWS* is actually the nation's—probably the world's—first homeschooling magazine. It was started by John in 1977. Now that *GWS* is available online and soon in print and as ebooks, you can read many of the articles by Holt, but there are some issues about unschooling, homeschooling, and putting John's ideas into practice that I'd like to address.

John Holt has been criticized for being unrealistic, because he had no children—how would he know how challenging it is to stay at home? I heard that criticism when John was alive and I've heard it since.

The longest-serving editor of *Growing Without Schooling*, Susannah Sheffer, doesn't have any children. The editor who took over after John died, Donna Richoux, didn't have children during her tenure and, when she did give birth, she stopped editing the magazine and moved out of the country. We were fortunate to get Susannah in Donna's place. Meredith Collins replaced Susannah, and Meredith doesn't have children. However, like John, they all enjoy young people and put themselves in situations where they can be with them and learn about them.

I really have a hard time understanding that criticism because what John was saying, first of all, was that school was not the best place for children to learn (he was speaking on the basis of his considerable experience as a student and teacher in high-end private schools and later in the homeschooling movement) not that only parents can homeschool children. The point of homeschooling, and unschooling in particular, is to have children learn from a variety of people and resources, not just parents.

John was a man who, for enjoyment, pretended to be reading a book while he observed children at play. Initially he would just sit on park benches and watch children, but by the time I met him in the early 1980s he felt uncomfortable doing that, given the weird looks he was getting from parents. The climate about children playing outdoors had changed so much from the 1960s to the 1980s, and seeing an adult on a park bench observing children at play was now a suspect activity. So, John would bring a newspaper or a book and pretend to be reading that, and continue his observations.

When I came on board at Holt Associates in 1981, John was doing at least two or three speaking engagements a month. Before that, when he was so popular in the late 1960s and early 1970s, he was on the road at least two weeks of every month of the year. He didn't like hotels, so John always looked for a family to stay with. Through homeschooling, he was able to make many connections with families so that he was always staying in homes. He enjoyed being around families and their kids, trying to understand what was going on with them. John actually had a wider experience of children than most people.

John didn't have the blinders and biases that we all have as parents. It is awfully hard to be objective about our own kids. One of the things that always impressed me about John, and even more so now that he's been dead and I've been reading his work and reflecting on my experience with him, is his absolute empathy and compassion for what it was like to be a young person trying to learn. He'd put himself in the shoes of a five-year-old, a two-year-old, a nineteen-year-old, and, in doing so, he sort of flipped the whole education paradigm around, looking at it from the point of view of "how does it feel to the learner?" John realized very early that students and teachers have very different experiences in school. His first book, *How Children Fail* (1964/1982), was based on the question that he heard in the faculty lounge all the time: "Why do I teach but they don't learn?" He wanted to figure out why.

To put John's ideas into practice, my wife and I have been following the lead of our children. What we realized, as we reflected back on our experiences from school, is that what we have found valuable and sustaining in our adult lives are the things that interest us the most. As John wrote and said many, many times, "the only difference between a good student and a bad student is that a good student is careful not to forget what he studied until after the test."

My wife and I were good students and we both realized the truth of that statement. We've really been trying to help our daughters gain confidence and experience in the world through following their interests, of which very few have to do with the standard school curriculum.

Probably the most controversial thing we've done, which bothers some unschoolers and homeschoolers, is that when

our children have expressed a desire and a good reason to go
to school, we let them. Some people feel that somehow
we've betrayed John's trust.

This issue is not new. John addressed it very early in
GWS. We have published many stories of families starting
and stopping and, often, re-starting homeschooling. John
noted that a child choosing to attend school is in a far
different relationship to that school than all the students who
are there solely because of their age. I would add, based on
our experience, that if the child knows they can leave school
at any time with their parents' support, it makes their choices
easier and helps build bonds of trust and communication.

My middle daughter, Alison, went to high school. She
wanted to go terribly; it became very important to her for
social reasons. She enjoyed homeschooling, but she
graduated from our local high school. Our philosophy is that
there's an open door between our home and the school, and
all three of my daughters have gone in and out of school as a
result. My seventeen-year-old, for instance, is pursuing a
non-traditional path through high school. My youngest, she's
eleven, loves Japanese and we found a Japanese speaker in
the next town over, she's taking Japanese lessons there.
She's taking pottery and voice lessons. These are all things
that, were she in sixth grade where she would normally be
for her age, she wouldn't be able to do. John's idea that
children learn best by learning what they're interested in
certainly has proven true for us.

One criticism I hear is that children are not going to learn
the important things, which we have found to be nonsense.
Through her study of Japanese, Audrey is learning about
Japanese culture, history, and cuisine. Through her study of
pottery she is learning math. When we tried to tackle math
head-on it was a disaster. When we just talked about how
you need this much clay to build something this big it
seemed abstract. But, when she sees her instructors and

professional potters doing these calculations and talking about these things, it means something to her. All of the math she needs to know to accomplish her task is embedded in the activities. They are not artificial constructs designed to be educational. Most of all, to me, is that we don't obsess over her weakness in math. We celebrate and nurture her strengths, so she'll have money in the bank, so to speak, so she'll have the confidence she needs, should she find a weakness that holds her back.

One of the things that has been really interesting, and gratifying to me, has been understanding the work of Ivan Illich and understanding why John Holt was such a big fan of Ivan's work. Illich wrote a book called *Deschooling Society* (1970/1983), which many people misinterpret, mainly because they don't read it—they just read the title and assume he's saying "let's eradicate all the schools." Illich is not saying that. His whole thesis is that we need to eliminate compulsory schooling. Schools make sense for having central locations where communal resources can be distributed, but school is not a true communal resource. It's become a private enterprise that is administered by professionals, almost as if it were medicine, and very expensive medicine at that. What Ivan pointed out is that learning is not a scarce commodity to be doled out like medicine. Human learning is abundant; institutional education is scarce.

Our economic system supports giving out rewards primarily to those who consume the most education credentials, but is that really learning? When Holt read and studied with Illich, he started exploring all sorts of ideas of how else can we help children and adults to learn?

In *Instead of Education: Ways to Help People do Things Better* (1976/2004), John outlines the reasons he thinks compulsory education is "the most destructive force on earth;" largely because it wastes so much of everyone's time

in busywork. This is borne out all the time when employers
say, "college graduates don't know how to do anything
except pass courses, and high school graduates don't know
how to write their names." Ivan pointed out, in 1971, that all
institutions seem to hit a point where they become counterproductive. Our institutions for transportation create traffic
jams, our medical institutions create iatrogenic illnesses like
the antibiotic failure we see now. We suddenly turn a corner
when these things get too big and, in education as Holt and
Illich claim, we have reached the point where schools create
stupidity in students.

Holt noticed, early in his teaching career, that children
are born learning. They come into the world eager, and full
of questions and full of adventure, and are fearless learners.
Parents of young children are exhausted from keeping them
safe from pulling things down and putting things in their
mouths—it's a biological imperative to learn. I believe it
was John who said birds fly, fish swim, humans learn.
Learning is part of our nature, but you would never guess
that once children reach school age. Then, all of a sudden,
we say, "Oh, there's this learning deficit," or "They must
learn certain things at certain ages and if they don't they
must suffer from learning disabilities," and so on. What's
going on here?

Deschooling Society (1983) and *Instead of Education*
(2004) are two cornerstone books that examine this question.
Now we've come to the point where education is the one
thing that is never questioned in society, as if it had nothing
but benefits.

John Taylor Gatto, an American school teacher who
wrote *Dumbing Us Down* (1992/2005) and several other
books, has been excellent at analyzing the history behind the
compulsory school movement and why alternatives such as
private schools, Montessori, Waldorf, home schools,
Christian schools, independent schools all have success, in

some cases more or better success than public school systems. Trying to analyze the whole question of schooling from the point of view of educationists always comes back with a standard solipsistic response: "We have to preserve the institution of school at all costs because what happens in school is what matters in education."

What John Holt did was to put the learner at the center of what matters in education, and then analyzed schooling from that perspective. Back in the late 1960s, Holt was writing that school should be a smorgasbord for children and they should be able to pick and choose what they want to learn, including the people they want to learn from. You can have a strong interest in Japanese as my youngest does. If Audrey didn't hit it off with that teacher; we would find another teacher. Alison cannot do this in high school. We got all these documents to sign before she started high school that said if she doesn't like her teachers, tough.

John and Ivan say: let's do away with conventional schooling that is enforced through compulsory attendance; let's do away with the system of education that simply rewards people who go through it. Just going through it and getting credentials doesn't mean that you know how to do anything, as we see all the time. We're led to believe that if we march through the grades of school or the rungs of education you will wind up as a well-credentialed, well-rounded citizen, capable of taking most jobs. In fact, most people end up more confused about how to find and do real work when they graduate college. Ironically, many learn the job skills they need on the job.

John was completely with protesting students. In the late 1960s he was a visiting lecturer at the University of California at Berkley. His 1969 book, *The Underachieving School*, ends with a letter saying, "I think we have made education, which should be something that helps young people move into the world and do useful work there, into an

enormous obstacle standing in their way, and I think we
need to find ways to remove that obstacle" (pp. 142-143).

That was one of the incidents which made him start to
realize that perhaps revolution was not the way things
change.

Indeed, in the very first issue of *Growing Without
Schooling Magazine,* John writes on the first page about why
he's starting this magazine, and what he calls it his nickel-
and-dime theory of social change. He decided that, after
many years of being in the anti-war movement of Vietnam,
and the school reform movement in the 1960s and 1970s, all
he saw was how quickly those were put down. The open
school movement had very few advocates, although listening
to education establishment talk you'd think the open school
movement was what undermined the entire country.
Subsequent studies have shown that less than 2% or 3% of
all classrooms in America adopted any sort of free school or
open classroom.

John realized that most people were against these
changes. He realized that having any revolutionary,
overnight change was just a fantasy. He then saw what really
changes people's lives, by looking at different movements of
the time, particularly things like breastfeeding, natural
childbirth, and the back-to-the-land movement in the 1970s.
John realized that when people actually do change their
lives, it's when they do something new in their daily life that
continues as a habit.

Is it really a movement when it happens this way? There
is an academic paper discussing whether or not
homeschooling is a movement because it's leaderless.
Certainly John Holt is a key figure, and so are Dorothy and
Raymond Moore, and many others who contributed to its
growth in the early years. John never wanted to be the guru
of the homeschooling movement. He was hoping that his
ideas of how children learn best would spread, but he did not

want anyone to feel that there was only one way to do it. John was open to alternative ideas, and he supported all homeschoolers, whether they chose it for conservative religious reasons or anarchistic communal reasons.

John wanted people to live and work with their kids, and allow the children to show how they learn best and how to best teach them. John wrote in *GWS* Issue One that, instead of yelling and arguing with people to change their ways about school, he would find a hole in the school fence and stand next to it and say, "here's a hole. If you guys want to get out of this rat-race you can go through this hole" (p. 1).

In the early issues of *GWS*, it's amazing how much time John spent talking about the legal and political ramifications of homeschooling, how to get around schools and compulsory education laws. John followed the stories of alternative schools that had experience doing this, as well families who had been homeschooling for years. The early issues of *GWS* are full of reports, letters, and analyses about school, court, and legislative battles. Homeschooling was still underground then, and it was like a whole bunch of mushrooms that suddenly came up when Holt started shining the spotlight on homeschooling through the magazine, his books, and radio, speaking and television appearances.

John's ideas about change developed over the years, and I've adopted his strategy. I'm comfortable talking to people who do school-at-home because I feel I'm putting a pebble in their shoe by sharing these ideas. I know that one day, when they are no longer energized by their studies and the way their family feels when homeschooling, they'll take off their shoe and look at that pebble and say, "That Farenga guy said something about what's been bothering me in this situation."

Social changes are embedded in our actions as homeschoolers, yet it's a much more gradual change of things than anyone wants. That reminds me of another

reason why schools are so resistant to change: they just have
to wait for the activists to graduate, then the pressure to
change lessens and it returns to business as usual. Education
institutions can pretty effectively outwait human beings. I
know this upsets some people in the homeschooling
movement and they would much prefer that we attack the
schools head-on and try to abolish the compulsory education
laws, but I think John was right.

Homeschooling is growing—there are at least 2 million
children being homeschooled in the United States and
Canada now, if not more, and that's substantial growth
considering that when Holt was alive he didn't think there
were more than fifteen to twenty thousand children being
taught at home. It's interesting that the numbers have grown
so much, but we have to remember that there are 57 million
children in the United States of America in public school and
perhaps another 12 million in private school. The vast
majority of those parents support "sit down, shut up, and do
as I say" as the primary means of educating their children.
Even if you do school-at-home, you can accomplish the
entire day's curriculum in about 90 minutes per child! I think
it's better to go slow and steady, and stay below the radar
until homeschooling's numbers are such that it would be
impossible to shut it down. That strategy has served us well
so far, though it is far more by luck than strategy. Some
people want laws to protect homeschooling, but laws get
revoked all the time. There was Prohibition in the United
States, and then there wasn't. That involved a whole
Constitutional Amendment, and it can happen again. Yet,
people talk about a Constitutional Amendment for
homeschooling, to protect it. That's not going to happen as
far as I can see and even if it did, once the powers that don't
like it get back in power, it could be revoked. The best
source for change is individual families deciding on their
own what is best to help their children to learn, and

defending their right to pursue that.

I don't view homeschooling as a hermetic movement, although a lot people portray us that way. It surprises people when they read *Instead of Education* (2004) and *Teach Your Own* (2003) carefully, that John still talks about schools. He talks about places like Berlitz language academies, karate schools, cooking schools, trade schools, hobby and sports clubs. Holt and Illich are not saying that these places should vanish, or that they are useless—it's the rules of use that matter.

We are not shunning our place in society. Our kids can get into college, and they do, if they need it. I think it is more important that we're showing that if you don't need college, or if college isn't right for you at this time of your life, that you can still be a valuable and productive citizen and lead a very good life without it.

High school is a little harder for homeschooling. Even committed unschoolers and deschoolers, I find, once the kids turn high school age, the game becomes a little different. Most homeschooling takes place between grades K through eight. A lot of people lose their nerve when their children become teenagers. It is a little more difficult, certainly, because at that point, statistically, there's a lot fewer homeschoolers for your kids to hang out with, and there is all that pressure about getting into college.

People are so worried about the high school diploma, but what we've shown over the years is you don't need a high school diploma to get into college. You don't need all the credentials. I think it is the parents who are worried about the credentials but there really isn't much need to worry.

I'll give you an example: just this past Wednesday, there was a local television show, *Chronicle*, which did a half-hour segment about homeschooling. It was quite positive, including the segment where the Dean of the Boston University School of Education claimed that educators should pay attention to what homeschoolers are doing, and why? Simply because they have had such great success, and educators should learn from it. I was floored to hear that from the dean of a school of education. I think we are having an effect, and parents can take comfort from comments like that.

On the same program, they showed a seventeen-year-old boy who had been homeschooled right up through to eighth grade, and then went to high school. The reason he went to school was social, purely social: he wanted to be in a band. They show him playing the drums in a rock band in a garage, which cracked me up because so much of this just isn't in school—you can be in a marching band perhaps—but he made friends. A lot of high school students go for the social reasons. Some leave high school, and realize they can still have social lives outside of school, or that high school social life isn't all it's cracked up to be.

There are so many other things our kids can be doing, other than sitting through boring high school classes. They could take community college courses, for instance. That's what my oldest daughter has done.

I'm happy when anyone decides to unschool for any amount of time: if it's for six months, or six years or forever; it's just good that they try it because it's very important for people to understand that you don't get an education, you don't buy an education, no one can compel you to be educated. You earn an education, and you earn it yourself. We forget that.

I am unschooling my seventeen-year-old and my eleven-year-old now. Or, I should say, they are unschooling me while my wife is the main breadwinner right now. She's teaching public school, ironically. I'm home with the youngest and the oldest while our middle daughter is in school.

One of the things I tell parents when they consider

homeschooling or unschooling through high school is, "if homeschooling through elementary school worked, why stop? Why stop what's working?" I guess it's because we've all been so schooled to think that anyone can learn what is taught in elementary school because it's just the basics. We think high school is so important. I mean, how are you going to teach chemistry? Well, the reality is, I don't teach chemistry. They can take chemistry courses, they are widely available—through the Internet, CD-ROMs, textbooks. You can buy chemistry sets. It's not impossible to do. You can learn alongside your child, or they can do it on their own.

I think fear is the biggest thing that drives most parents to stop unschooling and put their kids in high school. I'm amazed at how many parents have come to me over the years, at least five or ten a year, whose kids are in high school. Their social lives are a mess, and they are not learning anything. Or they are learning stuff, but they are completely disengaged from it. Those parents are saying, "What can I do? Is homeschooling going to be right?" I put that against the homeschooling parent, who has had a great experience homeschooling, but feels "now my kids should go to high school." It's hard seeing both sides of this. As someone who is now deep in the middle of it, I can appreciate the ambivalence parents have towards this. I really do believe, though, that homeschooling through high school is not only desirable, but it's probably better for children in the long run.

Unschooling does not work for everyone, but we've had a good history. Our kids have seen this, using school as a sort of test, I think. My younger daughter holds the record: she was in first grade for ten days; she was in third grade for six weeks; 5th grade for eight weeks. We did not hesitate to pull our girls out when they asked. Parents say things like: "Well, if you are going to choose to do school, then you're going for the whole year." A little more flexibility, creative

scheduling, and communication can alleviate a semester or
more of woe for a child.

I think La Leche League summarizes it perfectly when
they say children go from dependence to independence, and
you can't rush the process. Some children will stop
breastfeeding early, and others will go until they are four or
five. I see the same thing with learning. I can't say that any
child is going to learn everything that I teach. *How Children
Fail* (1982), by Holt, deals with that: you can't know what's
going on in someone's brain, and that just keeps getting
forgotten by educators, and parents.

This was brought home to me by the way my daughters
learned how to read. My oldest daughter showed all the
classical pre-reading behaviour, and then when she wanted
to read she was very amenable to sitting down and having us
talk to her and point out words, read out loud, and use flash
cards. She wanted to do some flash cards, so we didn't buy
any major phonics programs, we just used index cards. By
third grade-age, she was completely reading on her own. She
is still an active reader and loves to read.

Our middle daughter, Alison, enjoyed being read to, but
phonics was a complete bust. She just could not pronounce
things. Phonics drove her crazy because of all the
exceptions. With Lauren, we didn't even think about the
exceptions. It just seemed to work. With Allison, she
questioned everything: "Why don't we use 'ph' to spell
fish?" That stuff used to drive her crazy. As a young child
she had meningitis, so she had a speech delay and some
hearing issues, all of which made it difficult for her to
pronounce words phonetically. For her, the whole language
method worked beautifully. We found that by simply
reading to her she started recognizing words, reading them
when she saw them: exit, stop, the classic things you see in
whole language. She learned to read easily by the time she
was seven or eight. She remains an active reader now.

2. PAT FARENGA

Our youngest, she just started reading when she was four. We don't know how that happened. We loved to read out loud, and we still read out loud to her, but she just pretty much taught herself. We didn't teach her. Maybe she saw us working with Alison, but we didn't have a reading program for any of them.

Education is more and more becoming a commodity sold to people. I'm seeing this with early childhood stuff. Having access to early childhood centers and teachers and resources is fine, but to compel children to use them, that's a big issue.

When I meet parents, and this comes up, I tell them, "You didn't teach your child how to walk or talk, but they learned to do it." Every now and then, someone will raise their hand and say, "No, I taught them to talk. I taught them to walk." I say, "What do you mean?" and they talk about doing lessons every day, at set times . . . Oh my gosh! Is that necessary? There is this mindset, this guilt, that if we don't do it they won't learn it, and that is so wrong. Everything that we see in human nature, in the way humans have passed knowledge on for centuries, if not from the beginning of human kind, is that it's through conversation, it's through living together, it's through observation and reflection. And yes, having a well-designed course to learn something that you choose to learn is certainly beneficial, but that's only one mode.

An audio version of this piece appears in podcast and can be found at:
Farenga, P. (2003, November 12). Interview by B. Ekwa Ekoko [Podcast]. Pat Farenga, The John Holt Legacy; Radio Free School. Hamilton, Ontario.
Retrieved from
http://radio4all.net/index.php/program/8082

References

Farenga, P., Ricci, C., & Tedesco, S. (Eds.) (in press).
    Growing without schooling. Medford,
    MA: HoltGWS LLC.
Gatto, J. T. (2005). *Dumbing us down: The hidden
    curriculum of compulsory schooling.* Gabriola Island,
    B.C.: New Society Publishers. (Original work
    published in 1992)
Holt, J. (2005). *The underachieving school.* Boulder, CO:
    Sentient Publications. (Original work published 1969)
Holt, J. (2004). *Instead of education: Ways to help people do
    things better.* Boulder, CO: Sentient Publications.
    (Original work published 1976)
Holt, J., & Farenga, P. (2003). *Teach your own: The John
    Holt book of homeschooling* (Revised ed.). USA: Da
    Capo Press. (Original work published 1981)
Holt, J. (1982). *How children fail* (Revised ed.). USA: Da
    Capo Press. (Original work published 1964)
Illich, I. (1983). *Deschooling Society.* New York, NY:
Harper & Row Publishers. (Original work published
    1970)

———————————

Patrick Farenga worked closely with the author and
teacher John Holt for four years, until Holt's death in 1985.
He is the President of Holt Associates Inc. and was the
Publisher of *Growing Without Schooling Magazine (GWS)*
from 1985 until it stopped publishing in Nov. 2001. *GWS*
was the nation's first periodical about homeschooling,
started by Holt in 1977.

Farenga and his wife have three girls, ages 23, 20, and
17. In addition to writing for *GWS* for twenty years, he has

written many articles and chapters for diverse books and has also published and edited several popular books about homeschooling including his own book, *The Beginner's Guide To Homeschooling.* Farenga also appears on local and national television and radio shows as a homeschooling expert; he has appeared on *The Today Show*, *The Voice of America, NPR's The Merrow Report,* and *CNN's Parenting Today.* Farenga has been quoted as an expert on homeschooling many times in the national media. Farenga has addressed audiences about homeschooling and the work of John Holt throughout the United States, Canada, England, and Italy. Farenga now works as a writer, speaker, and education consultant.

http://www.patfarenga.com

CHAPTER 3

AN EDUCATION IN THE AGE OF CLIMATE CHANGE

SATISH KUMAR

Once my mentor and friend, E.F. Schumacher, was standing outside London and saw a lorry full of biscuits coming from Manchester to London. A few minutes later Schumacher saw another lorry going from London, full of biscuits made in London going to Manchester. "Now," he said, "I'm an economist, I've been to Oxford, I'm a mathematician. I must be able to find a logic in understanding why biscuits made in London should be sent to Manchester and biscuits made in Manchester should be sent to London." All these drivers driving these lorries eight hours on the motor ways and you have to build motor ways and highways and freeways for these biscuits to travel from London to Manchester and Manchester to London. He thought and thought and thought: this great Oxford economist could not make sense of this. Then he came to the conclusion, "Maybe I am not a nutritionist and by taking biscuits from London to Manchester and Manchester to London it must increase the nutritional value of the biscuits."

We have built an economy of free market and globalization. Simply put, free market and globalization is the cause of global warming. If we want to reduce global warming, if we want to mitigate climate change, it is not going to happen by technological fixes. It is going to happen when we are prepared to have a new worldview and a new way of life, like Mahatma Gandhi advocated.

3. SATISH KUMAR

The New World view has to be based in our relationship with the natural world, a relationship of respect and reverence. A *reverencian* ecology or a spiritual ecology, or a non-violent ecology, where nature is not there for our use. There is intrinsic value of nature, or in nature. Trees are there standing. They are useful to us because they give us fruit, they give us shade, they give us wood, and they give us oxygen, and therefore we value them. But there's more value to the trees, and to the forests, and to the lakes, and to the mountains, and to the animals, and birds, and all life than their usefulness to humans. Recognizing the intrinsic value of nature, that's the first big shift, the paradigm shift, we have to make. This idea of human superiority and all the rest of the species and nature for the benefit and use of humans: that has to change. We have to have equity with nature; an understanding and relationship with nature, where trees have as much right—your lake here, the wonderful Lake Ontario—has as much right to remain clean, unpolluted water as your home. You have a right to have your own home, unpolluted. You would not like me to come and throw my rubbish bin into the courtyard or living room of your house. If I do not have the right to put my rubbish in your living room, what right do I or you have to put our rubbish into the living room of the lake? Or living room of the forest?

Second, we have to develop a positive view of living in harmony with the natural world. Living in harmony in such a way in that we live happily but not wastefully. We live elegantly and simply, but not extravagantly. This extravagant wasteful lifestyle that we have built, as if there is no tomorrow, cannot continue. Gandhi came to believe that a simple life is a freer life. When we have this kind of materialistic society, materialistic culture, this creates more bondage and less freedom. We think that we are a free society just because we can write an article in the *New York*

Times or your *Globe and Mail*. Or, just because you can publish some books, you are free. Freedom is much more than just saying something. Therefore, if you truly want to be free then you have to be simple. It's a blessing to be simple, it's a blessing to be free. That is a Gandhian idea.

Living a simple, elegant lifestyle—that was Gandhi's idea of *swadeshi*. Gandhi coined three beautiful ideas: *sarvodaya, swaraj and swadeshi*. The first was *sarvodaya*. *Sarvodaya* is different from socialism and capitalism. The two dominant philosophies in our political system and thinking are socialism and capitalism. Socialism is concerned with the benefit of society, human society, a purely anthropocentric philosophy. Capitalism is not even concerned about society. It is concerned about capital. As long as your capital is safe, you are happy. Capitalism and socialism both do not take nature into account. *Sarvodaya* is the well-being of all, literally all. Even in socialism, you do not have the idea of all human beings. The socialist idea is the greatest good of the greatest number. *Sarvodaya* says not greatest good of the greatest number, but greatest good for all.

When you bring economic development, where do you start? With the poorest of the poor and the weakest of the weak. Gandhi started to work with the Untouchables, not just by preaching at them and telling them what to do and how to live, but by identifying with them. Gandhi said, "How is it that I go to toilet and somebody else, an Untouchable, comes and cleans it?" Gandhi started to clean the toilets. Gandhi took a broom in his hand and went out from his ashram and cleaned the streets. In that way, he incorporated the principle of *sarvodaya*—the well-being and upliftment of all, and that included not only humans but other species. The well-being of the animals, the way our farming works, the factory farming, that is not non-violent. You cannot have *sarvodaya* if animals are treated with cruelty. The well-being of all includes the welfare of animals and forests. If you clear-cut a rainforest in the Amazon to grow more corn or soya so that you can make biofuels or so you can have hamburgers or something mass-produced, that is violence to the forest. Forests have rights, as I said before. Gandhian thinking will lead you to understand rights of nature. *Sarvodaya* brings that philosophy into our politics and sociology so they give rights to all living beings, and well-being of all living beings.

The second principle that Mahatma Gandhi coined was *swaraj*. A Hindi word, *swaraj* means self-organized governance. Governance not coming from top to bottom, someone telling you how you live but *swaraj:* where communities, villages, towns, neighborhoods, and individuals, and families, bring governance that is self-organized. This is how nature works. How the forests are organizing? Is there any military force there? Do they have any courts? How lions, tigers, snakes, and eagles, and birds, how do they organize their governance? Do they have any president or prime minister or parliament?

Gaia, the earth system, is a self-organized system. Gandhi learned from Gaia, from Earth, from nature, to put that system into human society, the governance must rise from the inside. Development should come from inside out rather than imposing from outside. Take again learning from nature: Where does a tree come from? You have a seed, an acorn. And you put that acorn into the soil, into interrelationship, a symbiotic relationship, an interdependence. The moment that acorn goes into the soil the sun works at it and gives energy; the water works at it and gives nutrition; the soil works at it and gives nutrition. From inside the seed, a plant is emerging. That plant is emerging, and becoming mature and becoming a tree. And out of that little seed—that acorn—a mighty oak tree emerged.

That is inside outward. That was the Gandhian idea of education—instead of thinking that children are empty vessels, empty buckets, empty baskets, and the teacher saying, "You children! You are ignorant, empty not knowing anything. I'm going to tell you maths and technology and sociology and sciences and all the other subjects." Thereby treating children like an empty vessel. Instead Gandhian education would be that you don't do anything until you have understood the child. You have to look at the aptitude, and the tendencies, and genius, and the imagination, and the creativity of that child. Is this child interested in singing or gardening? Or in what kind of activity is this child interested? You try to help promote that particular interest of the child. That is called basic education.

The Gandhian idea of basic education is to observe the child, to help like a gardener helps the acorn, or the seed, an apple seed, or a tomato seed, or a potato seed, or whatever seed it is. A gardener does not tell an oak to be an ash. A gardener does not tell an apple to be a pear. A gardener says, "Apple if you are an apple seed, be an apple, and I will help you: I will water you, I will put some stakes so that you are not blown away in the wind."

The work of a teacher or a parent is to give support and help the child to be who the child is. That is the idea of Gandhian basic education, the idea of *swadeshi:* self-organized, self-disciplined, self-managed, and self-controlled. And in that way you come to self-realization. Self-realization means you become who you are, your true potential.

The third idea of Gandhi's is *swadeshi:* the local home economy. The home economy is where your maximum economy is local. Gandhi was not an extremist in any way. He would say if you want to do some trading it should be in goods that are not available locally, and that should be the icing on the cake. Small amounts, so not too much transportation is required. Maximize economic activity is at the local grassroots level. In your villages, in your towns, in your neighborhoods within 50 or 100 miles, where you can walk, go on horses, have a small public transportation system like trains or buses. But these huge lorries traveling from north to south, from east to west, from California to the eastern part of America, or Vancouver to Ottawa—long-distance traveling of goods—Gandhi said that is not *swadeshi.* That is not a sustainable, durable economy. A durable economy is one that is always renewable, and local, and available, and you have control over it.

You can see on a philosophical, political and economic level, he had a whole new vision, a whole new paradigm on which sustainability is built. Gandhi was talking at a time when nobody was talking about the environment and nobody was worried about global warming, but now we can see the relevance of his thinking in our age of global warming.

We need to think about our way of life, which is based in three words: it should be *beautiful*; it should be *useful*; it should be *durable*. I call it the *BUD* principle. Our Western Civilization is very much deprived of beauty. If you go back to the native people, the native people considered beauty essential.

The place of beauty is essential to nourish our souls. In our materialistic, violent civilization, we have to recognize that the violence is in-built, institutional violence, poverty, and waste. In Gandhian thought, they are all violent and so we have built a violent society, a violent culture. And if we want to create a culture of non-violence, beauty has to be at the center.

If we are to escape from the consumerist, materialistic, global warming, climate-changing culture and civilization of the industrial world, where do we go? Where do we take refuge? In the Buddhist language you say, "I take refuge in the Buddha; I take refuge in the Sangha; I take refuge in the

Dharma. *Buddham saranam ga chami; Dhammam saranam ga chami; Sangham saranam ga chami.*" In the age of ecology, from the Gandhian perspective, I would say I take refuge in the arts and crafts and a beautiful way of living. That will be feeding our souls in the greatest satisfaction and contentment and joy in our lives, *ananda*—in Sanskrit, "joy."

At the moment we are an industrial system, so busy, busy, busy that the industrial system has taken the beauty and joy from our lives.

I would say in this age of climate change and global warming, love-driven action is essential, without that we will come to a sorry state. After beauty, when we take refuge in the arts, whatever we make, we must make something that is satisfactory to our soul. Useful, but satisfactory. Which brings satisfaction to our imaginative, creative qualities.

What the system has created has taken the creativity and imagination out of our hands. You are working in the office and the computer is controlling everything. You are working in a factory or working in a supermarket, Wal-Mart or something similar in Canada or something similar in the United Kingdom, you are a cog in the machine. Human beings are turned into cogs in the machine. Human beings are creative, imaginative beings, and if our imagination and creativity is gone, then what is the good of airplanes, motorways, freeways, and cars, and computers, and iPods, and all the other gadgets that we have? Let us go back to that creativity and imagination and arts and crafts. This is why Gandhi said spinning the spinning wheel, weaving your cloth, tapestry, making your pot, beautiful things that you make, your garden, your home is a spiritual practice. Every day living is a spiritual practice, if you do it with imagination, and creativity, and a sense of beauty, and a sense of the sacred. That sense of the sacred give us food for the soul.

So friends, I would say that even though my own country, India, is forgetting Gandhi, and we are like a tsunami of consumerism, a tsunami of materialism, sweeping the entire world, we could take a different route. We are forgetting Gandhi, but maybe there will be another revolution, and Gandhi will go from Canada back to India. Gandhi will go back from Europe, and America, and Western countries where you have seen what this kind of consumerist culture brings to the society and how it kills the creativity and imagination and beauty. Perhaps you will set another example, and press my country to learn from the wisdom of Gandhi.

An audio version of this piece appears in podcast and can be found at:
Satish, K. (2007, June 27). Recorded by R. Kay [Podcast]. Satish Kumar: Gandhi in the Age of Climate Change; McMaster University for Radio Free School. Hamilton, Ontario.
Retrieved from
http://radio4all.net/index.php/program/23685

Satish Kumar has been a Jain monk, nuclear disarmament advocate, and is the current editor of *Resurgence & Ecologist* magazines. Now living in England, Kumar is founder and Director of Programmes of the Schumacher College international centre for ecological studies, and of The Small School. His autobiography, *No Destination,* first published by Green Books in 1978, has sold over 50,000 copies. He is also the author of *You Are, Therefore I Am: A Declaration of Dependence*; and *The Buddha and the Terrorist.*
Satish is on the Advisory Board of Our Future Planet, a

unique online community sharing ideas for real change and in recognition of his commitment to animal welfare and compassionate living, he was elected vice-president with the RSPCA. He continues to teach and run workshops on reverential ecology, holistic education, and voluntary simplicity, and is a much sought-after speaker both in the UK and abroad.
http://www.resurgence.org

CHAPTER 4

A LEARNING SYSTEM FIT FOR A DEMOCRACY?

ROLAND MEIGHAN

For many years, I was a double-agent in education. On the one hand, I have been researching home-based education since 1975 here in the British Isles, and on the other hand, I was involved in the school learning system itself: training teachers, but trying to produce a different type of teacher who would share power with learners. This double-agent role gave me a very interesting basis of comparison between the two learning systems.

From our home in Nottinghamshire, we run two organizations. One is called Educational Heretics Press and, with my wife Janet, we have produced 91 publications. We have spent some of our time commissioning books and writing books, which are of a radical nature asking questions about education and what we should do with it, and where it should go. One exciting thing about our press is that we have commissioned writers to write books for us who would never have had their books published by the normal commercial publishers. In fact, I do not think any of our books and booklets would ever have been published, but for us. We are rather proud of what we have managed to do, in terms of keeping ideas flowing that the mainstream presses do not want to know about.

The other organization we run from here is called The Centre for Personalised Education. This is a trust that has been devoted now for many years to the idea of promoting and developing all of the logistics of personalised learning. One of the things about personalised learning is that home-based education is one of the contexts where you are most likely to find it. There is no guarantee that you will find it in home-based education, because some home educators work to quite formal programs. But there are plenty of home educators who do personalize the learning, and the learners do take over the management of it and have a great deal of say in what is learned, when it is learned, how it is learned, and why it is learned.

Democracy and Learning Systems

One has to say quite a few things about democracy, because it is much more complicated than meets the eye. First, paraphrasing Winston Churchill, is that democracy is the worst form of organization except for all the others. I think that is quite an interesting observation, because it proposes that we cannot expect democracy to be an ideal or perfect system, but it is, nevertheless, an improvement on the other forms of organization, which can be any of the standard tyrannies of dictatorship or totalitarianism or fascism or theocracy or monarchy or bureaucracy or capitalism. All of these are forms of authoritarian domination and dictatorship, and if you do not have democracy, you have one of these. Despite the limitations of democracy, you are usually worse off with any of the others.

There are perhaps three or four things you can say about democracy and education. The first is that there will be a variety of provision for learning rather than uniformity. In a democracy, we are talking about taking choice seriously. If you are involved in something, for example if you are a tax payer then you should have some involvement in the government that taxes you; you should be able to vote it in or vote it out. In education, if there are options to what you can learn, then these should be made available to you rather than imposing one set of ideas on you whether you chose them or not.

The second idea is that in a democracy you are allowed to have critical thought, rather than just believe what the rulers tell you. You are able to question what is on offer, and to question the questioners. The other systems do not encourage that. Whether it is totalitarianism, monarchy, theocracy, or bureaucracy, they do not encourage question-asking. They actually want you to believe that there is one right answer and that they, the people in charge, know it.

Then, in democratic education, you operate some form of power sharing rather than having things imposed on learners from above. You will be looking at the situation where people can choose from a catalogue of ideas, what it is they learn, and maybe choose to learn it together, or maybe choose to learn it on their own.

The fourth feature of democracy in education is that it promotes flexibility, rather than rigidity. I think one of the things we experience here in the United Kingdom is the enormous rigidity in the system, and very little flexibility, and it's getting more rigid rather than less. Professor Bengu, Nelson Mandela's minister of education, made this observation about democracy, which I really treasure: "Democracy means the absence of domination." You can go on to say the maximization of consent. The schools here in the United Kingdom are riddled with domination. First you are forced to go there, then you are forced to learn the curriculum, which you have imposed on you, then you are punished if you do not learn it properly, then you are tested. The school-based learning system is riddled with domination, from start to finish, and I am sure that there are elements of this in Canada, too.

This is the whole point of democratizing education, that

children are people too, that is, they deserve human rights, they deserve consultation, they deserve the dignity of doing things with consent rather than by being bullied into it. It is a radical idea, but we have to regard children as people worthy of consultation and worthy of being involved in democratic processes, and worthy of having choices in a variety of things on offer to them.

There are many other things you can say about democracy. One of the important things is that democracy can be around in a very shallow form and it can be a deeper form, and a very deep form. There are degrees of democracy, and this is the kind of thing that politicians hate us to say, but we have in Britain a very shallow form of democracy: indeed very little power sharing, and very little participation in decision-making in society in general, let alone inside institutions like schools.

If we wanted to make a deeper democracy, then we have to take power-sharing seriously, and take participation seriously, however inconvenient this is to the people who rule. Indeed, one of our politicians says that our rulers in Britain actually hate democracy, because it is so inconvenient having to consult people and involve them in decision-making. It is so much more convenient to be a dictator and to say "this is what we will do."

This extends to parenting. One of our writers, Jan Fortune Wood, has written a book called *With Consent: Parenting for All to Win* (2002). It is about parenting. She is advocating that parenting should be about the whole idea of achieving consent from all concerned: the parents and the children agreeing on the rules, agreeing how they can do things together. Operating on the basis of consent and agreed rules and not on the parents saying "because I tell you so."

Democratic institutions do exist. I think the most prominent example of a democratic institution is the public library. The point about the public library is, first of all, it is professionally organized. It is not a random collection of books and learning resources. Professionally trained people properly organize it, but the professional activity stops there, at the point of having organized the places where books and things are available in a systematic way. The librarians then say, "It is over to you now, you are the learner, here are the resources, we have organized it for you. You choose what you want to learn, when you want to learn it and take the books away, or read them here. We shall not be testing you, we are not keeping records of what you are learning and it is your private business what you learn." This is a deep-democratic learning institution which says, "We respect you as the learner to decide what to learn, and how to learn it, and when to learn it." The librarians do not devise a national curriculum. They actually organize a catalogue curriculum, and you make your own way through it as fast as you like, at any age, via any pathway, any time, and any place. That is the philosophy of the public library. That should be the slogan of all the education systems, in my view. The best home educators do it that way.

I am a great fan of John Holt, and met him over here in England and we became good friends. We were collaborating on a few projects before he suddenly died of cancer. I have written two books about his ideas: *John Holt: Personalised Education and the Reconstruction of Schooling* (1995), and *John Holt: Personalised Learning Instead of 'Uninvited Teaching'* (2002). I think John Holt was one of the people who are committed to this idea of taking personalized learning, and personalized education, and making it the cornerstone of education.

We have to point out to people that we are not talking dreamland here. We do have public libraries; they have been going for over 100 years operating on exactly this principle. We just have to adopt those principles to the other places of learning. I do think this means that we have to, eventually, recycle all our schools into better learning places. Places that are learner-friendly, places that invite people to come and learn rather than command them to come and learn.

Now that takes a big shift in thinking, but the idea that we cannot do it is nonsense when you think the public library does it without even blinking. We can do this, but it does mean that we have to abandon some of the ideas that currently operate within the system.

Recycling Schools

The Centre for Personalised Learning had an inspiring weekend on the whole theme of recycling our schools. We came up with many different ideas for increasing the variety of choices for learners. Some of these ideas are very familiar: First, we should make home-based education properly available and supported rather than a kind of odd thing that some odd people do, and it should be declared that this is a valid form of education. People can choose to do some home-based education anytime they want to. Second, home-based educators working in cooperatives are also a valid form of education. There are arrangements operating in North America called the City Colleges. They are places that do not have an actual building because they are organized on the basis that people will learn in the city and in the places for employment, in the museums, and library, and elsewhere. They will choose the kind of experiences in the city that they think are important and construct a program out of that.

Then, there was the idea of flexi-schooling, where people can spend some days in school and some days learning at home and work the two together as a program.

There is currently a program here in Britain called Notschoolnet. It is interesting because it takes people who have been rejected from the system, or excluded from it, and starts by consulting them, asking what they would like to learn. Then it says, "We are not going to call you students anymore, we are going to call you researchers. As researchers why not start researching the kinds of things you want to find out about. Now, we will help you. We have got people we can contact and put you in touch with, we have got resources that we can put over the Internet to you. Start learning the things you want to learn, in the way you want to learn them and we will help and support you." The interesting thing is how this program turns ugly duckling into swans. It takes people who are supposedly hopeless in learning, and by using the personalized learning approach, they gradually become turned on to learning and become better and better at it. Some end up where you would not have expected, in colleges and universities later on. There again is evidence that we can do it. The Notschoolnet program is not an impossible dream: it has been going for over ten years.

The other idea I would like to see adopted, on the basis of personalised education, is an idea used in a number of USA schools called Year-round Education. Year-round Education recycles schools by being open 8am until 8pm everyday of the year, weekends as well, and offer choices about the kinds of things learners can come to learn, sign up for, and get interested in. Learners choose which they want to do. But also, say at the moment the program is not offering a certain thing, and some would like to have that, learners can ask for them to organize it. The answer has to be, "Yes, we will make it available to you if we possibly can." When I was at school, I wanted to learn Esperanto, but Latin was imposed on me instead. Now, I would hope my choice would be made available to me.

I think when you start doing all these things together, properly supporting home-based education, supporting home-based education cooperatives, and supporting the public libraries, the City as School (again, this is not the same as City Colleges, and the only references I could find on Google were for bricks-and-mortar campuses—it's a cool idea, but I'm pretty sure there is no real example of it yet), the Notschoolnet programs, flexi-schooling projects, and Year-round Education, you can see that this can offer the learners a whole portfolio of ideas they can build into their learning programs. Over a period of time, say ten years, they might include quite a few of these into their own learning.

There is another idea that I would like to see, which is from Denmark, where adolescents and others are invited to spend a year in a residential community focusing on one activity. It could be dance, it could be music, it could be ecology, it could be drama, it could be languages, or it could be one or two of these.

Another idea is that a learner could choose to study their locality. Their program would be for a year studying everything in the area: the history of it, the operation of it, the businesses, the facilities, and going to places of interest and seeing what's going on there. The project would be to get to know the locality in more breadth and depth rather than the young learners spending yet another year in the day prison.

I regard schools as day prisons, a really unimaginative and dull and anti-democratic kind of idea. As John Holt put it, school is not a good idea gone wrong, but a bad idea from the start. The best we have achieved so far is a national chain of day prisons in the name of education. Why are we fooled into thinking this is a good idea? Well, as Everett Reimer observed, some true educational experiences are bound to occur in schools, but they occur despite school rather than because of it.

School is such a convenient place for parents to leave their children and teenagers, that critically thinking about what is happening there is suppressed. As the contemporary writer John Taylor Gatto says, schools operate to dumb us down using weapons of mass instruction. I think we come back to home-based education because it does some learning very effectively, not always. Home-based education is much more part of a solution when it operates as personalized education than when it tries to ape schools. When it is practicing personalized education, it is pointing to all sorts of things about the way we can go about things: how the learners can understand learning; how they can be involved in consent-based program, an invitation-based program; how they can use a catalogue curriculum to make their way around the whole world of learning; how they can operate a learner-friendly situation as against learner-hostile situation; and how they can use purposive conversation as a tool of learning, which is a much more efficient way of learning than, say, formal instruction.

Formal instruction has an efficiency rating of between 5% and 10%. Purposive conversation, which is used a lot by home-based educators, has a 50% efficiency rating. You remember 50% on average, of what goes on in a purposive conversation, whereas you only remember 5% to 10% of a formally taught presentation.

There are many things in home-based education that are pointing the way and becoming part of the solution. Unfortunately, I do not think school is part of the solution, it is actually part of the problem. This is why we have to consider the whole idea of recycling schools into more intelligent arrangements for learning, developing a learning system fit for a democracy.

An audio version of this piece appears in podcast and can be found at: Meighan, R. (2006, December 13). Interview by B. Ekwa Ekoko [Podcast]. Edu-ocracy: Education Fit for Democracy, Radio Free School. Hamilton, Ontario.
Retrieved from
http://radio4all.net/index.php/program/20894

References

Fortune-Wood, J. (2002). *With consent: Parenting for all to win.* Derbyshire, UK: Education
Now Publishing Co-Operative (ceased to trade).
Available at Educational Heretics Press.

Meighan. R. (1995). *John Holt: Personalised education and the reconstruction of schooling.* Nottingham, UK: Educational Heretics Press.

Meighan. R. (2002). *John Holt: Personalised learning instead of 'uninvited teaching.'* Nottingham, UK: Educational Heretics Press.

Roland Meighan is a writer, publisher, and consultant/researcher on learning systems, past present and future. His work on *The Next Learning System* has been translated into more than twelve languages. He is Director of Educational Heretics Press, and Director/Trustee of the Centre for Personalised Education Trust Ltd. Roland began researching home-based education in 1977, appearing as an expert witness in key legal hearings. He continued as a 'double agent' by training teachers for the school system at the same time. This gave him a unique comparative perspective on the two learning systems.

http://www.rolandmeighan.co.uk/

CHAPTER 5

AN INTERVIEW ABOUT A SENSE OF SELF

SUSANNAH SHEFFER

Beatrice: How did you become involved with homeschooling?

I worked with Holt Associates, the organization John Holt founded, for fifteen years. John Holt was an educational writer and critic who is probably best known for his books *How Children Learn* (1967/1983) and *How Children Fail* (1964/1982). In 1977, John Holt founded a little magazine called *Growing Without Schooling (in press)(GWS)*. Soon after his death, in 1985, I came to join the folks who were continuing to put out that magazine, and eventually I became the editor and remained so until the year before we ceased publication, when I passed on the editorship to Meredith Collins. Unfortunately, it was always tough to sustain the magazine financially, and in 2001 we ceased publication after 143 issues.

Working for Holt Associates all those years, I got to keep in close touch with John Holt's philosophy and his ways of looking at children's learning. I kept in contact with people who were practicing growing without schooling all over the U.S., and in other countries around the world. After several years of editing the magazine, I wrote a book about homeschooled adolescent girls in particular. That book is called *A Sense Of Self: Listening to Homeschooled Adolescent Girls*, and it was published in 1995.

AN INTERVIEW ABOUT A SENSE OF SELF

Beatrice: What led you to that specific focus on girls?

I was interested in looking at the experience of homeschooled girls at a time when the experience of girls in school was getting a great deal of attention. In the early and mid-nineties there were a number of books and studies and reports coming out that looked at the experience of schooling for girls and found that girls were suffering in school in some very particular ways. For example, there was a study called "How Schools Shortchange Girls," which was produced by the American Association of University Women, and other related studies (1995). Girls' experience of school was being looked at very closely, from their general emotional experience to specific examples of discrimination, like studies showing that when students raised their hands, teachers called on boys much more frequently than they called on girls. Teachers were often not consciously aware of their behaviour. They might say, when being interviewed, that their classrooms had no discrimination based on gender, but when they'd be videotaped and then watch the video of their own classroom behaviour, teachers would realize to their shock that in fact they were favouring the boys.

That's just one example of the kind of research that was being done. Also, there was some important research that was looking not specifically at girls in school but more generally at adolescent girls' psychological growth and development and their inner experience. In this work, there was a lot of discussion about girls "losing their voice." That was the phrase that came out of the Harvard Project on the *Development of Girls* (1992), the sense that adolescent girls really were losing trust in themselves, doubting their own voices, doubting the validity of their own goals, perceptions, and experience. Those words sound kind of general but they meant a lot of important things. Adolescence is a hard time for many young people, but these studies gave attention to the particular ways that it was hard on girls, the messages that the culture sends to girls, the ways in which school sometimes reinforces those messages.

Here is something that I can paint with a very broad brush, and it is kind of a generalization, but I think it will resonate with a number of people. For example, if a boy is struggling in school or struggling in general as an adolescent, there is often very visible evidence of that struggle. Again, it is always dangerous to generalize, and of course there are numerous exceptions to any generalization, but classically and typically a boy might be, as they say, "acting out." A boy for whom school was not working might be the disruptive one in the classroom, the one who makes trouble in class, interrupting the teacher, in some way misbehaving, so that it would be very, very obvious that the boy is having trouble in the school set-up. He might be the one getting constantly sent to the principal's office. The girl in school, on the other hand, might look fine on the outside: she's the one sitting quietly in the corner not making any outward trouble. But her internal experience might be one of disconnection and suffering.

I'll tell you a quick story that illustrates this vividly. It's about a girl I came to know well, who chose to leave school and become a homeschooler at age 15. The final straw for her mother had been when the girl came home from school one day and her mother asked how her day had gone—you know, making ordinary conversation with her teenager. The mother asked, "What are you doing in science class nowadays?" The girl said, "I don't know." The mother said, "Well, how can you not know? What do you mean you don't know what you are doing in class?" The girl said, "I don't pay attention. I spend the class staring out the window."

It's a simple anecdote, but therein lies what so many

people were asserting was the issue with girls: that here was a girl whom the teacher probably didn't even give much thought to, would probably not have cited as one of her problem students. After all, a girl who is looking out the window, with her mind drifting in class, is not necessarily making the outward trouble that draws the teacher's attention. But here is a girl who is not being served by that experience, not getting anything out of it and not making her needs or her problems or her struggles manifest in a way that gets any attention from adults.

The adolescent girl studies and reports were getting a lot of popular attention—these were university studies but in the way that sometimes happens, these things were getting picked up by the popular press, and so there was lot of discussion about the issues. What I noticed, as I was following these things closely, was that the school context was assumed as a given. One of the studies even said in passing that all girls go to school, that was simply the assumption. The conclusion the study came to was that, therefore, we need to look at the way schools treat girls, which is an extremely valid point. But meanwhile, I knew, of course, through my work and my interactions with homeschoolers, that there were girls who didn't go to school; in some cases, girls who had never gone to school a day in their lives, who had grown completely outside of that experience. I was working with girls not only through the magazine *Growing Without Schooling,* but also through discussion groups for teenagers and through mentoring young writers. I had a lot of contact with teenagers of both genders, but I was aware of the girls that I knew well, and they didn't fit the descriptions that I was reading so much about. I would read about girls who were losing their voices, getting less confident, distrusting themselves, feeling alienated from their own goals. That just kept not fitting the girls that I knew well, it seemed that they were having a very different experience. I thought that it would be interesting and worthwhile, as a contribution to this whole discussion, to study girls who were learning outside of school, and ask them many of the same interview questions that girls in these other studies had been asked, and see how that all came out. That's what *A Sense of Self* (1997) was ultimately about. It was the result of 55 interviews with homeschooled girls age 11 to 16 across the United States. They were in-depth interviews—this was not a statistical study, it was what they call qualitative research where the focus is on the answers that the girls give as they are talking and reflecting in conversation. I did indeed find that the homeschooled girls' experience was in many ways quite different from the experience of their peers in school.

Beatrice: Can you summarize some of those differences?

The summary is that they were not experiencing the same kind of decline over time that was demonstrated in some of the other studies. What I'm going to say about the other studies' findings now is something that I think does resonate with a lot of adult women: the idea that at about age 10 or so, a girl often feels very confident and on top of the world, and then as the girl begins to absorb the messages about what's expected of females in this culture, things begin to get much harder. As Carol Gilligan (1992) and her Harvard colleagues describe it, the girl entering adolescence "goes underground." She doesn't feel comfortable saying what she really thinks, and focuses much more on what others want. This is all very much shorthand about a complicated psychological phenomenon, and I don't want to come across as being overly glib about what was being observed, but the girls I was talking to were reporting the opposite. A 15-year-old homeschooled girl might report that she felt more sure of herself, more trusting of her own experience than she had felt three years before, for example.

Another really classic distinction was this: the other studies had found that girls became increasingly uncomfortable with disagreement among friends. For example, think of the classic sense we have of social life of girls in school, that it's very, very important to conform, to fit in, to go along with what the norms are, what the leader of your clique demands. One of the interview questions is, "Do you speak up when you disagree with a friend?" That was a place where the homeschooled girls were almost unanimous. There were maybe one or two exceptions in the 55 girls I interviewed. Almost across the board, they expressed comfort with disagreement. They expected to disagree with friends about one thing or the other and didn't assume that that precluded friendship. After all, these are girls who are doing something so different with so much of their lives, and so often having to explain themselves, that if they needed to agree about everything in order to be friends, they would have a very limited pool of possible friends. They become much more comfortable with being different and yet having relationships with people. They don't assume you have to be the same in order to have a close relationship.

Beatrice: Why do you suppose the educational setting is what makes the difference in these kinds of things?

Although many of these interview questions look at internal, emotional experience, I believe that the responses are actually very much connected to a girl's external experience, to the circumstances she's in. For example, in some of the other discussions and studies, there is a frequently quoted story of a psychologist sitting with a girl from a prestigious private school and finding this girl to be very alienated from her goals. In other words, outwardly successful but not really identifying with that success, not really seeing the goals that she is meeting as her own goals. The psychologist in this case asks, "How can we help girls to identify with their goals?" The way I saw it—and this is really the heart of the book—was that conventional schooling is not really based on that idea. Schooling is not about helping people to identify their own goals and pursue them. On the contrary, school tells students, "This is what you need to learn. This is how you are going to go about it, and then we will test to see if you have learned it." That sort of thing. In a homeschool environment, on the other hand, in a setting where you are learning outside of school, or at least in a setting that is based on this premise, you are being asked to reflect on your own goals. You are learning to ask the question, "What do I want out of life?" Not just "What do I want out of education?" but "What do I care about? What seems important to pursue? What do I need to know in order to pursue that?" Those are the questions that, as homeschool teenager of any gender, you are being invited and supported to ask. So, if those students eventually feel more able to identify with their goals, it's not actually surprising. There's a relationship, a crucial relationship, between the structure and assumptions of their educational environment and the way they end up feeling.

Beatrice: Some parents might want to homeschool their teens but believe they don't have the time to do so because they have to go to work. Can you comment on that?

Potentially, a teenager doesn't need the same kind of direct custodial care that a five or six year old does. In other words, teenagers can safely be outside their parental line of vision for long stretches of time, as long as they are in a general sense supported and helped to develop a full and meaningful life. If we stop thinking of school as the only place for young people to be during the day, it becomes an interesting societal question, "What are the options? What do we do with young people?" So let's say we have a 15 year old who is not in school, is homeschooling. There are all sorts of things that that young person might be doing with her life. She doesn't necessarily need either parent to be at home instructing her for six hours a day. In that family set-up, both parents might very well work outside the home, or it might be a single parent. I always tell the story of the time when I was facilitating a discussion group of five homeschooled adolescent girls and three of them were at that time living in single-parent families. It was not a problem in terms of whether homeschooling was an option for them or not. They certainly needed their parent's involvement and care and support—every teenager needs that, ideally, or at least something equivalent to it—but they didn't need a parent to be teaching them all day long because they were learning from a variety of experiences and people.

Now, in a long-time homeschooling family there frequently might be more than one child, and so you might have a homeschooled adolescent girl around 13 who has a couple of younger siblings. The family might have in the early days arranged things and done what they could and chosen to live on a limited income and so forth so that one parent could be at home during those years and be available to the children. That adolescent girl might be living in a family in which the mother was home, or this family might have worked out something where the parents might split shifts, work in different kinds of ways, so one parent would always be available. They might be working from home, as is increasingly common now. They might be doing some kind of work in which the kids could be there or be involved some of the time. People work out all sorts of creative solutions to this logistical problem. In many ways, it is more of a challenge when the children are younger than it is when they are older and involved in all kinds of different things. A

16-year-old told me that she is out and about all day long as a homeschooler and so, in that sense, what her parents did or did not do was not as directly the issue during the day time.

Beatrice: I have had the experience where a few girls have told me, "Well, mum can clean; she is not doing anything else." It is a negative impression they have of their mothers because their mothers aren't out of the house, working at a job.

That comment could reflect a number of things. It could reflect a cultural bias against all the work that needs to happen but that our society doesn't value or doesn't reward monetarily. Or the idea that things that are traditionally woman's work are less valuable.

It is interesting that a number of girls I interviewed almost made the reverse comment because they did see what their mothers did at home, let's say even in those more traditional ways—and again I don't want to imply that the gender roles were always split so conventionally that it was always the mother who does the cooking and cleaning and so forth—but whichever parent does it, a child who grows up much more aware of that because the child who is not off in school all day long can develop a keen sense of what that work actually is, and therefore develop a respect for it. A girl might say, in answering the interview question, "What kinds of work do you parents do?" "My father is a (whatever his job was) and my mother works plenty hard at home." In other words, the girl would take care to acknowledge each kind of work, whether or not it was paid employment.

There's a lot in all of this about how the mother sees the homeschooling life. Over the years at *GWS* we certainly had a number of mothers report that it was through homeschooling their children that they developed a sense of their own interests and goals and things they wanted to pursue. It might be that they all took up an interest in a foreign language (or whatever) together, and as a result of that shared family activity, the mother discovered her own interests. It might be that the mother, through the process of undertaking this alternative to schooling for her children, began to reflect on her own path and her own schooling.

Sometimes a very beautiful thing happens, which is that the young person, having been given the respect and attention to her work all her life by her parents, then extends that back to her mother. A classic story would be a mother who treated her children with a great deal of respect and then was trying at some point in her children's childhood to give some time to her own writing, to build her own career as a writer, and was struggling with taking herself seriously. In the story like this that I'm thinking of, a young daughter encouraged her mother in that effort, and would hang a sign on her mother's room saying, "Do not disturb! Writer at work." The daughter really returned the respect and the serious attention that her mother had given her. In some ways, it's a journey of discovery where both mother and daughter together are having to talk about the cultural assumptions and to figure out how they're going to see their lives and what they are going to give value to.

Beatrice: There definitely is the idea that homeschooling is anti-feminist. What are your thoughts?

There is so much to explore there, probably more than we can discuss now, about how feminism is defined. Certainly in *A Sense of Self*, there is a discussion of that to some extent. Anticipating that question, I drew upon something that was outside the scope of the interviews for that book but that grew out of work we had done at *GWS* around this issue of homeschooling and feminism. We had a feature in which mothers had written in speaking to that claim that homeschooling is anti-feminist. Many of them challenged, very eloquently, the claim that homeschooling is not a feminist cause or a feminist experience. It was interesting that at a time when many women in the U.S. were actually reluctant to define themselves as feminists, for whatever complex reasons and again outside the scope of this discussion, these mothers writing to *Growing Without Schooling* would say, "I consider myself very much a feminist." They would say this in some cases as full-time homeschooling mothers, not actually having any other paid employment. There is a beautiful line from a single mother who wrote to us and said, "Homeschooling gave me my voice and the language to speak." Sometimes it's through homeschooling that parents and specifically mothers become activists, become advocates, learn how to speak up on their own behalf. Homeschooling often involves and requires a great deal of trust in oneself. Sometimes it also involves standing up to authority, depending on what the family's particular story has been and what led them to homeschooling. The point here is only that one cannot assume any one thing about homeschooling in this regard. One has to look closely at people's actual experience and at how they see themselves.

Beatrice: You explained at the start that you got involved in homeschooling through editing Growing Without Schooling *magazine, but how did you come to the whole idea of homeschooling and unschooling in the first place?*

Well, I had read John Holt's books when I was a young person myself. I was not thinking about homeschooling in particular then. Most of John Holt's books are not specifically about homeschooling; they are his experiences as a school teacher looking at what children's actual experience of school is like. That is what *How Children Fail*

(1964) is about. It's a journal of his years as a fifth grade teacher. (Fifth grade is ten to eleven year olds in the U.S.). Holt was someone who paid close attention to children's experience. I read that book and I thought, "This is a teacher who knows what children's experience is. He understands what school is actually like for kids." So few teachers seemed to be paying that kind of close attention to what school is really like for kids, as opposed to what adults think it ought to be like. John Holt was one of the people who really noticed that difference. One of the things he observed, when he was watching his students closely, was that their experience of school was very different from what he as a teacher hoped it would be, thought it should be, and thought it might be. That is where I began, with that kind of close attention to children's actual experience of school, of childhood, of their relationships with adults, and of learning. When I gradually understood that John Holt had turned a lot of his focus to helping people who wanted to learn outside of school, and was publishing the magazine, I became interested in that as well.

Beatrice: It's not common to hear about a youth taking interest in reading about education, is it?

It is interesting that people sometimes respond that way, saying it is amazing. I want to speak to that. First of all, to want to read the thoughts of someone who is writing about one's own experience is really pretty understandable, pretty natural. I make this point because there is a lot of writing out there about education and about school reform, and about what is wrong with schools and how we can make schools better and all that sort of thing. When we step back for a minute and take a broad view and think about that, we might ask the question, why wouldn't young people want to read about that? In other words, turn that around and acknowledge that, after all, young people are certainly among the key stakeholders in any kind of discussion about schooling and education and so forth. We could say that, in fact, it is the most natural thing in the world that a young person would read literature about schooling and about education.

Then, John Holt was an extremely clear writer. He was a wonderful prose stylist, and so it was not hard for a young person to find his work accessible. John Holt would have taken that as a great compliment. He wanted to write clearly enough that young people could follow him easily. Sometimes we think that to write clearly enough you have to be simplifying ideas, and John Holt didn't believe that. I just came at it from a different angle, that takes the focus away from whether it was or wasn't unusual for me personally to pick up a particular book and get interested in it. Increasingly, I think that young people are having input into discussions about school reform. You do see more and more that there will be articles or collections of interviews where adults will turn to young people directly to ask their opinions. *GWS* magazine certainly continued that tradition, where we always had young people's writing integrated right in there with the adults' writing. Whenever we posed a question about education or homeschooling or children's learning or whatever it might be, we always posed it to young people as well. They responded, they were just right in there at the discussion table.

Beatrice: So from learning about education, you came to learning without school?

I went to conventional schools. Homeschooling was not really on my radar screen, the idea of actually leaving school. Again, I was interested in Holt's critique of schooling at that time, and matching what he said to my own experience. Nowadays, things are different in that there are so many books about teenagers who are actually leaving school. Grace Llewellyn's book *The Teenage Liberation Handbook: How to Quit School and Get a Real Life and Education* (1998), for example, is addressed to young people and is specifically saying, "If you are unhappy at school, there is another option." There is also a community of teenage homeschoolers now. So nowadays, if someone is reading a critique of schooling, they have more of the potential to question whether they need to be there at all, and to step out of school into a welcoming community.

Beatrice: How can parents continue to support their homeschooled girls, find mentors and role models?

There's a philosophical answer to that and a very practical answer. The philosophical answer is right there, embedded in that word "support" that you mentioned. It can be confusing, because those of us who have been to school are used to thinking in terms of figuring out what kids need to do and then figuring out ways to get them to do it. As colloquial as that might sound, that's what much of the discussion on education really is about: What should kids be learning and how can we cleverly devise ways to get them to learn it, to get specific pieces of knowledge into their heads?

Then when people begin to critique and question that model, as many, many people have, sometimes there's a tendency to swing to a false other-end-of-the-spectrum, where the assumption is that instead you should just entirely leave kids alone. That is, I think, a very superficial and ultimately false understanding of alternative education: that the alternative to making kids do things is for the adult to do nothing at all. In fact, there is a profound third alternative to either making kids do things or leaving them entirely alone.

That alternative can really be summed up by the word

"support," where there is quite a role for an adult in the life of a young person who is self-directed and not forced to learn particular things.

There is, after all, a whole big world out there, and helping young people navigate through it, to understand what their options are, to figure out what they want, and to know what's available, is really valuable. There's so much in that regard that an adult can do.

That then gets into the very practical part of the answer. I'll just take a specific example: suppose a girl expresses a very general interest in working with animals. She may not be at all sure what she means by that. She may not be sure what the options would be. One of the things an adult might do in that situation is let her know what the options are: talk to her about how she could be reading about animals; she could be apprenticing; or, volunteering. What does she mean by animals? Does she mean training guide dogs for the blind, does she mean working in a veterinarian's office? There are so many different things you can do, and sometimes by throwing out those specific scenarios in the conversation with the girl—or boy, of course—adults can help young people figure out what it is that they really do want. As well, an adult can offer very practical help like placing the phone call to the veterinarian to begin to explore those possibilities.

The easiest way to sum this up is with some very wise words of some friends of mine, who run a resource centre for young people. The way they would always pose a question, to little toddlers and right up to teenagers, was, "What's the part you can do and what's the part you need help with?" This phrasing really shows that help is not an "all or nothing" kind of proposition. A young person might say, "I really need help with placing that phone call to the veterinarian because that's a really scary thing to figure out as a thirteen-year-old: how I place that cold call to a stranger and figure out if it is possible to volunteer there. But then once you place the call, Mom, I would be comfortable going to the first appointment by myself," or whatever it might be. In other words, there are parts that kids want our help with and parts that they feel able to do themselves. It's so important not to butt in and help with the parts that they don't want. Think of a toddler saying, "No! I want to do it myself!" It's so important not to interfere with that. It's also important to extend the help and support when young people do want it. That's kind of an overview that I think really shows what kind of help we can offer.

Beatrice: Can you talk a bit about the significance of role models, and mentors?

"Role models" is an interesting concept. What gets me nervous about the phrase "role models" is the idea that an adult would be doing an activity specifically for its hoped-for effect on the young person. In other words, an adult saying, "I'm going to make a point of doing this so that my child can see that it's important." Having that pedagogical intent. What I'm interested in is something a little more authentic than that. Adults should be doing what they think is important and what they care about, and then figuring out how to give young people access to that, how to let young people see it or hear about it or join in.

John Holt's classic answer to people who would say, "I want to work with kids," was, "Find some work you think is worth doing and then put your mind to figuring out ways for young people to join you." In some way, we are all engaged in the task of figuring out what we want to do in this world. Of all the things that there are to do, what seems to us to be important and meaningful? How do we want to make our contribution? We're all engaged with these questions, or could be so engaged. Adults can, in many ways, help

65

children by simply engaging with those questions for themselves and then sharing that with young people.

There will be a lot of homeschooling families where, because the kids are not shut off in school away from these concerns, the kids are joining in whatever the work is. Meaning that the family is in some way volunteering somewhere or in whatever way engaged with what they believe is important, and the kids are getting to do that, or at the very least are aware of it. A mother at home who has decided that she wants to take up a particular activity, maybe learn a musical instrument because she's always meant to do that, she should just do it for herself because she actually wants to. Whereas, if she is doing it because she thinks that it will be a good example, but she actually finds it miserable and she's resenting it and gritting her teeth, there's no need for that! Whatever the mother takes up because she truly wants to and cares about it, that would be what is valuable. For example, I am a writer. That's what I do for a living and that's what happens to be the thing that I care about and am drawn to, and so I then extend that to helping young people who are interested in writing. I'm doing it as someone who is a working writer and who is willing and delighted to devote some time to sharing that, passing that on, and helping young people with their own writing. Naturally, you can imagine that it would be absurd for me to do any kind of writing just so that it would be a good example for young people. The point is one has so many good examples to offer just by pursuing one's own life. You have your own work and concerns and then you just work on making that visible.

Beatrice: Can you talk about what "real work" means, and might be?

Work is so often stigmatized for young people, because we have a historical situation in which compulsory schooling laws were ostensibly instituted to protect young people from being exploited at work, from having absolutely no protection and spending many, many hours working in factories and so forth. The thing is, we made school compulsory. Instead of saying it's illegal to impose these kinds of working conditions on children, we made it so that it's illegal for them not to go to school. Of course, it's important to protect children from exploitation. On the other hand, though, there is young people's real desire to do what matters, to be doing the things that adults find important. Think of the toddler who rejects the toy, who is not interested in playing with the toy, when the adults are doing some real thing near by. The little kid wants to get his or her hands on what the adults are clearly using for their own real concerns. The question is, do we shut kids out of that? Do we always try and deflect them by giving them a toy version of the thing or do we try and help them to participate in whatever ways they can?

Then, when you get up to teenagers, people talk a lot about teenagers' alienation from the adult world and so forth. Well, we alienate teenagers by putting them in special places called schools and saying that only after quite a long time of preparation can you get out and join what we call, no surprise, the "real world." Students will jokingly say, "When I get out and join the real world," with the assumption that the world they are in is not yet real.

The premise of homeschooling, of growing without schooling as a teenager, is that you don't have to wait to join the real world, and for that matter that the real world is not any one thing. You get to figure out what you think that means, and so you are getting to do things that matter. Real work, as one young person defined it, is work that, if she didn't do it, someone else would have to do it. It's something that actually has to get done and isn't just invented for supposedly pedagogical purposes. This young person was volunteering at a nature education centre, and she was doing this as a young child of about seven or eight. She was given tasks to do that were not necessarily extremely complicated tasks, but she knew that they were real because if she wasn't in that day to do them, one of the other people there, an adult, would have to do the task. The tasks were real in that sense, and she knew it. At the Holt Associates office, young people were always eager to do whatever they recognized as real work, always asking if they could run the photocopier, put letters through the postage meter—all those kinds of things that they saw us doing. They could tell that the stuff mattered. That folding letters to go into an envelope for mailing was very different from randomly folding paper. It had that aura of real adult work surrounding it. These are just some examples of many, but absolutely, *Growing Without Schooling* always had stories of young people working with adults in almost any capacity you could imagine. I mentioned volunteering in a veterinary office, but also kids were helping in labs, working with artists, with political campaigns. Almost anything that they might be interested in, there can be a way to get involved with people who are doing that sort of thing.

An audio version of this piece appears in podcast and can be found at:
Sheffer, S. (2004, October 20). Interview by B. Ekwa Ekoko [Podcast]. Susannah Sheffer: A Sense of Self, homeschool girls, part 1, Radio Free School. Hamilton, Ontario.
        Retrieved from
http://www.radio4all.net/index.php/program/10292

        Sheffer, S. (2004, October 27). Interview by B. Ekwa Ekoko [Podcast].
Susannah Sheffer: A Sense of Self,homeschool girls, part 2,

Radio Free School. Hamilton, Ontario.
Retrieved from
http://www.radio4all.net/index.php/program/10351

References

American Association of University Women. (1995). *How schools shortchange girls: The AAUW report, a study of major findings on girls and education.* New York, NY: Marlowe & Company.

Farenga, P., Ricci, C., & Tedesco, S. (Eds.) (in press). *Growing without schooling.* Medford, MA: HoltGWS LLC.

Gilligan, C., & Brown, L.M. (1992). *Meeting at the crossroads: Women's psychology and girls' development.* Boston: Harvard University Press.

Holt, J. (1983). *How children learn* (Revised ed.). USA: Da Capo Press. (Original work published 1967)

Holt, J. (1982). *How children fail* (Revised ed.). USA: Da Capo Press. (Original work published 1964)

Llewellyn, G. (1998). *The teenage liberation handbook: How to quit school and get a real life and education.* Eugene, OR: Lowry House Publishers.

Sheffer, S. (1997). *A sense of self: Listening to homeschooled adolescent girls.* Portsmouth, NH: Boynton/Cook Publishers.

Susannah Sheffer edited *Growing Without Schooling*, the magazine founded by John Holt. She is also the editor of the book *A Life Worth Living: Selected Letters of John Holt* and of *Heinemann's Innovators in Education* series, which brought several progressive education classics back into print. Her other books about young people and learning are

A Sense of Self: Listening to Homeschooled Adolescent Girls and *Writing Because We Love To: Homeschoolers at Work.* These days, she is project director and staff writer at an international non-profit called Murder Victims' Families for Human Rights, and she also works with young people at North Star: Self-Directed Learning for Teens in Western Massachusetts. Her latest book is *Fighting for Their Lives: Inside the Experience of Capital Defense Attorneys.*

http://www.vanderbiltuniversitypress.com/index.php/books/523/fighting-for-their-lives

CHAPTER 6

TRUST, NOT EDUCATION

AARON FALBEL

I have had the great privilege of having known and befriended the late John Holt, the educational and social critic whose books people might remember from the 1960s and '70s, as well as the late Ivan Illich, historian, philosopher, and theologian, who was a friend of Holt's and one of the few people who really influenced Holt in the early seventies. Illich wrote books like *Deschooling Society* (1970), *Tools for Conviviality* (1973), and *Medical Nemesis* (1982). My thinking was definitely influenced by both of these people.

Holt came to question the efficacy of schooling early in his teaching career. Through keen observation and self-reflection, he saw that teaching (his own, in particular) did not necessarily produce learning, and that fear and anxiety—largely due to tests, grades, and the competitive environment of the classroom—essentially slammed on the brakes on learning. He became a central figure in the school reform movement of the time. But after encountering Ivan Illich in 1969 or 1970, he came to see that the problem wasn't merely figuring out how to reform the schools so that they were more humane or more effective, he came to question the very purpose of schooling and the idea of education itself.

6. AARON FALBEL

Education is Not the Same as Learning

Let me try to define some terms: I like to make a distinction between learning and education. Of course, many people don't make such a distinction; they use the words pretty much interchangeably. I think John Holt tried to make a distinction in several of his books. He wrote a book in 1976, called *Instead of Education*. A British journalist once asked him, "How do you define education?" This is what Holt said:

> It's not a word I personally use. . . . The word "education" is a word much used, and different people mean different things by it. But on the whole, it seems to me what most people mean by "education" has got some ideas built into it or contains certain assumptions, and one of them is that learning is an activity which is separate from the rest of life and done best of all when we are not doing anything else, and best of all where nothing else is done—learning places, places especially constructed for learning. Another assumption is that education is a designed process, in which some people do things to other people or get other people to do things which will presumably be for their own good. Education means that some A is doing something to somebody else B. (as cited in Hern, 2008, p. 61)

That's what I think education boils down to. It's a technical process, or some kind of treatment that somebody does to somebody else, presumably for their own good. The person who receives the treatment comes to believe this as well, to internalize the need for that process or that treatment and feel deprived if they don't get it or get enough of it.

TRUST, NOT EDUCATION
Learning is Natural

Learning, on the other hand, is a natural process—a biological process really, similar to breathing: we do it all the time. From the moment they are born, babies are already learning. They are good at learning, their learning does not need to be developed or improved or enhanced in any way. The notion that people need to be taught how to learn or need to go to school in order to learn how to learn—phrases we hear all the time—is preposterous and deeply insulting to babies who are prodigious learners. I don't use the word "learning" very much, because I think we get into trouble when we make such an issue out of learning, particularly when we try to control it or direct it. Why do we need to make such a fuss out of something we all do naturally?

John Holt (1981) wrote, in the introduction of *Teach Your Own*, his book about unschooling, that he wanted to get away from talking about learning. If we were in a society where everyone talked about breathing: How are you breathing today? Okay? Are you breathing better? Are you breathing well enough? We would assume that everybody was sick!

Today, with all this emphasis on learning and whether we are learning as best we can, we also assume that people are somehow impaired, that they are not able to learn and they need some type of assistance or treatment or arrangements to ensure that they are learning everything they need to learn, or are learning as well as they should be learning. I would like to get away from this way of thinking and speaking, and instead talk about activities, on doing them, on people doing things, participating in the life around them.

6. AARON FALBEL

The True Purposes of Education

Education has many functions aside from anything that has to do with learning or the welfare of children. I suspect that many of these functions have to do with the fixation that the authorities in Canada (or virtually any other country) have with having to separate the sheep from the goats, so to speak. That is, having a way to sort people into winners and losers. Most of us live in societies that are organized hierarchically, with very few good jobs or winner slots at the top and many more loser slots (bad or menial jobs) at the bottom. Society needs some mechanism, if it's shaped that way, of deciding who gets into the high places and who doesn't. Education is the way most industrial societies achieve this slot allocation. Historically, privilege had to do with inheritance or lineage, but now education does the job. Of course, we know that it does not do so in a fair or just manner. In every society where such things are measured, educational achievement correlates almost perfectly with socio-economic status. The people who already have those scarce winner slots make sure that their children are the ones who succeed in school (and who have a leg up to succeed in school) so they get into the good schools and get into those good slots.

There are exceptions where some poor kid gets into Harvard or Yale, but that's an exception. That's one in a thousand, maybe one in ten thousand, who gets to do that. Education is necessary to distribute privilege unequally. Education thus upholds a systematic injustice that our society needs in order to keep functioning smoothly. If everyone were to be winners, if everyone did all the work that schools says that they're trying to get them to do, society would fall apart because society needs winners and losers, and more losers than winners.

Most teachers believe that they are in the classroom to

provide equal educational opportunity to everyone. If they look at the results of what they actually do, they will see that they have to give a certain number of people A's, other people B's and C's and so on down the line. For if the teacher gave everyone an A, very soon the principal or supervisor would come and say, "You can't do that. Your standards must be too low. You have to be stricter and raise your standards and make sure only a few people get the A's." Here is the sorting mechanism at work. It's not equal educational opportunity. It's a way of creating a system of 16 or 22 levels (or however many levels there are) of dropouts. Each successive layer informs people where they are, where they are situated, and what their social status is in society.

Rather than being an equalizer, school is the great discriminator, the great sorting machine. Ivan Illich saw the educational process as pernicious, not only because it enforced this systematic injustice, but because it induced a form of self-inflicted discrimination. That is, you internalize the process to such an extent that you blame yourself for not having made it, for not being a successful student, for not making your way into one of the winner slots—which of course only a few people can get into, by definition.

The questions I wish to ask are: Why do we have education? Why do we have the idea of education to begin with? Why do we have to make special arrangements for learning if learning is a biological process that happens in every human being?

Education, Scarcity, and Needs

I think Illich tries to answer these questions by putting his finger on the notion of scarcity. He defines education as "learning under the assumption of scarcity." The very idea education conveys to people is that valuable learning is scarce in society. Valuable learning, in this way of thinking, is not something that happens readily. On the contrary, special arrangements must be made to impart it. If we just left it up to chance or up to the personal initiative of the learner, most people would not learn those things due to their scarcity. Education is an institutional, deliberate, arrangement whereby scarce knowledge is held. It's basically an institution that says to children, we don't trust you to learn, we need to make sure that you learn, we have to compel you to learn, coerce you to learn, and if you don't learn then it's your own fault. We gave you an opportunity, we gave you our best shot.

It's almost second nature to believe that human beings have educational needs or learning needs, indeed that they are born with learning needs. Illich created a Latin phrase to describe this type of human being: he calls it Homo educandus. You know, we speak of Homo sapiens as the species that scientists say that we are. Illich says we have evolved into a subspecies called Homo educandus, which means the human being born in need of education, in need of educational treatment. This is a fundamental belief of most people today: Just like we have a need for food and shelter, we have a need for education, and if we don't acquire it we are deeply deprived, stigmatized, and disadvantaged.

Illich calls this whole enterprise into question. He insists that we don't have educational needs, that we are natively equipped with all the resources to learn. We have sense organs, we have eyes, ears, mouths, and brains that are curious!

Anyone who has watched a two or three-year-old (or even smaller children) knows that they hunger for learning or, more accurately, they hunger to be involved in everything that is going on around them. They want to be a part of it, and are very much upset and insulted if they are not allowed. If you try to stop a baby from doing something, perhaps for safety reasons, they'll scream with rage. They get upset if they are stopped from trying to do things they see other people doing around them. This yearning to be a part of things is a powerful biological urge and it is the clearest evidence we have that we don't have "educational needs," but do have powerful learning desires that are built into the essence of our beings. Rather than being Homo educandus, we are human beings that are good at learning, are good at finding things out, are innately curious, and all we need is to be included, to have access to the world around us.

Education, Success, and Consumer Society

Many people express the concern, "if kids don't 'get' an education, they won't be successful, they won't be able to make it in society, and they will become a burden to us all." But what does "successful" mean here? Obviously, the word "successful" is a concept that refers to the type of society in which success will be achieved. Our societies are materialistic, consumer societies. I live in a society that is extremely wasteful and extremely violent, to nature, to other people, and to other cultures. I know that our way of life here in the U.S. is extremely exploitative, and that we are living on the backs of people all around the world. To be a success in this type of society might be the worst thing we could wish for our children—and for ourselves.

This whole notion of "being successful" raises a lot of red flags and question marks in my own mind. I don't have children, but if I did I would think twice about wishing them to be successful in such a society. I would much rather see them be "failures" and live what I would call a decent life, but that choice would be up to them.

Another function of schooling and education is to habituate young people to live in this type of exploitive, wasteful, violent, and consumer society. How does it do that? Education teaches the lesson that the more we consume, the better we are. That's the lesson that our society needs people to imbibe for them to be successful and obedient consumers, which is what our economy needs. The more consumption, the better. That's the lesson.

You won't find it printed in any curriculum plan. It's the form and structure of education that inculcates this message, not the content. I think the people who are starting to pay attention to the results of this ideology of consumption are horrified by its effects. We simply can't go on consuming at this rate for much longer. We have already done possibly irreparable damage as a result. The lesson that education teaches, the lesson that is reinforced by our economy—the more consumption, the better—is not only unjust, it is suicidal.

If you were to ask me, "What is the cause of all these wars and violence the U.S. has been involved in, especially in recent years?" I would say that the root cause is limitless over-consumption. It's the injustice that constitutes the U.S. (and other over-developed countries) in consuming far more than is our share. I know that in the United States we consume between 25 and 30 percent of the world's resources, whereas we comprise less than 5 percent of the world's population. That type of injustice has to be backed up by brute force. Sadly, it's education that prepares people for that level of consumption.

Ivan Illich talked about schooling as an initiation ritual for life in a consumer society. Earlier societies had different types of initiation rituals that marked the transition from childhood to adulthood. In our society, adulthood means primarily a life of consumption (having a job, earning money, buying things), so we introduce this idea early in children's experience by having them go through this ritualistic process of graded consumption that we call education. It's a lesson that is learned, I think, to people's detriment as they grow older.

Work vs. Subsistence

We are also an expert-worshiping society, so we are taught that we need to specialize in something. We need to find our line of work, whatever that is, mostly in exclusion to everything else. If we go to college, we need to declare a major. If we don't go to college, we need to find our line of work or trade, and that's what we will specialize in, perhaps for the rest of our life. This is something relatively new in human history. Most people did not live that way, did not have to find their work, their trade. I wrote an essay for the last issue of *Growing Without Schooling*, called "Questioning Work." (pp. 28-30). I mused that questioning work might be a sort of unschooling for adults. Just like school is the rat-race for children, the world of work and employment is the rat-race for adults. Earlier societies did not function this way; they were not organized in this way.

There are languages still in existence today that have no word for "work" the way we use it. I remember reading Jean Liedloff's book, *The Continuum Concept* (1975) about her experience living with the Yequana people in South America, whom she called Stone Age Indians. The Yequana lived what we would probably dismiss as primitive, but nonetheless beautiful life. They have no word for "work." Liedloff tried to describe to them what she meant by "work," but they couldn't understand it because they made no distinction in their own lives between activities that were useful and those that were not. What we call "work" is just a part of daily life, of the many tasks that needed to be done. They make no distinction between work and play or leisure; all are intermingled with the others.

Most people are unaware of how recent a concept

education is. They assume it was always around, that from time immemorial people had ways of educating their children.

Not so. The idea of education as a sphere separate from the rest of life, or disembedding it, as Illich would put it, is a relatively recent invention.

Most people participated in the subsistence of the household. They were hunters, or farmers. They had to tend the animals, gather or plant the crops. They created the clothes that they wore and built the dwellings they lived in. These were, for the most part, the activities of people. In the Middle Ages, there were some trades: stone cutters, barrel makers, shoe makers, but not everybody did that. A village needed only one or two blacksmiths. Most of the activities that people engaged in were totally separate from anything that we would call money economy. They lived a life of subsistence, and Native Americans in our continent led that type of life for millennia. As we moved toward the modern era, money acquired increasing importance in people's lives—or perhaps I should say over people's lives. Things people formerly did for themselves, they now had to purchase. People increasingly needed money, so more and more people had to specialize. This constituted a radically new way of organizing society and organizing people's lives. As specialization grew, so did education—the idea of education that, again, rides piggyback on the notion of scarcity.

A War Against Subsistence

When I think of growing without education, I think of such a society where it would be easy to learn things, easy to find activities that are worth doing for their own sake, because they are so obviously necessary. As I said, growing one's food, tending to children, making one's clothing, fetching water and fuel, building one's dwelling, etc., these are the primary activities of life that now are commodities or services to be purchased. It wasn't always this way.

Most people in the over-developed countries don't know how to grow their own food; they think food comes from a supermarket. Housing comes from construction companies. Taking care of children is purchased from a childcare provider or through the educational establishment. All these tasks are delegated or outsourced to other people who, supposedly, have professional training and this training convinces us that they can do these things better than we can. This is another concept that Illich talked about: modernity as being a war against subsistence. Namely, that those type of primary activities that people did for generations were progressively disembedded and taken away from them, and put in the hands of professionals, so that subsistence in the modern economy is extremely rare, if not impossible.

There are communities where people still know how to do these things, and I think that this is where our efforts need to be put. Not into education, but into what I call rejuvenating local culture. To rediscover what Wendell Berry (2001), one of my favourite writers, calls "the domestic arts" of living well within a place. By living well in a place, I don't mean having increased access to consumer goods. I mean actually participating in our own subsistence. That may be small: it could start with a small garden, learning to spin your own yarn, with building a small addition to your house, and so on. These are the types of things people need to rediscover how to do if we are to get away from the consumer society. How to rediscover how to live in a place, to derive sustenance from a place, to disengage from the global economy in which we find ourselves today. If they asked me for my advice, I wouldn't try to urge people to take a place within that global economy. I would encourage them to go in the opposite direction. I would try to find ways in which to embed myself in the remnants of local culture and try to nourish those remnants the best I can, so that they might be able to grow.

I think we need to ask the question, "What activities do we want to do in society?" Not, "What should people learn" but "What should we do?" Then open up those activities to people of all ages—not just children. There's another excluded group in society that we tend to shunt off into age-specific homes for their own good. I'm all in favour of re-embedding people into the life of society that's going on around them. That means we have to ask the questions, "How do we want to live in this place? How do we change the way we are living, our patterns of consumption? How do we get out of the rat-race of the consumer society for which education prepares us?"

I believe the power of stories is important. I think of a book by Helena Norberg-Hodge, *Ancient Futures* (1991) in which she describes the people who lived in Ladakh, the area of Northern India adjacent to Tibet, high up in the mountains. Until relatively recently, their culture was untouched by Western civilization, by modern society, because it was physically inaccessible. Helena Norberg-Hodge is a Swedish woman who was in Ladakh, mostly doing linguistic research, but she happened to be there exactly at the time when technology evolved to the extent that people could start to reach those high mountain villages. Little by little, Western Civilization encroached upon Ladakh. It's a sad read, because she chronicles what happens to a subsistence-oriented society that suddenly comes into contact with a market-oriented society. The Ladakhis were the happiest people she had ever met. When consumer culture arrived, this began to change.

These people lived in a subsistence culture. They had no educational needs, had no notion of the idea of work, as we understand it. By modern standards, we would call them poor—but they were happy. They had no idea that they were poor, because they had nothing to compare themselves to. They had enough to eat, they had decent shelter, they had music, entertainment, and a thriving local culture, even in that harsh climate with long, severe winters. Then all these influences started to arrive: consumer goods, television. Suddenly, they learned that they were poor, that they were deprived. Norberg-Hodge saw that people were gradually becoming dissatisfied with their way of life. They became angry, even violent with each other. The notions of competition and scarcity slowly started to make their way into Ladakhi society. It is amazing how fast this long-stable culture fell apart, once these influences entered their lives.

The Importance of Limits

The story of Ladakh teaches us an important lesson: the ability to be satisfied within relatively narrow limits, to live well while consuming as little as possible, and to develop what Ivan Illich called "the virtue of enoughness," (Illich & Sachs, 1989, Spring, p.16) that is knowing when is enough and when it is more than enough, and when is too much. This is another of the themes that pervade Ivan Illich's books: the notion of limits. Limits not only to the physical world, the ecological world, but also to the social world, and the way we live our lives.

Illich defines culture in a rather idiosyncratic way: culture is defined as those arrangements that a society puts into place to limit exchange relationships, commodity relationships, market relationships. They might say, "We can have some of that, but very little, and we will put it at the margins of society. We will not let that way take over the way we live our lives and the way we relate to each other." An intact culture prevents the tragedy of Ladakh (which may still prevail, thanks to the work of Norberg-Hodge's organization, International Society for Ecology and Culture.)

The Amish are an example of a society that still exists in North America, where there are strict limits on the lives of their members. They place limits on their use of technology; they ride around in horses and buggies; dress in very plain, handmade clothing; grow their own food for the most part; and they have a vibrant and alive culture—which may not be a culture that we find attractive. It's religious based, patriarchal, and very strict, and confining in many ways.

We don't have a true culture today in our society, we have patterns of consumerism. We have a homogenized culture where every place looks pretty much like every place else in the United States. Everywhere one sees the same stores, the same malls, the same commodities, and our freedom, which we like to parade about and put in our anthems, has been reduced pretty much to the freedom of choice between similar commodities. I think we are hemmed in by the institutions of our society. Today, people are afraid of not having enough money. That's the big risk in a consumer society. If life entails consumption, if we don't have the entity with which we need to consume (money), then we are in a bad way.

Education is a process that tries to get us, or make us, or manipulate us, or coerce us, consume knowledge, and here knowledge is akin to capital or money. (One can view educational "credits" as a type of proto-money). We are to consume knowledge, and the more we have, the better. That prepares us for other types of consumption and other types of coercion and manipulation.

Trust, Not Education

Today, of course, education is no longer unique to schooling but it happens in many areas of our society:

through the media, through advertising, through the games we play, the consumer goods that we buy, and the toys that parents buy (they always have a description of how good it's going to be for your children). Everything is educational these days. That's why I want to think not just about growing without schooling, but growing without education. After all, one can avoid school but still operate under the ethos and mindset of education.

People get confused when they hear me talk this way. Am I saying that there is no role for teaching at all in such a society? Does growing without education require that nobody shows anything to anybody anymore, nobody explains anything? That's not what I am saying. If someone asks you a question, you answer it if you know the answer. Nor am I saying that one mustn't influence people. One has to pay attention to the way one's interventions are received by the person who is asking the question or is subject to your influence. Teaching is fine as long as it's asked for, as long as the person who is being taught welcomes it. If it is not welcomed, if it's the for-your-own-good type of teaching, then, yes, I am against it.

Indeed, it is a great joy and privilege to help someone do something that he or she wants to do, when asked to help. It's when that help or that teaching is not wanted that the unequal aspects of our relationships come into play. That's where this idea of access comes in, which I mentioned earlier. We don't leave young people in a vacuum. We put within their reach those activities, those ways of life that we believe in ourselves, and then we wait for them to take advantage of those opportunities. Mostly they will. Remember those babies, eager to get into everything?

There are no guarantees, of course. When we try to guarantee an outcome, no matter how good our intentions, that's when we get into trouble. As my friend John Holt knew so well, and exemplified so well in his life, it all boils down to trust. That's what he (and Illich) believed in: trust, not education.

An audio version of this piece appears in podcast and can be found at: Falbel, A. (2005, February 2). Interview by B. Ekwa Ekoko [Podcast]. Aaron Falbel: Why "Education"? Why "Learning"? Radio Free School. Hamilton, Ontario. Retrieved from http://www.radio4all.net/index.php/program/11084

References

Berry, W. (2001). *In the presence of fear: Three essays for a changed world*. Gt. Barrington, MA: The Orion Society.

Falbel, A. (2001, November/December). Questioning work. *Growing Without Schooling, (143)*, 28-30.

Hern, M. (Ed.). (2008). *Everywhere all the time: A new deschooling reader*. Oakland, CA: AK Press.

Holt, J. (2004). *Instead of education: Ways to help people do things better*. Boulder, CO: Sentient Publications. (Original work published 1976).

Holt, J., & Farenga, P. (2003). *Teach your own: The John Holt book of homeschooling* (Revised ed.). USA: Da Capo Press. (Original work published 1981)

Illich, I. (1970). *Deschooling Society*. New York, NY: Harper & Row Publishers.

Illich, I. (1973). *Tools for Conviviality*. New York, NY: Harper & Row Publishers.

Illich, I. (1982). *Medical Nemesis: The expropriation of health*. New York, NY: Pantheon Books.

Illich, I., & Sachs, W. (1989). A critique of ecology: The virtue of enoughness. *New Perspectives Quarterly, 6*(1), 16.

Leidloff, J. (1975). *The Continuum concept: In search of happiness lost.* Toronto, ON: Penguin Books.

Norberg-Hodge, H. (1991). *Ancient futures: Lessons from Ladakh for a globalizing world.* San Francisco, CA: Sierra Club Books.

––––––––––––

Aaron Falbel considers himself extremely fortunate to have known both John Holt and Ivan Illich personally, as these men have greatly influenced his outlook on learning and society. Aaron's writings have been published in *Growing Without Schooling, Peacework, Plain Magazine, Mothering,* and elsewhere. He is currently an organic farm worker and part-time librarian in Western Massachusetts.

CHAPTER 7

A CONVERSATION ABOUT THE MAGICAL CHILD

JOSEPH CHILTON PEARCE

A great neuro-scientist, Paul Maclean, who was head of brain development research here at the National Institute of Health, came up with three needs. He calls them a trio or trinity of needs. From the moment of birth on, they are: audio-visual communication, nurturing, and play. They are all equally important, and they are all interdependent. It's interesting that play is included as the most important thing that a child could have, not only for the development of their body, but their whole neural system. Play begins almost immediately at birth.

The child catches on quickly when the adult is willing to play. Play can take place only in what Michael Mendizza and I (2003) call "the safe place" (p. 69). A child must feel secure to play. That's what audio-visual communication and nurturing is, a safe space. Given that safe space, the spontaneous reaction is to play, and to turn every activity into play.

Children, I don't think, have much connection with work. They will turn work into play, or they will play at their work; which is exactly what they should do.

In Montessori schools, they use the term "work," but if you look closely, you'll see that there is the same spontaneous freedom of movement, speech, and play. A critical part of all learning is the ability to approach it playfully. Literally, this has to do with the structure of the brain itself.

When people are in a totally safe space, feel completely secure, safe, and nurtured, the center of neurologic action shifts to the forebrain, which is the latest evolutionary development in brain structure, the structure for creating imagination, the one that will lead us to metaphoric, symbolic thinking, which underlies all of our great subjects like science, mathematics, religion, and philosophy. All those depend on metaphoric, symbolic capacities, which are developed in play, and play is the only way that this metaphoric, symbolic capacity can develop.

Play can only take place in a safe space. If the child feels at all insecure, a good part of their energy of their brain and body centers around the defensive areas, which are the sensory-motor, what we call the hind brain. Activity moves back into the more ancient animal structure, the reptilian brain, the oldest part of the brain systems. You can clearly see, with the new scanning devices, when the child is shifting from the forebrain, the highly-civilized mind, into the more ancient animal brain structures, when they are concerned about their safety.

Play, in the first seven years, develops this creative forebrain, which sets us beyond all the animals. The most important form of play arises from storytelling, after about the first year of life. Up until then, it's any repeated interaction between the infant and the parent. For example, hiding, peek-a-boo, little surprise movements, repeated over and over. The child immediately interprets this as play and goes into a state of hilarious delight. They do this from very early on. After about a year, when they have their language pretty much under control, storytelling is a primary impetus to play, because, having been told a story, they create internal imagery in keeping with the story, that activity brings about neural development. They want to play that inner image out in the world. That's when you get metaphoric and symbolic play.

A child will pick up a spool of thread, and that will become an automobile, or a match box will become a bed, or a chest of drawers: where one object can stand for another. That's the basis of metaphoric thinking for the rest of our lives. It is the neural foundations for metaphoric symbol, so when they begin to see that the little twist of cloth around a clothespin gives them a doll to play with—seeing one object in another—it enables them to look at numbers and alphabets and see what they stand for, what they mean. Imagination is the key to all higher human intelligence, and imagination is developed only in play. No one has ever found a culture that does not have a whole repertoire of stories to tell the children in the first seven years. They are surprisingly similar, the cultural stories, and they are to develop this capacity of metaphoric, symbolic thinking.

Peers

Generally, children's models are at the next level of age. The five-year-old will be fascinated by the seven-year-old. They want to see how they should behave, what to think and so on. We have a model of imitative play. I think a profound error is made, in thinking that the young child must be given a great deal of social interaction. Social interaction really unfolds with the huge shift that takes place in development around six and seven. By then, they need and look for some kind of social interaction. From about seven to eleven, where there is another big shift in the neural structure, one dear friend is all it takes. Children will have very passionate close friends at that point. They don't need a whole bunch of children. Certainly, the early child doesn't.

When two early children, say a four- and a five-year-old together in a room, they'll look like they are playing, but they are simply sharing the same stage. They are each playing out their entirely private world. They don't need a lot of social interaction. They do need interaction with adults, and some older children but not a great deal. We make this error in thinking that we have got to fill the child, from early years up with all kinds of busy social interaction, and it's just not the case.

We do well to remember Burton White, one of Harvard's greatest. In 1975, he published a book, *The First Three Years of Life*, and he wrote of the critical need, in the early years, of giving the child vast periods to themselves. He said there was a study of children in literate societies. There were about 3% of the children that he considered really brilliant and happy, who had spent an enormous amount of time in their early childhood in blank, open-eyed staring, doing nothing at all. If you look in their eyes, in these periods of blank, open-eyed stares, there's no one at home! That's hard for parents who are inclined to say "Do something!" But, this is a critical part of the balance of their whole inner life with the outer world.

Jean Piaget spoke of "the child of the dream," that child from three or four up to about seven—a beautiful term really, "the child of the dream"—one foot is in the dream-like world of the pre–conceptual and the other is in the physical world. They have to be allowed to spend lots of time in both. Rudolf Steiner spoke of the child in the ethereal world in that period. If you make them attend to the physical world too soon, you'll have an unbalanced and disturbed child.

We all need time of quiet solitude with ourselves and, given that, children's development is much, much better. When they need interaction with other children, they'll make that clear. You have to honour where the child is at each stage of their development. Out with the business of slapping them in a desk at school and demanding hours of abstract thinking from them. It's a tragedy at that stage.

That doesn't mean that some children don't spontaneously read just from being read stories. I had two of my children who were spontaneously reading by the time they were four. Why? Because their mother had read to them from the moment they were born. They wanted to read that magical world.

The great Hans G. Furth, the Austrian child psychologist, said that the primary reason for spontaneous reading in children is to keep that inner world going, around which the inner response to images is formed. The idea of teaching them to read and write at that age doesn't work. Maria Montessori was horrified when people used the term "teaching" her three-, four-, five-year-olds. Paraphrasing Montessori, she said, "We don't teach them at all. We give them a loving, nurturing environment and their absorbent mind does what it wants to, what is suitable. People were beginning to take her "techniques" for reading and writing and applying them in our school system. Of course, they don't have the same results at all.

Taking your cues from your child is a critically important thing. If we are thinking more of "what needs is the child expressing?" and picking up from the cues that they are expressing, and following through with them, then learning will take place. If we are looking at the child with the idea of imprinting them with our notions of what they should be doing at that point, we are then looking at them through a grid of what we think our cultural needs are, rather than the signals being sent by the child. When you take your cues from the child they nearly always indicate the areas of interest, the areas they are opened to, and ready to absorb.

David Albert's book on homeschooling, *And the Skylark Sings with Me* (1999), is a remarkable work because he points out that it was his real education. He had a Ph.D., when he started, but said his learning from trying to stay one jump ahead of that child was the most exciting and exhilarating and difficult job he'd ever undertaken, because they are moving at lightening speed when they are getting their cues met.

I think Jean Leidloff's book, *The Continuum Concept* (1975) is the greatest model we'll ever find. She speaks of how these little children, the Uquana in South America, want to take part in every social activity practically from birth. They just want to take part in it, to get a rough idea of the activity, and the parents always let them. If mama is stirring something, she lets them stir. They are not going to keep at it for very long. They want to rough-in the pattern of that kind of activity in their minds. They want to stick their finger in everything going on, but they don't necessarily have to be kept at the task in that early period.

The Uquana let children follow their own interest and inclination. As the children grow older, they want to complete tasks to please their parents, to please and take part in their society. I remember her saying that, among the Uquana, they might say to a child, "get some wood for a fire," and the child always does it. The people have no word for disobedience. They have no word for obey. The adults assumed that the child wants to take part in any activity they were capable of, which they always do.

Here, we have people assigning their children work and then this great nagging that they must complete the task!

A very important item about children in the social ages— eight, nine, and ten—is to earn some money, which is a thrilling thing for them. We used to shovel someone's side walk, get a nickel for it, and we were thrilled. Any kind of activity that we could get paid for, particularly from a neighbour and not our parents, we loved. Later, teens need meaningful employment, so to have a newspaper route, or drugstore job after school, is not bad at all. It gives them a feeling of competence, of security that they can take their place out in the world, and that they can earn money. The age that the child is determines the nature and the character of the work that they can do.

I have been asked what do we do when, for example, we have three children, five, six and eight, and we try to get them to help, take a turn with the dishes, say, and there is fussing. We all go through that. I have had four children, bringing them up alone because their mother died, and the way I solved that problem was to turn it into play. You'll find if they are drying the dishes, they will start flicking each other with the towel. They'll convert the work into play, but they will get the job done. You have to have a lot of patience and tolerance with them, and not turn it into painful labour that they are going to be censored for if they don't do it a certain way.

Treat the work as a joint venture, a playful working at something. I really think it's a mediated thing. Doing it with them, acting as a role model for how to do it right, and then easing your hands off and letting them take over. When it's approached with the word "work" it is kind of dangerous. Children tend to live out our intentions. When our underlying intentions are that they must learn to do this in order to mind, behave, and obey, they sense that. That's not play, and they resent it. They'll object to it, drag their feet and balk. When your underlying intention is to enjoy the work as a joyful venture for the family, they will pick up your intention and live it out. Jean Leidloff makes this clear, how the underlying intention with which we approach our children can be seen in the attitude of the child.

Let me say one more thing about our teenagers. We have, as a nation here in the USA, for a long time regarded teenagers as trouble. A bad, bulky, troublesome age. The underlying intent of our approach to them is one of expecting trouble. They will act that out without even being aware it is what they are doing. It's the looped effects between parent and child, and between society and child.

If that underlying intent is to maintain the interaction of play with them, a lot can be done. I don't think the concept of minding, that they must learn to mind, should ever enter into it. Minding is cultural conformity. We are insisting that they conform to a culture's behavioural pattern, lest we as parents be censored for their failure. They pick up that fear, that their parents will be censored if the child doesn't behave in a certain way. There is no love and play and nurturing in that fear.

One quick thing about role models. Greenfield and Tronick, part of Jerome Bruner's team of child psychologists at Harvard University, years ago came up with something that we've since overlooked. They called it the cycle of competence, which underlies all learning (1973). The cycle of competence is that first the child must have a rough overall idea of what a new activity is. They must rough-in this basic framework for any new activity.

Then, the brain itself will be cued toward filling that empty category in with material. They will attend to all the parts and bits of information that might help with this roughed-in idea that they have seen from a role model. Once they have filled that in, through their own exploration, they'll want to practice the completed pattern over and over.

From that comes the ability to transfer. When you can transfer that particular kind of activity over to other roughly-similar activities, which is the third and final stage of learning.

That first stage of learning, in which we rough-in frame of reference for the learning, comes from role models. Children can't become who we tell them to become, they become who we are, and so it behoves us to be what we want our child to become. We must be the models we want them to be. This is about resonance. The way the brain seems to work is through resonance. It has to be shown a resonant source of that finished product to initiate its own learning.

The tragedy of school is that the child's mind/brain will not learn incrementally. We think that in school each day we can give them another bit of information about this subject, in mathematics and so on, add it all together at the end of the year and they have this subject under their hats. The brain doesn't work that way. Even in mathematics, something so abstract as that, they must be given an overall idea of each one of those processes to understand.

To rough it in makes a ready pattern in a neural field in the brain, ready to receive that kind of information, and learning takes place. Rudolf Steiner understood this particularly well. Waldorf school curricula is really applicable at home, and they are beginning to adapt Waldorf programs for homeschooling.

Being the best model you can be for your child is critically important. The child will become who we are, not what we tell them to be, and that really ought to scare the bejeebers out of us. You can't act one way and then think you can turn around and have them behave in a different way. None of us became who our parents demanded or expected us to be. We became some variation of them. It is also a tremendous opportunity because each of us can break the vicious cycle that's been handed down.

The parent's modeling is critically important, but they are going to hit the world out there, and they are going to have to make adaptations to it as well. I wouldn't worry about that. I've heard of people who will not send their children to Waldorf or Montessori school because they're child is happy there. They say, "It's a jungle out there, we've got to toughen them up ready to meet that jungle." And I say, "That's the equivalent of saying that it's a mad world out there and you must drive your child mad in order to live in it." I say, "The strongest, greatest thing you can do for your child to deal with the mad world is to be absolutely whole, and sane."

An audio version of this piece appears in podcast and can be found at:

Pearce, J.C.(2004, July 7). Interview by B. Ekwa Ekoko [Podcast]. The Magical Child: Conversation with Joseph Chilton Pearce, Radio Free School. Hamilton, Ontario.

Retrieved from http://www.radio4all.net/index.php/program/9546

References

Albert, D. (1999). *And the skylark sings with me: Adventures in homeschooling and community-based education.* Gabriola Island, BC: New Society Publishers.

Bruner, J.S. (1973). *The relevance of education.* USA W. W. Norton & Company inc.

Leidloff, J. (1975). *The Continuum Concept: In search of happiness lost.* Toronto, ON: Penguin Books.

Mendizza, M., Pearce, J. C. (2003). *Magical parent magical child: The art of joyful parenting.* Berkley, California: North Atlantic Books.

White, B. (1975). *The first three years of life.* New York, NY: Prentice-Hall Publications.

_____

7. JOSEPH CHILTON PEARCE

World-renowned thinker, author, and advocate of evolutionary child-rearing practices, Pearce has expertise that spans a broad range of disciplines: psychology, anthropology, biology, and physics. He has been a seminal figure in the study of human consciousness and child development for over a quarter century. His greatest publishing success was the national bestseller, *Magical Child*, in which he delineated an exhaustive and visionary approach to child rearing, especially focused on support for the nonviolent birthing approach revived by LeBoyer, Lamaze, and Odent, and popularized by Sondra Ray. For over thirty years Pearce has written and lectured internationally on human development and the changing needs of children. He has recently completed *The Biology of Transcendence,* which explores the biological foundation for what we think of as spiritual development. He was a faculty member on child development at the Jung Institute in Switzerland. More recently, he has become a certified HeartMath trainer, further developing his already extensive insights into the heart-brain connection. This connection between the heart and brain is not merely neurological and autonomic, or romantic and metaphoric—it is central to our full development and total health. He is also a member of the Scientific Advisory Board of the Institute of HeartMath, and a faculty member at the Omega Institute.

http://www.enlightennext.org/magazine/bios/joseph-chilton-pearce.asp

CHAPTER 8

HOLD ONTO YOUR KIDS

GORDON NEUFELD

Attachment—holding on to your kids, collecting your kids—
and at the same time allowing the kids to stretch their wings,
fit together very, very beautifully. If you think of it, the way
you enable somebody to let go is that you hold on. Our job is
to do the holding on. The idea is that you create a home base
for them where they are secure, where they are attached,
where their connection is not at stake. Then they can venture
forth to become their own persons. The two go together
hand-in-hand.

Our problem is that we think our job as parents is to help
them let go, to push them away, to foster independence. Our
job is not to work at that, but rather to be able to provide for
their dependency needs: their needs for contact, connection,
closeness, love, affection, and mattering. These are what we
need to nurture.

The research is unequivocal on this, in a very concrete
way: Those parents who pick up their toddlers generously
have toddlers who want to stand on their own two feet.
Those parents who, in a sense, say to their toddlers, "You
can walk by yourself, you don't need me to pick you up, I
don't want to do anything for you that you could or should
do by yourself," have children who are absolutely
preoccupied with being picked up, and who don't want to
walk on their own two feet.

As a young psychologist (and I've been in this field for

thirty-five years; I have five children of my own, and three grandchildren), I used to focus on the same thing: independence. I eventually realized it was a huge mistake. I used to talk about how parents need to let go. That's very rarely the problem. It's only the problem when parents are taking their own attachment needs to their children. The reality is that we need to assume we are the answer to their needs for contact and closeness, love and affection, then they can become their own persons without losing that connection with us.

One frustrating question that many homeschoolers get asked ask is, "Are your kids getting socialized?" Even when it is clear that, really, the kids are meeting with all kinds of folk.

My thought on this is that even if they didn't meet with many others, this assumption that they need to, is really a misunderstanding of how development occurs. The most important issue—relating with others, and being socially integrated—is to be able to treat another person as a separate being, with their own boundaries, their own thoughts and values, their own decisions. You can't do that unless you become a separate person yourself. So the question becomes, "How do individuals grow up to become their own persons?"

The answer is very clear: in the same way as it was in the womb. In order to become viable, as a separate human being physically, you need to be thoroughly attached to your mother through the umbilical cord. When you are thoroughly attached, you receive the nurturance you need so that you can become viable—you can become a separate person. The same thing is true psychologically: The more connected a child is to the parent, believing that nothing can come between them and the love of their parents, the more free they are to become their own persons with their own boundaries, and the more they spontaneously come to relate to others as separate human beings.

It's the opposite of what people think: the womb for socialization is actually a very, very strong attachment to those responsible for the child. When you look at it this way, it becomes apparent that homeschooling is not only the best bet for the child, but for society as well, and the research bears this out. One piece of research, for instance, concludes that those children who prefer to be with their parents at age eight, nine, and ten years of age are the ones who show evidence of more psychological maturity, and who are also more likely to get along with others in the true meaning of that word: togetherness without loss of separateness. Homeschooled children will tend to be the favoured among some of the Ivy League universities, not only because they are more mature and independent, ironically, but because they are more socially sensitive. This is the opposite of what people assume!

In my book, *Hold Onto Your Kids* (2005), I write about creating that attachment village. The question becomes, "How to develop a relationship?" The main thing is, first, to assume responsibility for the connection, and, second, to nurture the need for contact and closeness. We need to remember that the relationship is the most important factor in the parenting equation, not behaviour. If we remember that, and our children fall deeply into attachment with us, including giving us their hearts, wanting to matter to us, sharing all that is in their hearts with us, their secrets, that sense of closeness is what makes them easier to parent.

We are making huge mistakes in parenting today. The prevailing method of discipline is to use the relationship against the child, for example, the time-out. When children misbehave, we are saying to them, in effect, "Your behaviour is more important than the relationship, you can't count on me to hold on to you when you misbehave, you're in charge of the relationship, of preserving the contact and closeness." This deeply wounds children, and provokes instincts to detach from us rather than attach to us.

Another mistake we make in parenting is that we use what children care about against them. Imagine, if we ever did that with our spouses! We euphemize this as logical consequences, as natural consequences, but we are doing this because when children are not strongly attached to us, they don't have a natural desire to be good for us. As soon as we lose that motivation in them, we look for something to be able to bring them into line: we look to the outside for something they care about, and we use that against them. This makes children not to want to be dependent upon us.

We need our children to depend upon us. That's what attachment is. We need them to look to us for the answer, for a sense of love and connection, for assistance and guidance and cues. The whole purpose of attachment is dependence. Dependence has become a dirty word, and we are doing things to harm that in our children.

We get ourselves completely out of perspective. Children must be in right relationships with their parents in order for everything to work. We put behaviour before the relationship, we give cues about what it is we don't like, but we forget that it is far more important that we give the cues that we like them, and that we like them despite the fact that we may not like what they do.

The most fundamental need in all of us is to have the invitation to exist in somebody's presence. That's true for us as adults. We want to know that we matter to somebody, that they want to be with us. We want to know that our heart is in safe keeping, that they won't wound us. Children need to know this from their parents. They need to see that twinkle in the eye, to hear that warmth in the voice. They need that fundamental invitation to exist in our presence and to know that nothing—nothing they do or can say—could sever that connection.

If children feel that secure, if we have their hearts, (and we need their hearts, even if they are adolescents), then we have enough natural power to be able to do our job, because we have their desire to be good for us, to please us, to measure up to our expectations. When we have that, we have all we need to parent. It needn't be contrived. It needn't be manipulative.

Sometimes we confuse demands with needs, but this is largely because of child-led parenting. We take the cues from our children in terms of what they demand instead of assuming that we are their best bet, and that what they need is love, affection, a sense of significance, to be known, and so on. If we meet their needs, they are far less demanding, but if you don't meet the needs of a child they become very demanding. You often hear parents say, "Don't give heed to him, he is only going for attention." Well, first of all, what else is there to go for? It's fundamental that children would want the attention of those that they are in attachment with. Second, why would we ever withhold it? It's like saying to somebody, "Oh don't feed him, all he wants is food. . . ."

An audio version of this piece appears in podcast and can be found at:

Neufeld, G. (2005, October 26). Interview by B. Ekwa Ekoko [Podcast]. Hold on to Your Kids, plus Halloween Show and Crazy Show, Radio Free School. Hamilton, Ontario.

Retrieved from http://www.radio4all.net/index.php/program/14769

References

Neufeld, G. (2005). *Hold on to your kids: Why parents need to matter more*. Toronto, ON: Random House Digital Inc.

———————

Dr. Gordon Neufeld is a Vancouver-based developmental psychologist with over 40 years of experience with children and youth and those responsible for them. A foremost authority on child development, Dr. Neufeld is an international speaker, a bestselling author *(Hold On To Your Kids)* and a leading interpreter of the developmental paradigm. Dr. Neufeld has a widespread reputation for making sense of complex problems and for opening doors for change. While formerly involved in university teaching and private practice, he now devotes his time to teaching and training others, including educators and helping professionals. His Neufeld Institute is now a world-wide charitable organization devoted to applying developmental science to the task of raising children. Dr. Neufeld appears regularly on radio and television. He is a father of five and a grandfather of three.

http://neufeldinstitute.com/about/gordon

CHAPTER 9

THE PRICE OF PRAISE

NAOMI ALDORT

Q: Some children seem to study more, and even behave better, when praised. Yet, I have read your article in Mothering Magazine about the harm of praise. Parents say that their children do achieve more with praise, and don't do much without it. What do you suggest to do to nurture the child's engagement instead of praise?

There is nothing to do "instead" of praise. Words that intend to make the child feel and do what we want are manipulative, and carry the same price as other coercions: loss of intrinsic motivation, loss of self-trust, damaged parent-child relationship, lowered self-esteem, dependency, insecurity, disinterest, getting by with as little as possible, and more. This does not imply that we become indifferent. On the contrary, when free of the intent to impact the child's actions or behaviour, a parent can generously express her appreciation and joy with her child.

Positive feelings and thoughts about a child or his actions can be expressed in four ways: validation (empathy); unconditional appreciation; gratitude; and feedback, when requested. None of these include praise-as-evaluation. It is not about good or bad, nice or ugly, but about using the opportunity of a child's self-satisfaction to be part of his joy, to appreciate, love or respond to his need for feedback. In this part on praise, I will address the way to express feelings of joy and appreciation of your child: validating his feelings of self-satisfaction.

A child wants to know that we are aware of his success, and he wants to have a shared experience of his joy with us. When you praise with the intention to make an impact on your child's feelings or actions, you are manoeuvring his emotions, not relating to him. To connect with your son, while appreciating him, you need to empathize with his expressed feelings, rather than try to manufacture feelings in him.

Cheering and evaluating a child can be confusing in variety of ways. A child's yearning to please her parents is so potent that she can be easily swayed away from her own path, in her quest to live up to expectations. Her own sense may be far from your words, so she may feel disappointed in her creation, embarrassed about her behaviour, resentful that she has to do something, or puzzled by the undue fuss, and then doubt her own ability to know herself. A father related to me his memory of sitting on the top of a big slide, contemplating coming down. He sat there for a while and then turned on his belly, feet first. The second he took off his parents cheered and clapped. He was still serious when he arrived at the bottom, but not anymore due to contemplation but because he concluded that something was seriously wrong with him or else his parents wouldn't consider it a big deal that he could go down a slide. This conclusion limited him as an adult in many ways.

The question is, "What could this man's parents have done to express their appreciation without contradicting his inner experience?" They could have validated the feeling that was already there, contemplation. After he made it down, they could have waited for him to express his self-satisfaction, and if he did, they could have then joined his joyful expression without exaggerating or dramatizing it. Maybe he would have laughed with delight, and they would then laugh with him. Maybe he would have said, with a grin on his face, "Did you see me coming down so fast?" and they could have smiled and said, "Yes, I saw you sliding fast all the way." They can ask, "Are you feeling excited?" And yes, if he didn't express anything, it would have been best to say nothing. Later they can ask him how he enjoyed himself.

If your son stops studying when you don't praise him, he is evidently not interested. You may think that praise helps a child's self-esteem because he appears joyous. Yet, he is not happy, but only relieved that he has again succeeded to get approval. He is becoming skilful, not at studying, but at living inauthentically.

There is no difference between the common kind of praise (evaluation) and punishment, in terms of being methods of manipulation. The fear of not getting the approval is just as intense as the fear of punishment. As with any manipulation method, the child does things for the wrong reason: to get the praise or avoid its absence. The only "benefit" is to the adult who gains temporary control over the child. It is temporary because, being inauthentic, the action or behaviour can only exist as long as the approval is dished out.

When your child expresses his joy with himself or his creation, you can empathize. You do so with words that convey your feelings, without evaluation. You don't try to generate a feeling in your child, but to reflect his joy and join his victory. For example, if your child expresses joy in his artwork you don't evaluate the picture, but mirror the feeling that is already there, with a smile or with words. "Are you excited about your picture? Would you like to hang it on the wall?" You can also express your feelings freely, "When I look at it I feel calm."

If your child is already conditioned to look for your evaluation and asks, "Is it good Dad?" you can mirror his need for your approval, "Are you feeling doubtful and do you need to know that your art is beautiful?" and you can add, "When you ask me to tell you if I like it, I feel concerned because I need to know that you can be pleased with yourself on your own." The weaning process can include open discussions on the topic.

When instructed, "look at me," or "listen to my story," simply follow the instructions. After all, you were not asked to evaluate, nor to pump good feelings. Look, listen, and give attention. Children know what they want and they are assertive by nature (which parents often complain about).

Even when your child chooses freely to study or to develop a skill, you need not use praise to support him in his endeavour. When sensing our investment in his path, a child may lose his own passion for it. More than once I empathized with parents whose child stopped his art, sport, or music after receiving even one dramatic praise from the adults around him.

Using praise to modify behaviour means that the child is not choosing to do what we wish, but only acting to please us while her needs are not being met. Such manipulation builds walls between people, regardless of the method. Needing approval is a human quality that can benefit us all when it is not used as a tool to direct the actions of another, but as a way to connect with each other. Do not attempt to create a feeling or a behaviour in another human being. Instead, celebrate the way he is by reflecting the feelings that are already there.

Q: I understand your guidance not to praise the child's achievements, and to validate his expressed self-appreciation instead. However, what about praising when he helps, or what about giving positive feedback when a child is practicing music or doing something else well?

We want to let a child know that we appreciate his help,

and we wish to give useful feedback when he practices music, sports, dance, and so on. Praise is an evaluation, so it misses these intentions. Anytime we give our opinion or judgment (no matter how great) on the behaviour or accomplishment of another, we appear as though we are one up—which is the reason it is perceived as patronizing. Such praise is likely to elicit annoyance, shoulder shrugs, or rolled eyes because it does not meet the need of the child for respect and equality. If such praise is accepted, it can lead to dependency and insecurity.

When Your Child Serves Your Needs

A mother told me about her twelve-year-old son who one day, on his own, mowed the lawn. She praised him, "How wonderful, you are becoming helpful and it looks so nice." Three months later, she reported that he hasn't helped since, even though they have done a lot of yard work. After the session with me, she empathized with her son and said, "You haven't participated in our yard work since you mowed the lawn. Are you feeling thwarted because you wish to help out of your own free will?"

"I don't want to get grades for my work," he responded.

"Do you need respect and autonomy?" she asked.

"Yes," the boy answered, "when you praise me I know that you are trying to make me do it again, that just kills it for me."

When a child serves your needs, she does not want evaluation; she wishes to know that it served you, and how you feel about it. The relevant response to the service is gratitude. Saying "thank you" may be enough for minor help, but not for an involved or lengthy action. You can generate a greater sense of appreciation by sharing your feelings, and acknowledging what needs of yours were met. For example, to a child who surprised you with dinner made, you can say, "I feel such relief, now I will be able to enjoy dinner and we will still be on time for the party. Thank you so much."

In a similar way, children want to know that your needs were met when they are being considerate. Praise words like, "You were so nice to stay quiet while I slept," provide evaluation, not gratitude. What the children want to know is: did you benefit from their effort? How are you feeling about it? In the case of your afternoon nap you can say, "I feel refreshed and am grateful that it was quiet in the house. Thank you."

Giving Feedback

Feedback consists of facts, not value judgments. It is not about good or bad, but about specific details. Saying, "That was good," tells a student very little because she has no way of assessing what caused the "goodness" or how to improve her performance. Yet, providing feedback does not have to be dry; your validation of the child's self-satisfaction, as well as your feelings, can be expressed in connection with feedback. Expressing feelings can be the actual feedback, when the child asks you to tell her how her creation or performance impacts your emotions.

As a parent, give feedback only when you are asked to, and only precisely what you have been asked. Adding a "lesson" will, most likely, generate annoyance, as it is not respectful. If your child does not know yet to request feedback and he asks you, "Was it good Dad?" you can acknowledge, "I feel confused because I don't know what you wish to hear." Ask for direction, "Can you tell me precisely what you need? Would you like me to tell you if your legs were straight?" "Shall I time your run?" "Would you like me to tell you if any notes are out of tune?"

Once you receive a precise instruction, you can provide

feedback. To a dancer, "Yes, your legs where straight twice and the back one was bent on the third leap." To a cellist, who asks if his bow changes are smooth, "They were smooth on the C- and G-strings and stiff on the D- and A-strings." If instructed to report your feelings, do not use value words, only feelings: "When I look at the painting, I feel absorbed."

The relationship with a teacher is different in only one detail: the teacher need not wait for the student to ask for a feedback. By coming to the lesson, the child has declared his desire to get feedback and instruction. At the end of a productive lesson, a teacher can express general appreciation because it is naturally-connected to the specifics that occurred in the lesson. She can say, "I see a great improvement in the quality of your sound," or, "I have enjoyed today's practice. You are becoming a fine tennis player."

While you may feel overwhelmed, and wishing that you could be more spontaneous, realize that what feels to you like your "real self" is more likely a set of habits. While changing such habits, the intention of the heart is by far more important than the perfect wording. You can flunk the "vocabulary" test and throw in a few words of praise, which will get lubricated by the vital connection you create.

Replacing praise with validation, gratitude, and feedback is bound to generate autonomy for your child and a sense of ease for you. The child's sense of worth must not depend on her achievements, service, or behaviour. In the next section, I will elaborate on creating a context of love and appreciation—unconditionally.

Unconditional Love and Appreciation

What about my own authentic need to delight in my child, and how else can I nurture his self-esteem?
We need not hold our awe inside. Appreciation and love (not

praise, which is evaluation), can be shared abundantly. Ask yourself what touches you more, when someone says to you, "You are great," or when she says, "I feel inspired by your words." It is the emotional impact we make on the people we love that matters to us the most. Express your love and appreciation unconditionally when one-on-one with your child, or, when a child shows a need for recognition in her worth (often through disturbing behaviour).

Use those precious moments when you feel a deep bond. Share whatever is present and real for you at the moment: a smile, a hug, an action, and/or words. Instead of vague expressions of praise, share how you feel and how her presence inspires you. While taking a nature walk together you can say, "I feel joyful walking with you. Your interest in nature inspires me." While helping your child wash his hair, "I love washing your hair, I feel so close to you and that is so important to me." Giving your full attention is one of the loudest ways to express love, and recognition of your child's importance in your life. Do so by listening, watching and serving her with joy (rather than annoyance).

When you don't mean it, don't say it. Finishing a phone call with a mechanical, "I love you," or "You are great," lacks respect and drains the meaning out of these words. If your child rolls her eyes or seems annoyed when you say something wonderful about her, you are probably not respectful of her preferences (not here Mom, or, not now) or, you are dishing out praise instead of sharing your feelings.

It is when children behave in ways that are difficult for us that they need our love and adoration the most. When they express their needs in desperate ways, we may feel angry or bewildered. Sensing our distress, a child may fear that we don't love him and his despair escalates. Therefore, when your child expresses herself in ways that stimulate your own "bad" behaviour, you have the opportunity to choose between fear and love. Being afraid that your compassion will "condition" your child to behave badly, you might stop your love and miss the opportunity to provide for her, and to resonate with her magnificence. A child who acts out-of-control needs assistance, it is as though she is drowning. When you offer her the rope to pull her out of the water with empathy, love, appreciation and care, she will rise out wet, but inspired by her own magnificence.

I recall when my children and a couple of friends were having a ball in the bedroom jumping on the bed and laughing. Every now and then I heard screaming. Suddenly the door opened and out came one of my children. He walked over to me: "I disturbed," he started hesitantly, "they said that if I disturb five times I will have to leave the room." I opened my arms and he climbed into my lap. "I disturbed five times," he continued. I kissed and hugged him. I said, "You wanted to stay and play but you couldn't help yourself?" He nodded. "I know how hard it can be to control yourself," I empathized. "I know," he said. I hugged and kissed him again. After giving him more empathy he became quiet and I said, "When you tell me what you did, I feel inspired by your honesty." His large eyes shone. I went on, "Sitting together, I feel so connected to you, happy to be with you, I love everything about the way you are." "Even when I disturb?" He asked, "Yes," I responded with a smile. "I love you because you are you." He looked at me and said, "Ah." He stayed with me for a short while drinking my unconditional appreciation and love. Then he got up and walked over to play by himself. He looked content and peaceful.

Some parents would wonder if, by treating a child so lovingly after he misbehaved, I don't reinforce the bad behaviour. However, there is no "bad" behaviour in the child, only in our judgmental thoughts. A child does what she does in order to meet her own needs. When we validate her feelings, find out what her needs are, and express our appreciation and love unconditionally, she thrives because she experiences that we care and that she is worthy and loved simply for being herself. In the process, the child learns compassion. She learns to recognize the goodness in herself and in others. She learns to look for the unmet needs instead of pointing what's wrong. She learns the taste of feeling deep connection and love, unconditionally.

Words of appreciation, as in the above example, have no evaluation to live up to or to feel confused by. If I said, "You are wonderful," my son may have doubted my sincerity and experienced me as vague or patronizing. Instead, I expressed my feelings of appreciation as related to the moment. It is not about telling the child "you are this or that," but about sharing how I feel in response to a specific experience of him. My son, in response, seemed to have felt confident in my love and in knowing that his value in my eyes has not changed. He may have then experienced himself in high esteem, not because I said so (which I didn't) but because being connected can shed doubts in one's worth.

We don't water a flower if it will bloom, we water it so it will bloom. Love is the water of the human soul. One of the many ways love shows up for the child is through the experience of knowing that his life matters. To fulfill this need, we must express love and appreciation unconditionally. We love the child because she is herself, and for no other reason.

References

Aldort, N. (2006). *Raising our children, raising ourselves: Transforming parent-child relationships from reaction and struggle to freedom, power and joy.* Bothell. WA. Book Publishers Network.

———————————

Naomi Aldort is the author of *Raising Our Children, Raising Ourselves* (2006). Parents from around the globe seek Aldort's advice by phone, in person and through her workshops, teleclasses, by reading her book and by listening to her CDs/MP3. She is an engaging public speaker who has lectured in conferences, colleges, and private events. Her advice columns and interviews appear in parenting, homeschooling, and other parenting magazines worldwide in English and other languages.

Naomi is married and the mother of three young people who have never been to school and are flourishing. You can see and hear two of Naomi's sons: www.OliverAldort.com and www.LennonAldort.com.

http://naomialdort.com/biography.html

CHAPTER 10

THE WORDS WE USE:

LIVING AS IF SCHOOL DOESN'T EXIST

WENDY PRIESNITZ

Schools sort, slot, categorize, package, and label. They teach students that those activities are important. Most of us learned the lesson well, even those of us who have rejected schooling for ourselves or our children carry those remnants with us.

However, few people fit as neatly into categories as our grade-four teachers would have liked. I'm no exception, and perhaps that is why I have long refused to label myself—especially with words ending in "ism" and "ist." Nevertheless, categories and the words used to distinguish them from each other, are convenient if we are going to discuss ideas.

As someone whose mission has long been to help create social change, I like discussing ideas. I also know that words are extremely powerful and can either help or hinder change. Since education and parenting are emotionally and politically-charged, and change involves the challenging of some very deeply-held assumptions and beliefs about children and their place in the world, I like to choose my words carefully.

There are many words used in reference to education without school, including, but not limited to the following: homeschooling, deschooling, home-based learning, home-

based education, self-directed learning, child-led education,
autonomous learning, natural learning, autodidacticism, free-
range learning, life learning, and unschooling.

The generic term is "homeschooling." For the first
decade or so of the modern homeschooling movement, that
word worked fine, since the few thousand of us living that
way shared a general understanding that we were
experimenting with something that was as far away from the
school model as possible. However, as the movement has
grown, the number of approaches used by families has
grown too. Now, the word "homeschooling" has come to be
identified with the parent-driven, school-at-home, end of the
spectrum. It no longer accurately describes a curiosity-based,
learner-driven, self-managing style of education, which uses
life and the world as its resources, and that doesn't look at
all like school.

Naming Learning Without School

Since school is such a part of our culture, it initially made
sense to describe a rejection of school (whatever one's
motivation) in terms of school. The word "deschooling" was
used in the late 1960s by author Ivan Illich, the author of
Deschooling Society (1970) to help people realize that
school is not the best way for people to learn, and to describe
the process of removing school from people's lives. It
remains a useful word for that process. Those of us who are
already living and parenting without school are at the
forefront of deschooling society.

The word "unschooling" has been used by many people
to describe what life looks like after deschooling happens. It
was coined in the late 1970s by educational reformer and
author, John Holt, to describe the learner-directed, trusting,
and respectful type of education (and attitude towards

children) that he championed. He said, at the time, that the word was inspired by a popular commercial for the soft drink 7Up, whose ad agency was differentiating it from the pack by describing it as unconventional, hence the UnCola. Unschooling was a useful and sometimes in-your-face challenging play on words that helped to differentiate not-school-at-home from school-at-home. In recent years, some people have begun to preface "unschooling" with words like "radical" and "whole-life" to further identify families who extend the trust in and respect for children beyond education and into their whole lives.

We are now seeing the next step toward a world without school. Web-based information and the devices to access it have become widely available, allowing learners to bypass schools altogether, even if they don't consider themselves to be "unschoolers" or "homeschoolers," or have never even heard the terms before. Nevertheless, the concepts of learning and schooling are still synonymous for most people. Most have yet to leave behind the belief that one gets (or is given) an education through attendance at school, and that "unschooled" therefore means "uneducated."

Moving Beyond School

So this is a good time to move beyond any terminology that involves the word "school." If we truly are living as if school doesn't exist, we can stop describing ourselves in school terms! We can de-couple learning—and the life we're living with our families—from the institution of school. When we use words like "unschooling," we are reacting to school, rather than leaving it behind as the short-term social experiment it was. I believe we will help society to move beyond narrow definitions of education when we stop defining our lives in terms of what we're not doing.

But there's more, especially relating to the use of

extensions to the word "unschooling," to describe family life beyond academics. To portray how we interact with children in school terms simply gives too much credence to the place of education in our lives. Learning is simply life. We are always learning and can never stop learning, no matter how hard we might try. Children emerge from the womb eager to explore and learn; they make no distinction between what we have come to call academic learning and the other pieces of the puzzle that make up their world and the way they relate to it. As parents, we are here to facilitate that: to trust, respect, support, and love. I think that's too big a role—and too big a paradigm change for most people—to describe by sticking "un" onto the front of a word that describes an institution of training.

I look forward to the day when the transition from passive learning to active living has ended and we all see the word "school" and its various forms as a strange little artifact of the past. That will be the day when there is no longer a need to label how we live (and inevitably learn) in our families, to devise parameters for those labels, or to judge those who disagree about their definitions.

Meanwhile, please help me popularize the use of different terms like "life learning," "self-directed learning," and "whole-life learning," because they put the emphasis on learning rather than on being taught, and signify moving forward rather than looking backwards. If you have any feedback on the use of these terms— or ideas for others—I'd be glad to hear from you.

References

Illich, I. (1970). *Deschooling society*. New York, NY:
    Harper & Row Publishers.
From "The Words We Use: Living As If School
    Doesn't Exist," by W. Priesnitz, 2011,
    LifeLearningMagazine.com. Copyright [2011] by
    Wendy Priesnitz. Adapted with permission.

Wendy Priesnitz is a Canadian alternative education and environmental advocate. She was leader of the Green Party of Canada from July 1996 to January 1997, when she abruptly resigned.

She is known for her advocacy of homeschooling/unschooling and home-based/green business. She founded the Canadian Alliance of Home Schoolers in 1979, and is the author of numerous books on homeschooling. Since 1976, she has co-owned and edited *Natural Life*, an award-winning sustainable lifestyles magazine. In 2002, she founded *Life Learning Magazine,* which she owns and edits. She is listed in Canadian *Who's Who* and *Who's Who of Canadian Women.*
    http://www.lifemedia.ca/

PART II

LIGHTS. CAMERA. ACTION! (THIS IS HOW IT WORKS)

CHAPTER 11

WE DON'T NEED NO EDUCATION, WE DON'T NEED
NO THOUGHT CONTROL:
REFLECTIONS ON ACHIEVING MUSICAL LITERACY
& THE IMPORTANCE OF UNSCHOOLING

JOHN. L. VITALE.

During a recent curriculum methods class, one of my
students inquired about my musical training. Since the vast
majority of my musical experiences transpired outside the
forum of formal music education, I was unable to answer the
question without getting into my life story. This experience
motivated me to chronicle, and subsequently reflect on, my
lifelong musical experiences. These reflections ultimately
substantiate that the process of rejecting formal music
education and engaging in self-teaching has been the
primary method that allowed me to achieve a high level of
musical literacy. The paper also argues that the process of
self-teaching in the musical arena is very similar to the
principles of unschooling (a term coined by American author
and educator John Holt) where learning is based on the
student's interests, needs, and goals.

The grammatically-incorrect double negative used in the
second stanza of Pink Floyd's "Another Brick in the
Wall"("We don't need no education/We don't need no
thought control") is, ironically, a reaction to the grammar
school teachers of lyricist and composer Roger Waters.

According to Waters (cited in Winterman, 2007), his

grammar school teachers were more interested in keeping
the students quiet, rather than teaching them[1]. The proverbial
wall, therefore, was the imaginary wall Waters built around
him, because he was not in touch with reality (Songfacts,
2008). I would like to think, however, that a quality
songwriter like Roger Waters intentionally used the double-
negative to read as a positive, indicating that we in fact need
an education, but not the formal and conventional pedagogy
that tends to be delivered in most Western institutions. If this
was in fact the case, Waters is making a very bold statement
about education indeed.

As I wear the multiple hats of musician, music teacher,
music education researcher, music education advocate,
university professor, and parent, the importance and
significance of my musical training and education becomes
lost in the shuffle. One of my current students, enrolled in
the Consecutive Bachelor of Education Program (a teacher
candidate), recently asked me about my interest in music
during a curriculum methods class, specifically inquiring
about what instrument I played and where I studied. Since
my experiences are rooted in multiple methods that
habitually focused on self-teaching, and the fact that I do not
have a degree in music, I had an exceedingly difficult time
answering the question. In fact, this very simple question
provided the motivation and inspiration to chronicle my
lifelong musical experiences from my earliest memories to
the present, and reflect upon them. The methods I employed
during the self-teaching process were very similar to the
principles of unschooling as established by Holt, himself a
self-taught musician.

The purpose of this paper is threefold:

[1] Winterman (2007) has stated, "Waters was inspired by his own
schooling in the 1950s. It was a protest against the strict regime he felt had
tried to suppress children, rather than inspire them."

(i) it will provide a detailed description of my lifelong musical experiences,

(ii) it will offer a critical reflection of these experiences with regards to musical learning, and

(iii) it will demonstrate how these experiences are mostly rooted in self-teaching—a product of the unschooling paradigm.

Prior to addressing these three items, however, it is necessary to engage in a discussion that tackles the age-old battle between taught and self-taught musicians.

The Age Old Battle Between Taught and Self-Taught Musicians

In the musical arena, the war of taught versus self-taught musicians has been waging on for centuries! Since there are many musical styles (classical, jazz, pop, etc.), there are many different perspectives on what constitutes a taught or self-taught musician. Another factor that contributes to this multiplicity is the lack of a unifying and governing body that regulates all musicians—after all, music is an art, and art simply cannot be regulated. The realm of classical music is perhaps the one entity that comes closest to some sort of regulating body. In Canada, and other countries, the Royal Conservatory of Music is such an example. The Conservatory very much functions like a regulating body having formal exams in performance, theory, and history, that all must be passed in order to move from one level to another. Hence the expression, "classically trained" or "formally trained." My experience as a teacher has revealed that music students who come from this approach are exceptional emulators. That is, they read music notation and perform music with great success. Many of these students, however, are not able to perform once the sheet music is removed. They struggle at improvisation, lack in

compositional skills, and quite often do not understand what
they are actually playing until the very high grade levels,
which most students never achieve.

In the realm of pop music, however, (which
commercially makes up the vast majority of the music
industry) such restrictions do not apply. There is no
governing body, other than the record buying and consuming
public who dictate what sells and what does not, which
changes almost weekly. Musicians in this field are often self-
taught, almost always engage in unstructured learning
typical of garage-band practices, and have little or
sometimes no formal training. This is the realm in which I
developed my musical literacy. None of the Beatles, for
example, knew how to read music when they started, and
Paul McCartney was the only Beatle to eventually learn
how. Yet, that did not stop them from being perhaps the best
songwriters of the twentieth century.

Being a self-taught musician, however, does not mean
that influence, motivation, stimulation, and prompting from
other musicians/mentors fails to exist. In fact, quite the
contrary. That is, it is other musicians who provide the
underpinning for all self-taught musicians to effectively
learn a musical instrument. In the technologically-savvy
society we currently live, these "other musicians" come in
the form of a variety of formats, including live music,
recorded music (radio, television, CDs, DVDs, MP3 Players,
and computers), and print-based materials (both traditional
and electronic formats). The principal difference, therefore,
between taught and self-taught musicians, is that the latter
lacks formal structure and instruction, but allows for richer
musical experiences representing a variety of methods and
formats, very similar to the unschooling principles as
described by Holt (1981) and Farenga (2003). Lebler (2008)
has stated:

Popular music is usually learned in the broader community as a self-directed activity, sometimes including interactions with peers and group activities, but rarely under the direction of an expert mentor/teacher. One Australian conservatorium has adopted the pedagogy of popular music through the creation of a scaffolded self-directed learning environment within its Bachelor of Popular Music programme.

My Musical Training and Experiences

My earliest memories as a child are imbued in musical contexts. I can distinctly remember as a four-year-old, for example, that specific melodies would make me laugh or cry. I discovered early on in my life, therefore, that musical ideas and themes greatly influenced how humans think and feel about the world. In terms of a hands-on approach to music, I would spend hours and hours as a child of six, experimenting with my brother's electronic keyboard—a small one-and-a-half octave keyboard with only one simple organ sound—a far cry from what children have at their disposal today. I can distinctly remember experimenting with intervals (although I had no idea what I was doing) and evaluating the difference in sounds between them. Despite the fact that I was a very young child, there was nothing formal about these initial musical experiences. They were rooted in curiosity, experimentation, and self-discovery (Bruner, 1961).

By the age of ten, I was actively watching/listening to the crude and unsophisticated sounds of my 16-year-old brother's band that rehearsed in our basement for a few years. The only thing better than attending one of these band practices was the opportunity to try all of the instruments, which could only happen in secrecy with a little coaxing of my mother when my brother and his band mates were not in the house. Since the band rehearsed almost every evening, the musicians often left their instruments in my basement, which was definitely to my liking. On most days after school, I would vigorously bang on the drums, strum the guitar, and tickle the ivories on my brother's full-size keyboard. It was the electric bass, however, that particularly captivated my interest. I loved the potent and powerful deep sound it made, which would always rattle the heating ducts in my basement. All of this experimentation and self-discovery was really the first major step towards musical literacy—all without formal instruction. Although I did not know the proper terminology at the time, I was actively teaching myself and becoming intimately familiar with a variety of musical rudiments and fundamentals, such as dynamics, rhythm, texture, melody, and timbre. All I needed was the right environmental conditions that allowed me to engage in this unstructured but highly efficacious approach to learning music, such as my brother's band rehearsing in my basement. It was at this time that I knew music would play a profound role in my life.

By the time I reached the 6th grade, my parents had purchased an electric guitar for me. Although I had preferred the electric bass, I was still ecstatic about receiving my very own instrument. Although I did not engage in formal lessons, I practiced that guitar (which hangs in my basement today) for hours and hours every day. I would try to imitate the hit records of the day (known as "lifting"), all the while honing my musical and compositional ear. Within a few months, I had started a band called TNT, with another guitar player and a drummer, and the first song we learned to play by ear was the theme to the television series *Hawaii Five-O* (1968), which we actually performed on a local cable channel. The thrill of performing on television at age 11 was, needless to say, euphoric! Furthermore, this was the first time that I experienced the educational benefits of playing in a band, including developing patience, discipline, teamwork, and communication skills to name a few. I rapidly realized that playing an instrument on your own represented one set of distinct skills, but playing your instrument as part of a larger whole represented a vastly different set of skills and abilities. Once again, all of this musical training and education was occurring outside the formal context of traditional pedagogy.

With the drummer moving shortly after the band was formed, TNT broke up, and it was not until two years later, in the eighth grade, that I got the call to play bass in another band. Since I did not have a bass, I eliminated the last two strings of my guitar (the high "E" and "B") and created a makeshift bass. We played a variety of songs, but I was considered to be the weakest member of the band, since I did not know how to read music and all of the other members did. This band continued for a total of three years (until the end of my grade ten year) and we actually played several gigs with remuneration. This was the first time I associated the fact that I could make money from doing something that I absolutely loved, which motivated me to further pursue my musical interests. Once again, there was no traditional pedagogy connected to this musical experience. Although I learned many things from my band mates, they also learned from me, as I had a more developed ear for lifting songs from recordings.

At the beginning of my grade ten year, I still could not read music and continued to play bass by ear. I did, however, take a course in instrumental music and played the alto saxophone. This was my first introduction to the world of formal music education on an instrument[2] where I learned to

---

[2] Previous musical experiences in my school-based education were restricted to vocal music, where we sang from words and learned melodies from rote style teaching.

read notation in the treble clef. Although this did not help me on my bass, I received a taste of what it was like to engage in a very structured form of music learning, which I found very stifling and suppressing. I felt as though my imagination was crippled through learning that was imbued by rote-memorization drills (Gatto, 2009).

The most significant aspect of my musical life at this time, however (particularly as a bass player), was discovering the Canadian rock band, Rush, and specifically the bass playing of Geddy Lee. The influence that Rush had on my musical outlook was so profound that I classified music into only two categories—"Rush" and "everything else." I would spend hours playing my bass alongside my Rush records, which made me feel like I was part of their band: I was Geddy Lee—plain and simple! This imaginary world of playing bass alongside my musical heroes was very real in increasing my musical literacy. Once again, my musical experiences (particularly on the electric bass) were curiously void of formal instruction. Perhaps the most important aspect of my teenage years, with regards to music, was the freedom informal instruction provided. I was free to play and listen to the music that was meaningful and significant for me. The magnitude of freedom in the life of a teenager cannot be underestimated, particularly when it comes to education. Teenagers often view traditional education as the antithesis of freedom—a very formal, rigid, and inflexible approach to learning, much like I found playing alto saxophone in the high school band. Llewellyn (1998) has noted:

> Part of my work in writing this book involved contacting all the unschooled teenagers I could find. I asked them, each as part of a questionnaire, what they considered the greatest advantages of unschooling. Almost

unanimously, they agreed: Freedom! (p. 43)

Furthermore, freedom[3] allows students the essential right of controlling their own thoughts and experiences. This notion is confirmed by the guru of unschooling John Holt (1990) who has stated:

> Next to the right of life itself, the most fundamental of all human rights is the right to control our own minds and thoughts. That means, the right to decide for ourselves how we will explore the world around us, think about our own and other persons' experiences, and find and make meaning in our own lives. (p. 4)

All of my spare time during my junior year of high school was spent playing bass in an original rock band (highly influenced by the sounds of Rush, of course). We wrote several songs, recorded demos, and played a variety of gigs, which were attended by our friends and family. Although I continued to play alto saxophone in the school band, I still did not know how to read bass music. As I entered my last two years[4] of high school, a decision was made by all of us in the band to attend university to study music (which was only a 30-minute drive from our high school). This of course made me very nervous, since I was not formally trained on the bass. With roughly a year and a

---

[3] Our current system of education was put in place to provide students the basic skills needed to be successful in the industrial age. This system of education is old, antiquated, and not in touch with individual needs and requirements. Harrison (2002, p. 6) has argued, "The education system that we have in place now came out of the transition from the agrarian society to the industrial society. Our education system was a way of preparing agricultural workers for jobs in industry. The great narrative, the story that we tell ourselves about public education, is that if our child is educated, he or she will be able to be successful."

[4] The province of Ontario, at this time, required an extra year (grade 13) of high school in order to graduate with a secondary school diploma.

half to prepare for my audition, I purchased every book I could find and taught myself how to read bass clef and execute the notes on the electric bass. Looking back, it was at this time that I started to embrace the skills of a schooled and formally trained musician, but I discovered, learned, and cultivated these skills on my own.

Although several aspects of my university audition did not go well, particularly those that addressed music theory and sight reading, I was admitted to the program based on what the audition committee members referred to as my "freestyle performance ability." I guess this was an acceptable way of saying I did not do that well on the formal things but they liked the way that I played. So, there I was, a first-year undergraduate music major and I absolutely hated it! I detested the History of Western Music; I despised sight singing; I loathed music theory and counterpoint; I hated the fact that the jazz program only allowed traditional bebop jazz and not the modern jazz fusion that was popular at the time, and I could not stomach the fact that my favourite band, Rush, was considered on the fringes of the musical arena! I felt as though I was expected to learn music the way that it was heard and processed by someone else. This was not my world, and learning music that was boring and uninspiring on the promise that it would help me in the long run was a pill I was not prepared to swallow. Llewellyn and Silver (2001) echo my position:

> For real learning to take place, the information must occur in a world. [. . .] The relationship of the information to reality—its context—must be apparent. People can be asked to absorb a certain amount of meaningless data in good faith, on the promise that eventually it will be related to a larger world and transformed into information. (p. 17)

Although I was reasonably successful in my courses, it was the focus of my original band that kept me going. By the end of my second year, however, a band member became seriously ill for a while and the band broke up. With a lack of musical focus, I dropped out of the music program at the end of my second year and transferred to the Geography Department in the Faculty of Arts, where I would eventually earn an Honours Bachelor of Arts, and a Master of Arts. The structured approach of the university music department boxed me in and did not cater to what I wanted and needed to learn. It was my original band that allowed me the freedom to discover and learn music the way I wanted to. When that band dissolved, so did my musical aspirations. This is why I made the drastic move to leave the music department and enrol in a completely different subject matter. There was, however, a huge silver lining in this decision.

Switching my academic focus away from music, ironically, allowed me to cultivate and nurture my musical literacy more than any other time in my life! I was no longer bound to the rigid and formal framework of the music department, but rather open and free to discover and experiment with musical stimulation in other forums—an opportunity made possible through the principles of unschooling: learning based on my interests, needs, and goals. What I discovered was a university that was brimming and overflowing with musical talent that was not formally associated with the music department. Rather, these were students (just like myself) who were majoring in various non-musical disciplines, but who had a keen interest in playing and composing music in their own way, shape, and form. It was the musical world I thought never existed on such a large scale. Simply put, I was in musical paradise, and the next five years were spent studying geography but

learning music! It was at this time in my life that I made the
largest gains in my performance and compositional abilities,
and used such abilities as a means of earning desperately-
needed money. I was actively working in the Toronto music
scene as a freelance musician, performing at bars, weddings,
private parties, and corporate functions. Life was good!

After completing my Masters Degree, I enrolled in a
Bachelor of Education Program, and would spend the next
14 years teaching in Ontario Schools (mostly at the
intermediate/senior levels), where I took a few years off in
between to tour professionally as a musician, as well as
commence my doctoral studies on a part-time basis.
Teaching allowed me a comfortable lifestyle where I earned
a good living and could still play professionally on
weekends, and even take semesters off in order to
professionally tour.

Despite my geographical training, I have spent the vast
majority of my teaching career engaged in music pedagogy.
Although I eventually learned the nomenclature of
traditional music theory, much of my pedagogical approach
was rooted in the unschooled approaches that imbued my
musical experiences, particularly in the latter[5] years of my
high school teaching career. I was respected and valued by
some colleagues, and I was also considered revolutionary,
radical, and dissenting by others. I even felt ostracized by
some of my music teacher colleagues, once they found out I
did not have a degree in music. Somehow the lack of my
formal training in music demeaned and belittled their formal
accomplishments in the arena of music education. In the
high school music classroom, I often worked with students
on the fringes of traditional music education (the so-called
Rock/Goth students of the school) and gave these students a

---

[5] It is very easy as a new teacher to fall into the trap of traditional
pedagogy for many years.

voice by allowing them to play the music that they wanted. Even in traditional orchestral settings, the selection of music I would perform at concerts was very atypical for secondary school.

As I write this paper, music continues to play an integral part in virtually all aspects of my personal and professional life. As I reflect upon my musical training over the years, the overwhelmingly vast majority of my learning was rooted in unconventional and informal pedagogy that mirrors the paradigm of unschooling. This learning was not attainable through traditional and conventional music education, but rather through an alternative and unconventional approach imbued in the principles of unschooling where I had the ability to choose what and when I wanted to learn, with regards to my musical education. This is very different from traditional schooling, which boxes students into a pre-existing framework rooted in the experience of others. Fitzenreiter (2003) has stated:

> The true aim of school seems to be conformity rather than learning. Schooled children have no say in what they do with their time; therefore they do not learn how to make choices for themselves. (p. 8)

As educators, it is our responsibility to foster an environment that is conducive to learners of all types, especially those who flourish in environments free of restrictions and boundaries. Creating such a free and unrestricted learning environment requires educators to gamble and take on risks, because the majority of educational forums do not embrace unschooling principles. Griffith (1998) has so adeptly stated:

> The first requirement [of unschooling] is that children spend bulk of their time in places where learning and

exploration are possible and welcome [. . .] children need to feel comfortable exploring those surroundings and using what they find around them. (p. 6)

At the end of the day, however, all of us (students and teachers) need to take risks, and metaphorically create a sculpture of who we are. No formal education can help us with that. In sum, I urge all people reading this paper who have had a similar experience, in either music or another field of study, to share their story and help expose the limitations and restrictions of conventional education.

First printed in the *Journal of Unschooling at Alternative Learning*, Volume 3, Number 2, (Issue #6) 2009, Nipissing University. Used with permission of the author.

References

Bruner, J. S. (1961). The act of discovery. *Harvard Educational Review, 31*(1), 21-32.

Freeman, L. (Producer). (1968). *Hawaii five-o* [Television series]. Hawaii: CBS Television Distribution.

Fitzenreiter, V. (2003). *The unprocessed child: Living without school.* Lake Charles, LA: Unbounded.

Gatto, J. T. (2009). *Weapons of mass instruction: A Schoolteacher's journey through the dark world of compulsory schooling.* Gabriola Island, BC; New Society Publishers.

Griffith, M. (1998). *Unschooling handbook: how to use the whole world as your child's classroom.* Roseville, CA: Prima Publishing.

Harrison, S. (2002). *The happy child: Changing the heart of education.* Boulder, CO: First Sentient Publications.

Holt, J. (1990). *Learning all the time: how small children begin to read, write, count, and investigate the world without being taught.* New York, NY: Da Capo Press.

Holt, J. (2004). *Instead of education: ways to help people do things better.* Boulder, CO: FirstSentient Publications Edition.

Holt, J. (1981). *Teach your own: a hopeful path for education.* New York, NY: Delacorte Publishing. revised and updated: Farenga, Patrick (2003). *Teach your own: The John Holt book of homeschooling.* New York, NY: Perseus Books.

Lebler, D. (2008). Popular music pedagogy: peer learning in practice. *Music Education Research, 10(2),* 193-213.

Llewellyn, G. (1998). *The Teenage liberation handbook: How to quit school and get a real life and education.* Eugene, Oregon: Lowry House Publishers.

Llewellyn, G., Silver, A. (2001). *Guerrilla learning: How to give your kids a real education with or without school.* New York, NY; John Wiley & Sons.

Songfacts (2008). Retrieved from http://www.songfacts.com/detail.php?id=1696

Winterman, D. Just another brick in the wall. *BBC News Magazine*, October 2, 2007. http://news.bbc.co.uk/1/hi/magazine/7021797.stm

––––––––––

Dr. John L. Vitale is currently an Associate Professor in the Schulich School of Education at Nipissing University (Brantford Campus), where he teaches Music Education and Curriculum Methods at the undergraduate level, and Research Methods at the graduate level. Dr. Vitale has numerous publications to his credit in the field of music education, and he has also presented his research at a number of international conferences. As a professional bass player, Dr. Vitale has performed at over 1,000 national and

international venues with four different Juno Award winning
artists. Dr. Vitale also has numerous compositional credits,
including the score to award-winning children's animated
film Attic-in-the-Blue (first place winner at the Chicago
International Children's Film Festival).

CHAPTER 12

WHAT DOES IT MEAN TO BE EDUCATED?

JOHN TAYLOR GATTO

Isn't it ironic, that the question, "What does it mean to be educated?" is virtually never asked? It dawned on me, when I set out to answer that very question for myself, that the elite private boarding schools—the ones that carry on the tradition of Westminster, Eton and Harrow—would be likely places to look. The ones that carry on that tradition would aim to produce an educated, managerial class, to manage the rest of us dopes.

So, I began to study them. There are about twenty in the United States. There are hundreds and hundreds that claim to be, but there are about twenty that produce streams of original inspiration. Take the upcoming American presidential election (2004). The challenger, John Kerrey, is from St. Paul's, one of the most prestigious boarding schools in the United States. The incumbent, Bush, is from Andover, one of the top ten.

If you go back to the last election, we have the current incumbent president being elected, and his main competition, Al Gore, coming from St. Mark's school in Washington, D.C.. St. Mark's is certainly on everybody's top-fifteen lists. We also had John McCain, who represents himself as a man of the people, but McCain went to Episcopal which is on everybody's top-five list. We had Steve Forbes who went to Kent, a school underwritten by J.P. Morgan.

WHAT DOES IT MEAN TO BE EDUCATED?

We're talking here about a mass populace that has been so numbed intellectually that it's incapable of responding to evidence right under its nose. You don't have to be a conspiracy theorist to say that in a nation of 300 million people, if two fraternity brothers, from the same fraternity chapter, at the same college in the same years, were opponents in the presidential election, something awfully fishy is going on. Yet that is the case in the current presidential election (2004).

What's most exciting (and depressing), to me, is that the press refuses to enlighten the public about the implications of this queer election, in our so-called democracy. How could it happen? Mathematically, what would a good London bookie put as odds against that happening? I think it would be billions to one, and yet, we have it in America. I dare you to find anywhere on radio or television with even a reference to that.

Let's get back to school. Schools were set up about a hundred years ago to act as psychological conditioning laboratories. To really train minds or characters in a mass population would be a dangerous social revolutionary thing to do. So schools don't do that. Bells, buzzers and horns, standardized tests, these are ways you train dogs or rats.

I don't want to hear that Burnaby South or North Vancouver is the greatest school, one jammed full of high-tech equipment. It's got the same bells, buzzers, and narrowing behaviour practices. All the rest of the stuff is window dressing. Teachers have no positive authority, only negative authority. They can constrain a kid from following a productive path, but they don't have power, legally vested, to encourage a kid along a positive one-of-a-kind path. Many, of course, find ways to sabotage the system a bit, to treat their clientele as human beings with personal destinies. But, if discovered doing that, they are toast. There is no sympathy, in most cases, no second chance. If kids like a teacher too much, that teacher automatically becomes a fringe person in school. I include colleges in that indictment.

That did happen to me, but I'm not a push over. I was raised in a Scotch-Irish community in western Pennsylvania, and basically taught how to fight, how to defend myself, how to inflict damage on people I opposed. The whole school apparatus is intensely cowardly, although it can bully a mother at home, or a kid in school. School people, in fact, have no seat themselves at the policy table. They are flunkies, relays in a system: if they call attention to themselves, get their names in the paper, it's the end of career ambitions for administrators, the beginning of heavy surveillance for teachers.

Think of the structure of systems: How can you have independent thinkers, or creative thinkers, (or an amalgam of both) and be systematic? It's not possible. That would assume the one right way to do things had been discovered, or even exists. Even someone of modest mental gifts knows it doesn't.

The great teachers are intensely observant and adaptable to the expression of one or another talent on the part of a student. That's the situation homeschoolers find themselves in, unless they try to imitate the school pattern. But if homeschoolers generate an educational diet the way scientists generate hypotheses, they become superior to the best institutional schooling in Canada or the United States.

The most prestigious scientific job in the world today, and nothing's even close to it, is heading up the human genome project. One of the two leaders was a homeschooler who didn't follow any balanced diet himself: you know the kind that includes a little history, a little science, and a little math. The method used by his mother (who had three other boys) was that they all voted on what they wanted to study and that was the only thing they studied until they got bored with it. And then they voted for something else. I seem to recall in the *New York Times* about four years ago, he said if the authorities knew what we were doing, my mother would have been thrown into prison and the boys would have been parceled out to the social workers. He had no trouble getting into Harvard; he had no trouble rising through the ranks of well-schooled scientists to his current position of awesome power.

Of all forms of homeschooling, unschooling would be my personal pick. How you choose to spend your time, I think, says a tremendous amount about yourself. The admissions officer at Princeton, (a long time ago) told me the first thing he looks for is hobbies.

I said, "Why do you look at hobbies?"

He said, "It's really the only way a young person has an opportunity to commit to something without being pushed into it. The choices they make, when they have choices, tell me all I need to know."

I asked, "What would it tell you? What would you like to see?"

He said, "We would like to see someone with an intellectual hobby, a social hobby, and a physical hobby."

"Wow," I said, "like what?"

He said, "It could be chess playing, it could be ballroom dancing, and it could be swimming."

"So what about sports?"

"It's got to be there, but people do not understand that individual sports like bike riding and sky diving, and long distance walking and stuff like that," he said, "are much more important than team sports."

"Why so?"

He told me, "Team sports enable an individual to hide behind other people. You can slack off and let your teammates carry you. Whereas, when you are out there alone, if you make a fool of yourself, or if you are inadequate, there's no place to hide. And people willing to do that," he said, "are superior people, the ones we want at Princeton."

So why aren't these ancient, well-understood truths the stuff of schooling?

In a corporate economy, you have one boss, twenty sub-bosses, and fifty sub-sub-bosses. That arrangement is only possible if people don't know how to escape their placements. You can lie, saying with Darwin that most of us are inferior and they couldn't escape their placements, but my experience teaching for 30 years is that is not true. Harlem kids are capable of exactly the same quality of intellectual production as upper-middle-class white kids. I don't say that as a romantic, or as a humanitarian. I say that as somebody locked up with children, who decided to do a first-class curriculum with poor ghetto kids out of personal boredom. I got in a lot of trouble, at first, doing that, but the minute the kids caught on that you actually meant what you said when you told them you'd treat them with respect, after the adjustment period, the quality of the work was exactly as high as it was with so called gifted and talented kids. And these were street kids from the ghetto!

I can't be the only one who's discovered that. But what would you do if 70 million kids graduated every twelve years in the United States, and every one of them had, as Napoleon advised, a field marshal's baton in his backpack? What if everyone was looking for an independent livelihood? What if everyone wasn't just willing to pick up a pay cheque, but brought principles and moral standards and aesthetic preferences to the job and said, "No, I won't do that!"

Let's suppose that tens of millions of kids tomorrow grow into a modern America in which employment will be part-time for many, and not well paid. That's cause for resourceful thinking, where you say, "How can I improve this situation?"

Don't you think kids have a right to know these things? To spend a respectable amount of their school time reflecting and researching and debating and coming up with personal answers that will help them in their lives? To leave them completely in the dark about this, until they are laid off and remain out of work for four years, such is the fate of many of our people. Why would you do this if you had any real concern for them? Truth is, the mass population in America is no longer relevant, except to man armies to suppress the rest of the world.

Kids, from first grade on, are set against one another. It's no surprise, then, when they become adults after twelve years of back-biting, competing, being placed in class/status relationships to one another, that they can't build a community. It's no surprise at all.

Community isn't built, intellectually, by saying, now wouldn't it be a good idea if we all worked together? Kids have had twelve years of never working together. These are truths so fundamental it almost embarrasses me to say them, except for the fact that people have been trained not to think of these things. They strike the virgin ear as some radical statement.

What can you do for the entire society? I think the answer is nothing, except doing your best for the principles you believe in. Struggle, argue, and don't expect any substantial change but what you can change for yourself, and your friends, and your neighbour. It's not easy, it remains a struggle but it's just so much more correct a way to live.

I mean you don't live that other, selfish way. You say, "I prefer not to act these other ways." And sometimes, you submit; because not submitting would exact a price way out of balance with what you would win from acting on principle. I think you develop the mind of a saboteur.

You look and move like everybody else, you don't draw attention to yourself, but from time to time you find where the gears are meshing and you put a nice handful of sand in them. The biggest handful of sand, though, will be your children. If they come to the age of majority with independent critical minds, with a good attitude towards things, without expecting change to come easily, enjoy the struggle of testing themselves, this gives them good lives.

In having good lives, they'll be helping me and you and everyone else. It will happen after I'm dead, I think, but at some point a critical mass of people will emerge who just won't accept bullshit any longer. Then things will change, as they did in 1776. Now, what I just described is very, very hard for a nation to do, but it's not that hard for a family, a neighbourhood, or a community.

To set children against parents, is, of course, another function of institutional schooling. It's meant to be, "divide and conquer is the rule." What you don't want is mothers and fathers who would die for their kids. You want authority to be vested in official management. You want people to be addicted to stuffing their faces. You want that because it makes them more manageable. Now the state has an incentive they control entirely. You can give it or withhold it, according to whether behaviour is compliant or not.

Is there a problem with an unschooled child who does nothing but read all day?

No, no problem with that, if the reading can be expanded into areas of writing and speaking. I think the inevitable result, down the line, will be a good one. If it's just reading though, if the kid's locked up and partly mute in the face of different people and different customs and idioms there, then there's a real disability. The way I would deal with that in the beginning is to actually talk with the kid, and say you are going to develop a huge repository of information and probably a wonderful layered complex mind, but now the product of that mind has to be heard! Expression!

It's not uncommon to find someone who is merely

developed in that reading area, who is roundly exploited by their co-workers who can speak and write fluently. But I wouldn't be worried about a single-minded passion, as long as it gives way in time to something larger.

I'll give you a radical example of that: Over the years, I would encounter a fraction of the male population in schools who did nothing at all but read comic books. That was it. They played games too, but comic books were the addiction. They would read comics through the school day. I would take them aside privately and I would say, "I'm willing to cut you a deal where you don't have to do anything but read comic books." Almost all of them wanted to draw comic books too. I said, "I expect that you'll develop professional proficiency in this, but right now there's no evidence of that." I would take a kid's comic drawing and he would be very proud of it and it would look pretty much like the drawing in the original.

But I would say, "Look at the original!"

"I don't need to I've drawn it."

"No you haven't, every one of your panels is exactly the same size. Look at the page you just copied, every panel is a different size. Every one of your panels contains all heads and arms and feet of the characters in the panel. Look at the original comic book. Hands shoot out of one side of a panel and heads out of another one." I said, "You're looking at that and you can't even see what you are looking at! That is a drastic sickness. And it's been conditioned into you by standardization. The comic books aren't standardized but you are standardized.

"Now I'll let you cut school legally. I'll give you a pass to do it. Go to the public library, but don't go with any friends. Take a stack of graphic art manuals off the shelves, open them, and start to learn what you are doing."

"If you reach the stage where you understand the structure of the comic book, the next thing to do is to begin to study the economics of it. Who reads Spider Man? Not everybody. Is it equally read in all the fifty states? I doubt it. Find out where it's read, what age group reads it, whether they have any distinguishing characteristics. And, they will have, and the comic book will know that profile inside out."

"Begin to look at this thing as a large complex business. Where does the ink come from? Where does the paper come from? What are the stages in the production of a comic book? How do you crack into the business? What does it pay? What about ancillary rights for ashtrays with the Hulk on them or whatever? You could spend the whole year and do nothing but comic books, as long as it isn't just sitting there reading them." So, year after year we'd have wonderfully individualized curricula. Was the kid only learning about comic books? Of course not. He was using the comic as an entry into a dozen different worlds.

You can understand how difficult it is to break the habit of lockstep schooling: mothers have been conditioned to think about a "balanced diet" concept of curriculum. They begin to worry (even though they've got their kids out of school) if they don't see an echo of the school day being duplicated. So I would say to mothers, "have courage, trust your kids, they will surprise you. Use your superior experience, your capability of seeing the big picture, to get them to do more than what they otherwise would do, but in areas they want to operate. Make sure your homeschooling doesn't become a mere re-creation of institutional schooling."

About Television

You have to show them, I mean you don't need to be crazy about it, but you have to show them the aspect of absolute death of the mind that lurks in television and the computer. As an addict, you are a semi-hypnotized subject

146

of a technology whose regard for you is to make money for its owners. There is no charitable impulse in any of it. It's built to become obsolete; it's built to humiliate you if you can't afford to keep up with the latest generations. It controls your time, controls how you think, what you think about, which buttons you press, in what sequence. It's a conditioning device, and a very, very, very dangerous one.

The biggest hype that comes through school is that the highest form of thinking is problem solving. That is far from the truth. Problem-solvers are valuable people who often cause hideous problems, because they don't understand that their problem is part of a much more complex context, that by solving their problem, they make things considerably worse.

The example I usually use is the problem that was set long ago to America's best biological scientists. It was to come up with a bug spray that kills all the bugs so we could double and triple and quadruple food harvests, and they did: They solved the problem. It was called DDT. By 1960, the whole food chain on the planet was being threatened by accumulations of this poison that didn't biodegrade, and past some point caused sterility. So, by solving the problem, which they did brilliantly, they put life on the planet in peril. You see what I mean about problem solving.

The great thinkers are people who think in contexts and understand the historical and the economic, the philosophical, the religious, the social aspects of what they are thinking about. So they can judge whether a problem should be solved, or forgotten, or lots of stages in between. That takes judgment, and, unfortunately, judgment is the last thing schools are about. How could they teach judgment and remain schools?

An audio version of this piece appears in podcast and can be found at: Gatto, J.T. (2004, December 28). Interview by

B. Ekwa Ekoko [Podcast]. Outing School with John Taylor Gatto Part 3, Radio Free School. Hamilton, Ontario.
Retrieved from
http://radio4all.net/index.php/program/10763

John Taylor Gatto (born December 15, 1935) is an American retired school teacher of 29 years and 8 months experience in the classroom and author of several books on education including *Dumbing us Down: The hidden Curriculum of Compulsory Schooling* (2005), and *Weapons of Mass Instruction: A Schoolteacher's Journey Through The Dark World of Compulsory Schooling* (2009). He is an activist critical of compulsory schooling and of what he characterizes as the hegemonic nature of discourse on education and the education professions.

Gatto's office is in New York City, his home in Oxford, New York, where he is currently at work on a documentary film about the nature of modern schooling entitled *The Fourth Purpose,* with his friend and former student, Roland Legiardi-Laura. For more information about this film, visit *The Fourth Purpose*. Gatto has been married for forty years to the same woman, and has two grown children and a cat. He hopes to build a rural retreat and library for the use of families pondering local and personal issues of school reform.

CHAPTER 13

DEMOCRATIC SCHOOLS

JERRY MINTZ

My name is Jerry Mintz; I'm the director of AERO, which is the Alternative Education Resource Organization. We've been going since 1989, and what we do is act as a networker of educational alternatives around the world. That means we help people who want to start new alternatives; we also help people who are looking for alternatives. What the schools in our network have in common is that they are learner-centered as opposed to curriculum-driven.

Our website is educationrevolution.org, and we have an e-newsletter that people can get free through the website. We also have had online courses for people who want to start new alternatives.

I think what we're talking about here are two paradigms. There is the one paradigm for learning, that most regular state or public schools have, and actually most private schools: Their paradigm is that kids are naturally lazy and need to be forced to learn. When you start with that paradigm, then you need to have homework that's required, and you need to have a set curriculum, and force kids to learn things that you think they need to know. You need all that stuff, including testing to make sure that they are learning the things you think they should be learning. That describes our current system, which is failing.

The second paradigm is that the job of the educator is to help provide the resources for the student, for them to learn the things that they are interested in. With that comes no forced homework, no set curriculum, and that allows kids to go off at staggering rates when they are really interested in things. All knowledge is ultimately linked, therefore, if you want to go deeply in anything, you're going to learn everything else that's necessary to go with it. You can't study mechanics or aviation without being able to read or do math.

How learner-centred education works varies from school to school. There are 12,000 schools in our network, which include Montessori, Waldorf, charter schools, public alternatives, and homeschoolers. In some cases, yes, there is a set curriculum; in other cases, no. We're more specialized in democratic schools, there may be 200 of those schools around the world, but it's a movement that's growing rapidly. In those schools, the kids are not forced to go to classes. They can choose what they want. They can do their own classes. They can teach their own classes, even. They can ask for classes they want, if they're not being offered. Then, whoever wants to, could go to those classes.

Let's talk about math for a second. At the school I ran for 17 years, there was no compulsory class attendance. Kids had to demonstrate, when they wanted to graduate, that they could handle a certain degree of academics. One of the things that the kids would do is take the GED test, or something else, to show that they could handle all these areas, including math. What they told me is that if they hadn't been doing much math before, they could learn a year's worth of math in three weeks. So, a motivated student could learn a year's worth of math in three weeks, that an average student gets force-fed for a year.

At democratic schools, there are parents, and volunteers, and other people, who can work individually with kids. The fact is, a motivated kid just learns faster, really at lightning speed sometimes, and goes way past what you would expect a kid to do.

Recently, I was walking around at Brooklyn Free School. I volunteer there once a week. It's just amazing, in every single corner, there is a beehive of activity. Sometimes when I go in there, I teach table tennis: I just set up the table and people will come over and ask, "Can I take lessons?" I have brought in equipment that is a game based on brainwaves, which helps people learn to meditate. The more you can produce the alpha waves the more you can light a fire, or make a ball move or something like that.

By the way, I have no problems with teachers bringing things in or offering classes. I don't think you have to wait around for kids to come up with ideas, but the key is that the kids aren't forced to go do that: if they're interested, they go.

There's unschooling, and I guess you could call democratic schools "anti-school." It's anti-the- traditional-school-model, but it's a chance for kids to learn what they're interested in learning. They're not going to do it in isolation as easily, without some help. One charter alternative school in New Jersey doesn't call the teachers "teachers," they call them "guides."

This is a rapidly growing movement, and many people ask how the students will be accepted into college. Interestingly, the colleges are falling all over themselves to get these kids, because they've discovered that they are the most motivated, top-performing students, because they didn't get their natural interest in learning squashed.

When I talk about the two paradigms, the first paradigm becomes self-fulfilling. If you take a kid and over six or seven years force him to learn things that he's not interested in, well then he will appear lazy. It is very hard to undo that damage, where school has actually extinguished his natural curiosity, his natural ability to learn. It takes almost as much time to undo as how long it took to do the damage. Which is why, for example, Summerhill (one of the first schools taking this approach, in England) won't take a new kid over the age of eleven. Brooklyn Free School doesn't take kids over thirteen. There are democratic schools that will take kids of that age, but they run into some problems.

The idea of unschooling is very simple: you believe your kid is a natural learner, you listen carefully to them, and help them do the things they're interested in. There's nothing wrong with you saying, "Hey I'm excited about this. Do you want to do this?"

The average homeschooler is in the 85th percentile on standardized tests. Sudbury Valley School is a school that really runs on the same ideas. It's been a school since the 1967, in Framingham, MA. There are about 25 schools that are based on Sudbury now, all around the world. At Sudbury, they have published a book about their graduates: Basically anybody who has wanted to go to a certain college got into that college.

I've gone to India four times. There's a big system of schools called Dayanand Anglo-Vedic (DAV), with 700 schools. These schools are huge, with 2500-3000 students. They've brought me over to try to help democratize those schools. I was just checking my email today and there's a girl in one of them who is working to help her school become more democratic, inviting people to come do workshops, to move in that direction.

In Israel, there is the Institute of Democratic Education, which has training programs for people who want to teach in democratic schools. Israel has twenty-five democratic schools. In the Netherlands, there are many new democratic schools.

Every year there is an International Democratic Education Conference, in a different country. AERO has an annual conference, at which we usually have people from about thirty states and about ten countries.

Some question whether young children can participate in

a democratic process, and make decisions. In short, yes. One thing that I recently discovered that's very interesting connects with this. We have an online course for people who are starting new alternatives. A group of four to five parents who were starting a new school in New Jersey were taking that course. They had established their school, and asked me to come demonstrate the democratic process with their children. The oldest child is five years old. I'd never done that before, but I have confidence in this process. On the way over, I was thinking to myself, "I'm going to have to come up with items on an agenda for these kids, because they're so young," but I still thought that they would come up with good ideas. When we got these kids together, sitting around this little table on little chairs, the parents around the outside, I explained, "You know that in this meeting you can bring things up to talk about, what are good ideas for the school to do, or you can talk about problems in the school." No sooner did I get the words out of my mouth and the hands went up with things for the agenda. One of the kids wanted to talk about healthy food. He said, "You know certain foods like chocolate actually have a caffeine-like substance in them. Should we ban people eating too much of that in the afternoon?" She was four-years-old! One of the other kids talked about clean-up and problems with clean-up and I asked, "What should you do with a kid who doesn't want to do clean up?" Someone said, "You just have one of the parents or teachers talk to them."

"What if they still won't clean up?" Another kid said, "Kick them out of the school." The other kids said, "Nah, that's too drastic!" so they passed a motion that said "If the kid didn't clean-up, they couldn't play with their toys until they did." The meeting went on for awhile, so much for the idea that kids can't concentrate. We had three items on the agenda and I thought, "Okay, you've got the idea so unless you have something else. . . ." They wanted more, they had other ideas. One of them brought up the problem of going outside when it was cold, and thought maybe that wasn't a good idea to go outside when it was cold. Several kids objected. They liked going out when it was cold. They decided that if you had a cold, you shouldn't be able to go out in the cold.

The idea of using the democratic process is important because the rules mean you have to listen, you have to make proposals, there has to be agreement.

Some wonder if public schools can adopt democratic processes. There is one in Vancouver, British Columbia, called Windsor House, which is a really radical school. It was doing really great for maybe 30 years, and then trouble: When you have a public school it can go for a long time and then administration changes cause problems, which has happened to Windsor House. It is a shame, but for all those years it had been very effective for all these kids who have gone through it.

It's hard to convert a school, because it's hard to change. Some of the old processes are almost like religious dogma: We do that because, well, we've always done that. But it can be done. There's one in Russia that was converted, a 600 student school. It's called the School of Self-Determination, and the kids have the constitutional right to leave any class they want without any explanation. I was at a conference in Russia. There was a kid from that public school and I said, "What did you think about that, Igor?" and he said, "We have much more freedom." I was shocked to think about a kid going to a public school in Russia with 600 students who said, "We have more freedom."

There is a spectrum of democratic schools. On the one end you have Summerhill, one of the most famous, at which there is a set timetable of classes, but no pressure at all for the kids to go to them. A lot of kids don't, but the ones who do, know that classes are going to be offered. On the other end is Sudbury Valley School, where there are no classes unless students ask for them. In the middle, there are the kinds of things I did at my school where anybody could offer a class, staff or student; there would be class announcements; everything was considered a class, and; there was no set curriculum. Students could choose to go, or not, do something entirely different, or do nothing.

I think that children are natural learners, and it makes sense for a lot of kids to learn in a group, and call that a school or whatever you want. I don't think there's an inherent contradiction. I think what has happened is that the people who created the public school system, according to John Gatto, actually had as their purpose not to create independent, strong thinkers who would be willing to stand up to the government, or who would participate fully and completely in a democracy. They wanted to indoctrinate students to become the kind of people who would be consumers, who would not rock the boat, who would follow orders. I think that's what we have got with our current mainstream schooling system.

Democratic schools are generally small. Sudbury Valley School is one of the bigger ones, at 200-250 students. My school was never more than 45. It's interesting that the Gates' Foundation once thought smallness was better, but, to them [Gates], a small school is 400. They moved in that direction, not realizing that it wasn't just the smallness, but the learner-centered approach that worked.

Democratic schools begin in various ways. They might be started by a group of parents, or by students, or teachers. That has an effect on what kind of school it is. I found that, ironically, parent co-ops don't seem to be that effective in the long run. The most effective schools have been ones that were started by a leader with a vision, someone who had the ability to empower the students to be able to make decisions.

The Free School in Albany was founded by Mary Leue.

She's not there anymore, and now the next generation of teachers is involved with running it, and so they've made a transition from their charismatic leader and founder. That strong leadership is also true of some Quaker schools; they have the Quakerism as a base. There is the Meeting School which is in Rindge, New Hampshire, and Arthur Morgan School (AMS), a boarding junior high school, in North Carolina. They each use the consensus model for making decisions.

When a group of parents runs a school without a clear leader, the parents are so invested in it that they try to live vicariously through it, which takes something away from the student's empowerment. That's because the adults are not the products of this type of system. Remember, a lot of democratic schools won't take a new student over the age of 12 or 13, because it's difficult to reverse their programming. Adults who have not had that experience often end up with splintering and infighting. I know this might sound controversial to unschooling parents, but it's my experience.

Summerhill School is a proprietary school. It's owned by the Neill family. Zoe runs the school now (her father started the school in the 1920s.) She's had 4 children go through the school, and now I think her grandchildren are starting to go. She feels very strongly that if it had been a non-profit organization with a board that they would have capitulated to the pressure from the government a long time ago, to force compulsory classes.

I ran a democratic school for 17 years. I couldn't then imagine that all the wonderful benefits of the democratic process and the interaction could be replicated in a home school situation, but I have changed my mind about that. From my experiences, I think that democratic schools and unschooling can work. A good homeschool/unschool situation is great, because the kids get plenty of interaction, out in the world doing things, like interning, joining organizations, and they have in their own minds the clear sense that they are the learner. I think that works fine. My school was almost like a big unschool, in the sense that it was a totally learner-centered approach.

Iroquois democracy is something that we evolved toward at my school. We started out with the typical Roberts Rules, sometimes called a "tyranny of the majority" approach, but we came into contact with the Mohawk Indians in our first year, when we visited them at their reservation at Akwesasne, New York. People may not realize it, but the democracy that is practiced in the USA really got its inspiration from Iroquois Confederacy, after Thomas Jefferson and Benjamin Franklin came in contact with it. In going there, we discovered that when the Iroquois Confederacy make decisions, if there was minority dissent they honoured the minority by letting them say why they were voting the way they did. Then there was more discussion, and then it was incumbent upon the minority to make a better proposal. This process could go on for a while.

This is how we made decisions in our school. It worked very well, so we have shown others, in practical terms that it's easy. Once a proposal is voted on, the minority is polled so that anybody who wants to can say why they voted the way they did, and there is further discussion. If nobody asks for that, then the decision stands. When the minority doesn't feel like speaking, then they "stand aside," in Quaker terms, that is, they disagree but are willing to try.

I'll give you an example: I went to the Home Education Seaside Festival in England, where something like 1000 homeschoolers camp out for a week by the sea. I was there to demonstrate our process. It was in a big tent and there were a couple hundred adults, and a smattering of kids. I had got about 10 kids to volunteer, to be in a fishbowl demonstration. We got in the middle, and we started talking about the process. They put squirt guns on the agenda, because it had become an issue: who could use them, when, where, and who was objecting to them.

A few of the kids left, which was okay, so we started the discussion. The kids who had left came back with all the rest of the kids. They had said, "You won't believe this, they're actually talking about something that's important to us!" The first proposal passed: That the squirt guns only be used in one certain field. When we asked the people who voted against it why, one said, "My children are young and pretty far away from that field. I really don't want them that far away." Another said, "That's where my tent is, I don't want that to be the only place!" Someone else said, "There's no water tap in that field." And so, a vote reversed it.

It was very instructive to realize that the decision was not set in stone, that it was a real discussion and change was possible. People sometimes have the idea from voting in elections that everything is predetermined, and what they say doesn't matter. So this was enlightening to people.

A few days later, the kids wanted to have more meetings. In the campground, there was a sweet store. A kid had shoplifted something, so the woman was now refusing to let any children in the store. The kids were very upset, and wanted to have a meeting about this, so we put it on the board. About 200 kids and maybe 25 parents attended.

With such a large group, a portable microphone made it so that even the quietest kid could be heard. There was a woman with her six-year-old, Alfie, sitting on her lap, and his hand went up. When we brought the mic to her, mom's expression was like, "Oh my God, what's he going to say?" He said, "I think that the woman in the shop finds it difficult to watch so many kids at once. We could offer to help her out, but I don't think that's the most important thing. I think we need to apologize to her, and I make that a proposal." Everybody was stunned, including the kid's mother, and we discussed it and it was passed.

Afterwards, about a dozen were going to go down to the sweet shop, and we had to decide who was going to represent us. It should be Alfie, and his mother decided not to go with him. I introduced him to the woman at the sweet shop, and he explained to her about the meeting, and spoke to her in the most beautiful way, and that was it. She totally melted and all the kids were able to come to the sweet shop.

One of our main thrusts has been to help people set up homeschool resource centers, where you're homeschooling and you take the basic responsibility for your child's education but you do it in a group, including hire resource people, if you want. Those parents who are free, can be there, so people who are working can homeschool or unschool their children.

One of the very first homeschool resource centres I ever saw was in Paris, around 1989. The Collectif Enfants-Parents, met every day, in a different house, with about 15 kids. Each family got half a day off work for each parent each week. There were two parents present at time, and they covered the whole week. The kids were the real continuity. They have been doing it for 15 years.

Of course, homeschooling doesn't have to be done at certain hours. I know one woman who was so desperate that she got a baby sitter. Both she and her husband were working, but she got a babysitter during the day and she worked with their son in the evenings and on weekends.

I knew John Holt quite well. I remember having a discussion with him about Christian homeschoolers, and the fact many do school-at-home. He felt that, eventually, the kids would teach their parents how to teach them, or the parents would get frustrated, give up, and send their kids to Christian schools. It seems that there has been an evolution in Christian education; there are now a lot of Christian educators who call themselves unschoolers.

I think that the parents do learn from the kids, and realize the kids bring the curriculum with them, it's the parent's job to listen well to what the kids say or show they're interested in. It isn't always verbal, it becomes an art. I don't necessarily agree with people saying "You can't do anything until the kid says they're interested." If you know your child, and you can see what kind of things they are likely to be interested in, I do not think that it is inconsistent with the idea of unschooling to present ideas and possibilities.

For those who question the need for the basics, well, it really depends on what you think is basic. It's interesting, if you talk about the real basics. I think one of the most basic things kids need to learn is how to get along with other people. Homeschoolers manage to do that better than public school kids. Kids in the public schools can't even look an adult in the eye. Adults are not part of the kids' world. They also can't seem to relate to many people beyond that one little age range they're stuck in. They don't have that experience, whereas homeschoolers, because their parents bring them everywhere, they get to relate to people of all ages. And so, that's one of the most important basics.

Another basic is to be able to find the answers to your own questions. In this age, it really doesn't matter what you specifically know. Albert Einstein was once asked what the speed of sound was and he said, "I don't bother memorizing things I can look up." The fact is that the least important thing today is what facts you've memorized. With the information explosion, you could never learn a millionth, a billionth, of what there is out there. What's important is that you know how to answer the questions that you have, and find resources. Those are the real basics. This emphasis on high-stakes tests, and standardized tests, are exactly antithetical to this concept.

The history of democratic schools goes pretty far back. There was once a guy, Bronson Alcott, who had a little school in the 1800s-1830 or so. He accepted a black girl into his school. Soon he only had six kids in his school, but one of them was his daughter Louisa May Alcott. That's where she got her inspiration for the books *Little Men* and *Little Women* (1868).

One of the key events in democratic school history was when Summerhill started in the 1920s. Another key event was when the book *Summerhill* (1960) was published in 1960. That started the Free-School movement, which led to the alternative school movement, which then led to homeschooling, charter schools and all that.

The thing to know is that this phenomenon is going on all over the world, this education revolution. We started the International Democratic Education Conference, back in 1993, in Israel; we have met every year since. We hosted the last (2003) IDEC in the United States for the first time. We had at least 600 people come to Troy, New York, from 25 countries and 25 states. We raised $65,000 for low-income and third-world people to participate. People came from India, Nepal, Thailand, Russia, Ukraine, Guatemala, Hungary, and Poland. It was an amazing, amazing event. We had 17 speakers, including Zoe Redhead, A.S. Neill's daughter from Summerhill; John Taylor Gatto; and Pat Montgomery from Clonlara. An amazing group of people. We have an mp3 recording of all those speeches.

This piece combines two audio versions in podcasts that can be found at:

1. Mintz, J.(2004, July 28). Interview by B. Ekwa Ekoko [Podcast]. Building Democratic Schools-Interview with Jerry Mintz, Radio Free School. Hamilton, Ontario. Retrieved from http://radio4all.net/index.php/program/21592

2. Mintz, J.(2007, January 31). Interview by B. Ekwa Ekoko [Podcast]. Democratic Schools with Jerry Mintz, Radio Free

School. Hamilton, Ontario.
     Retrieved from
http://radio4all.net/index.php/program/9712

References

Alcott, L.M. (1871). *Little Men.* Boston, MA: Roberts
     Brothers.
Alcott, L.M. (1868). *Little Women.* Boston, MA: Roberts
     Brothers.
Neill, A.S., Fromm, E. (1960). *Summerhill: a radical
     approach to child rearing.* Wocester Place, OX: Hart
     Publishing Co.

———————————

Jerry Mintz has been a leading voice in the alternative school movement for over 30 years. In addition to his seventeen years as a public school teacher and a public and independent alternative school principal, he has also founded several alternative schools and organizations and has lectured and consulted around the world.

In 1989, he founded the Alternative Education Resource Organization and since then has served as its Director. Jerry was the first executive director of the National Coalition of Alternative Community Schools (NCACS), and was a founding member of the International Democratic Education Conference (IDEC).

In addition to several appearances on national radio and TV shows, Jerry's essays, commentaries, and reviews have appeared in numerous newspapers, journals, and magazines including *The New York Times, Newsday, Paths of Learning, Green Money Journal, Communities, Saturday Review, Holistic Education Review* as well as the anthology *Creating Learning Communities* (Foundation for Educational

Renewal, 2000). Jerry was Editor-in-Chief for the *Handbook of Alternative Education* (Macmillan, 1994), and the *Almanac of Education Choices* (Macmillan/Simon & Schuster, 1995). He is the author of *No Homework and Recess All Day: How to Have Freedom and Democracy in Education* (AERO, 2003) and is co-editor (with Carlo Ricci) of *Turning Points: 35 Visionaries in Education Tell Their Own Story* (AERO, 2010).

http://www.educationrevolution.org/

CHAPTER 14

AWARE AND ALIVE

DAVID ALBERT

For every homeschooling mom, there is, at least in theory, a homeschooling dad. We define our family as a homeschooling family. I always insist that homeschooling is not only for the kids. It's also a chance for we, as parents, to reinvent ourselves in the process.

Sometimes I've called my wife the principal, but, no, I don't think there is a special role that has to be ascribed to the male or the female in this relationship. Though, I think that's probably true that there are more families in which the man goes off and becomes the breadwinner, the women tend to have part-time jobs, and are more likely to stay home with the kids and organize the life of the home.

I'm a great believer that education starts from the inside, not from the outside, and that as you go through life—as you grow and develop—you meet up with opportunities for action that stretch you, in mind, body, and spirit. As you are stretched, you meet up with new opportunities that move you in that direction. I was trying to find the simplest summation for what I think homeschooling should be about, and I think I have done it in five words: "Have fun. Learn stuff. Grow."

Although it does flow, we work hard to provide opportunities for the kids, for ourselves, and for the family. I think all my books strongly suggest that. The first thing to be said is that almost all of us who are homeschooling these days were not homeschooled ourselves, and so we carry around messages, and ways of doing business, and ways of thinking about education, that we learned in our 13 years of incarceration.

Almost none of us learned how to learn at school, but we all learned how to teach. We had 13 years of models in front of us, more often than not, bad ones. So we have to go through this business of unlearning how to teach, so that we can allow education to naturally occur. I have always had my own learning projects, independent of my kids. They have always been welcome to come on along on my journey, if they liked; I didn't insist on it. I don't necessarily join theirs either. I think the model of having an adult learner in front of them is extremely important.

When you go to school, whether you had a good teacher or a bad teacher, you almost never had the example in front of you of a learning teacher. No teacher, from what you could tell, ever learned anything. Children very rarely experience adults learning around them. When they see that example, of you trying new things, often failing at them, making mistakes and then, with time, energy, and effort, getting better at them, and finding they meet your needs and feed your spirit, kids are likely to do the same thing.

I was a frustrated musician growing up, and as luck would have it, I guess, I have two musicians as children—two very different musicians, but two musicians. In the process, I took up the violin at the age of 47. I'm not very good at it, but I helped found a little community orchestra that now has 55 members. At the age of 52, I made my operatic debut. There was a new opera company forming in our town, and we saw a little ad for it. My older daughter, 14, who had been singing since the age of 7, thought she would love to do that. I had no idea that 14-year-olds could join opera companies. I did know they always need bass singers in the chorus. I figured they would get us as a package deal. After all, we were going to be driving there and I would have to wait, so I might as well join. We both did. I later discovered that the vocal director had been singing since 14, and the conductor had been conducting since she was 12. They didn't think it odd at all, but what did I know? I had never sung opera before. I have been involved in five productions since. I just came back this weekend from Smith College, where my older daughter entered with a paid research assistantship, to work on a production edition of the first opera ever written by a woman, in 1626. It was performed to a sell-out crowd, some 2,100 people, over the weekend.

In my book, *The Curriculum of love* (2005), I write about being at home in oneself. Trying to feel at home in one's own skin, and I mean that skin as small as the epidermis that encases you and the skin being the skin of the earth. If you want aware and alive human beings, the best way to produce them is to have them around other aware, alive human beings.

Back in the seventies, Ivan Illich talked about education, and he meant institutionalized education, "Education is learning under the assumption of scarcity." When you think about school, from the way we do public education in our countries, the idea is there is never enough time; there is never enough space; there's never enough individual attention. The assumption is there couldn't be enough. Whether we are using our resources correctly is another question. I'm not an education reformer, and I never claimed to be, and never want to be. I wonder what would happen, if we simply went about assuming that education is learning under conditions of abundance? That's an idea that I try to keep in front of me, in thinking about how I want our family to be learning.

Kids need to have the space to learn to be themselves, they need the time to become themselves, and to learn specific skills. I always like to use the example of how I failed walking about 300 times at 13 months. I mean, I fell, I tottered, I teetered, I scraped up a knee here and there, I balanced myself against walls, I slumped down against chairs. I failed walking 300 times, every time. But, at 15 months, I would have had an A.

I say if you're doing the same-old, same-old with your teenagers, and assuming that they are simply a child with hormones, you can be pretty sure you're doing the wrong thing. They have reached a new developmental stage where they need mentors, not you, but other people in the community. They need to be able to try on future hats that they might wear in a future world that will be theirs and not yours. They need those opportunities to stretch themselves in new ways. It's very hard work and it's very enjoyable work at the same time.

Mentors are all over the community, you just have to get a knack for finding them. In one of my books, *The Healing Heart–Communities* (2009), my friend, the storyteller Doug Lipman, talks about games that he uses to teach children community-interviewing skills. My favorite technique is to get a pair of kids, who have no idea what they want to seek in the community, put them on bicycles with one of those throw-away cameras and a little notebook, and having taught them to do interviewing. Have them go out and interview the mayor, the person who runs the hardware store who may also be the mayor, a minister, a nurse, whoever, and as they do so, ask at the end of the interview whether they might allow an apprentice or somebody to shadow them for a couple of days, or provide mentoring. If you have a homeschooling group, you can take those opportunities back to them and end up with an entire community library of mentors.

My younger daughter is an extreme example, she's very sociable. She collects adult friends all over the community, but some kids aren't like that. That's why, if you teach them interviewing skills and get them out on bikes, they can find things that they would never have discovered for themselves. It doesn't come naturally to all children. As my older daughter, Aliyah, used to say when she was a young teenager, "It's kind of like being a snake, getting ready to shed its skin. When they are getting to shed their skin, their eyes cloud completely over and they have no idea where they are going."

I don't separate my views on religion and on the spirit from my views of education. They are really all-of-a-piece. I believe that the spirit reveals itself constantly and continually to all of us. We just have to be open to that happening.

The subtitle of my second book *Homeschooling and the Voyage of Self-Discovery: A Journey of Original Seeking* (2003) suggests that seeking behavior, the seeking for something beyond ourselves is built into our very nature as human beings. We don't know what it is we are seeking, it is beyond ourselves, yet we are involved in this lifelong search, it is our defining characteristic as people. This to me is a core tenet of my Quaker faith.

Our kids have been very, very supportive. Aliyah serves on a national Committee of Friends, and flies from college to meetings in Philadelphia and Maryland all the time. I don't know how she gets all her schoolwork done, but that's hers to figure out. Both of them have been heavily involved in both our Meeting's life, and in the larger Quaker community.

The basic, to me, is how much I have learned in the journey. I am, generally speaking, well-educated. I have more degrees than you'd ever want to know—I'll trade some for a musical instrument—but what's amazing to me is that so many of the things my kids became involved and interested in, I had no knowledge of whatsoever. I tell parents that ignorance is a great gift for the homeschooling parent.

When there are homeschooling problems, I have discovered that a vast number of them are simply cured with time. Whether it's, "I don't like him playing all those video games," or perfectionism, or whatever they come to me with, I often reply: "Two years from now, write me a letter, and you'll find out that you are laughing about the things you are concerned about now."

Children are not with us for very long, it's a very precious time in our lives. I can tell you now, with an 18-year-old and a 15-year-old, it doesn't last that long. I like to look at learning as a voyage: You don't know where the voyage is going to take you when you begin, but you can be sure that you're going to meet lots of new and interesting and intriguing sights and people along the way. That doesn't mean they are always going to be pleasant, but they are always going to be interesting. If you look at your learning journey as a family, again not something to be done to the children, but something that you do, together as a family, you end up exploring all kinds of mysterious islands that you never even knew were there.

When conflicts arise, my wife Ellen is always right. I don't tell her that when we are in the midst of a conflict, of course (but she knows that's what I tell everyone, and she agrees). I learned that from experience. She carries less schooling than I do, and usually that means she can see things about learning more clearly. Usually, when I'm having conflicts with children, it's because it's a kind of internal conflict that I'm having with myself, and I just haven't wrestled hard enough with it. Often, it is stuff left over from my own school days, or my days as a child that I haven't resolved for myself.

It's kind of like when you have arguments with people about homeschooling and it's very clear you can't convince them, they don't like homeschooling, and you are very upset about it. You are upset about it because of your own internal struggles. When a person has different views from your own, the simplest thing would be to say, "Oh, it's interesting that you think that. What made you think that?" and, "Thank you for your views." The fact that you feel conflicted, and may turn red in the face or come home feeling unsettled, often is a reflection of the fact that you have those conflicts in your own mind and heart.

I always like to look at the community itself as our total learning environment. I mean, my first book *And the Skylark Sings With Me* was subtitled *Adventures in Homeschooling and Community-Based Education* (1999). So much of what we did, first of all, didn't resemble school at all, but secondly, didn't take place at home. And, you know, we mined our community. In mining our community, we gave as much back, more than we got, in the process. We are in the process of helping to reinvigorate our communities.

I look at schools and I'm constantly upset by schools in various ways. They spend $2,500,000 on a new football field that only the football players can use, when the community is begging for park space. Or they'll start a new high school theatre program, which is great for the high schoolers, except there are playhouses and theatre groups all over the community that are begging for actors, and actresses, and set designers, and techies, and would be pleased as punch to take on some teenagers to learn new roles, take part in their productions, help learn to do technical theatre and whatever.

The enormous waste of resources in schools is extraordinary when you think of them not as school or education resources, but as community resources. If those resources were similarly available to the community, we could be living in better places for all of us. The first thing I think of when I hear the word "school" is a giant sucking sound.

I wrote, in *Homeschooling and the Voyage of Self-*

Discovery (2003) that the young teen years were the time for vision quests, walk-abouts, rites of passage, mentorships, apprenticeships, and bar mitzvahs in the Jewish community, all under the auspices of adult members of the community, never one's own family. We start with our family and move outward. This is a wisdom that's been learned by cultures around the world for two or three millennia, and when we reject it, we do so at our peril.

An audio version of this piece appears in podcast and can be found at: Albert, H. D.(2006, February 15). Interview by B. Ekwa Ekoko [Podcast]. Fun. Stuff. Growing with David Albert, Radio Free School. Hamilton, Ontario.
Retrieved from
http://radio4all.net/index.php/program/16601

References

Albert, D. (1999). *And the skylark sings with me: Adventures in homeschooling and community-based education.* Gabriola Island, BC: New Society Publishers.

Albert, D. (2005). *Have Fun. Learn Stuff. Grow: Homeschooling and the curriculum of love.* Monroe, ME: Common Courage Press.

Albert, D. (2003). *Homeschooling and the voyage of self-discovery: A journey of original seeking.* Monroe, ME: Common Courage Press.

Cox, A.M., Albert, DH., Mellon, N (2009). *The healing heart-Communities.* Gabriola Island, BC: New Society Publishers.

llich, I. (1970). *Deschooling society.* New York, NY: Harper & Row Publishers.

14. DAVID ALBERT

David H. Albert is a homeschooling dad, husband, writer, and storyteller. He writes a regular column, "My Word!" for *Home Education Magazine*, and is a featured contributor for *Life Learning Magazine*.

As founder of New Society Publishers, Albert was both editor and publisher of John Taylor Gatto's *Dumbing Us Down: The Hidden Curriculum of Compulsory Schooling*, and more than a 100 other titles.

http://www.skylarksings.com/

CHAPTER 15

FROM ALBANY TO NOW

MARY LEUE

The ideas we used at the Albany Free School are really beginning to catch on very nicely. It's somewhat like Summerhill. A.S. Neill who founded, and ran Summerhill for many, many years, and I used to correspond. He would answer with a one-liner, ordinarily. I asked him, "Would you do a school for working-class people?" And I got an answer back, "I'd think myself daft to try." So, I said to myself, "Right that's what we're going to do." I wanted to, because I've always been drawn to the inner-city.

The Albany Free School is a maximally-diverse population, we don't select anyone. Any kid whose parents let him come and visit for a week, and then he says, "I want to go to this school," we say, "sure." We've never turned anybody away; we've never had a waiting list. We take whoever comes. The student body is pretty well divided, in terms of the neighbourhood kids, between black, Hispanic, and a few Asian children.

The school is pretty much a democratic school, as it's defined now by the International Democratic Education Conference people. The children do as they wish. We don't have as much formal curriculum as Neill did, where the kids could come or not as they chose. The education here itself, I think, is different. When I visited Summerhill a couple of times, it seemed to me that the academic aspect of

173

Summerhill was rather boring. Our kids find it very exciting. They jumped right in on computers very early on and taught themselves reading and writing. Chris Mercogliano, who runs the school now, is a mathematician, so they get the three-Rs fine.

One of the unique things, which I adapted from Summerhill, is the meeting. That is where decisions are made at Summerhill. Our kids attend up until 9th grade— that's our state-defined mandate—then move on to high school. After a few tries to solve problems the Summerhill way, I set up another system, with the idea being that children really needed to take responsibility for their own problem-solving. It's much better done on a peer level than with adults. They'll run to the adults and say so-and-so hit me, and this kind of thing, and there's no need for it. What we did was set up a council meeting system, whereby any child, at any time, no matter what is going on, is entitled to run through the school yelling "Council Meeting!" That takes precedence over everything, including curriculum.

The kids all come together and we use Roberts Rules of Order, parliamentary procedure. The kids select a chairman, never an adult. They vote for a chairman who's going to run a tight ship, because they don't like to have to hang out solving people's problems for several hours. They want it to work efficiently, so they pick the kid who knows how to keep order. They did vote in, after I left, a provision that the chairman can relegate an obstreperous kid to the corner for a while. That seemed to work very well.

New kids coming in on the whole thing, very surprisingly, rapidly thrive on it, because their needs get addressed very seriously. With the council meeting, we use rules of evidence. We use witnessing. The interesting thing is that when you trace any of these problems back far enough, very often it turns out that the kid who was the initial aggressor came in to school that morning wiped out, or bummed out, or angry, or scared, because of something that had been going on at home during the night.

The kids are tremendously supportive of each other. They move very quickly now through this issue of blaming, into fact finding: what really happened. The new ones learn to trust quite readily. It's a brilliant system.

Unschooling

I think we are an unschool, basically. That's a term that Matt Hern uses. It's a matter of the term you choose to use, really. It's a question of finding out what works for you, with your kids. I think schools need to be totally individual, and adapted to what the parents, and the kids work out together. As long as it works, that's the important thing.

John Holt and I didn't see eye-to eye, but then, he never visited our school. He became very anti-school, for perfectly good reasons: He saw too many middle-class, rural alternative schools that catered to parents who already had options, and he saw what happened to kids in the public schools. He never put those two things together. He just had a personal experience of homeschooling, which was brilliant, and it worked. It worked beautifully. I was very skeptical in the beginning, but I'm a believer. I would never discourage parents from unschooling their own kids.

It's important that children understand, as early as they can discover it, that it's ok for them to be in this world, that they are important within themselves. That's a prerequisite. As Neill pointed out endlessly, but very few people got, freedom implies and involves responsibility for your acts. If you are free to act, then you have to own what happens as a result. Do you see? Your freedom must not impose on the freedom of other people. Children need to have a lot of freedom to roam, to move out of doors. Even here, in Albany in the winter, there is tobogganing, and skating, and skiing.

There are wonderful little hills right by the school, so even the smallest kids can sled or toboggan, so we go out. There is a nature preserve in the Helderberg Mountains to the west of Albany, and the kids have spent quite a bit of time there. The staff is wonderful with children, introducing them to species and so on. Kids who have freedom in their lives are naturally affectionate towards creatures in the wild, and curious about plants and trees and birds.

Our kids have always been very supportive of people who care about the environment. A guy in the New York State Department of Environmental Conservation, I think he was second in command, blew the whistle on how little the department was doing for the environment. The head of the department fired him, and our kids got so outraged that they collected a huge armful of wildflowers for him, called the TV stations and presented him with the award. They raised such a ruckus that he was reinstated.

When kids are comfortable within themselves and with each other, and enjoy what they're doing, it just naturally extends to the environment. They're all activists, natural activists, which continues after they get to high school, and to college.

Gabby, one of our kids who graduated a year ago, has just taken over an abandoned Italian church down the hill from our school. The diocese let it go and nobody was able to resurrect it. She's got it as a community centre. Our kid's just love to jump in. They have raised thousands of dollars. Two years ago they raised the money to go to an International Democratic Education Conference in New Zealand.

Children are loving creatures, and everything grows out of pleasure, enjoyment of their lives, and wanting to expand. No formal teaching is needed. Kids vie for the privilege of grabbing one of the handles of our great huge cooking pot that has had scraps from lunch in it, so they can feed the hens. The love of animals is a prerequisite for having spiritual sensitivity. When they become adolescents, they just expand their horizons in whatever way they choose.

Children will gravitate in the same direction their parents have gravitated. If there is no spiritual background there, the children will find one on their own. It's just being treated with love and kindness, and a lot of singing, and dancing instead of providing them with formal experiences. We take them to the cathedral up at the top of the hill; the kids are awestruck when they walk in. They get that kind of experience, but not in a formalized manner.

An audio version of this piece appears in podcast and can be found at: Leue, M. (2004, August 18). Interview by B. Ekwa Ekoko [Podcast]. From Albany to Now with Mary Leue, Radio Free School. Hamilton, Ontario.
Retrieved from http://radio4all.net/index.php/program/9846

References

Leue, M. (1994). *Challenging the giant: The best of SKOLE, the journal of alternative education*. Albany, NY: Down to Earth Books.

In 1969, Mary Leue started the Free School, a democratic, elementary school in inner-city Albany (New York), dedicated to the authentic lives of children. It is the oldest urban free school in the U.S. Other accomplishments include a community-investment organization, a magazine of alternative education *(SKOLE),* a magazine for empowering families, and a community enterprise renovating neighborhood buildings to finance the school. Mary has written many articles, published many magazines and books and continues to do so.

http://www.spinninglobe.net/spinninglobe_html/biomary. htm

CHAPTER 16

GUERRILLA LEARNING

GRACE LLEWELLYN

A lot of people find themselves looking around, looking within, and seriously thinking about defining themselves as human beings for the first time when they are teenagers. I see adolescence as a powerful time, and I felt drawn to work with kids at that stage. Certainly for me personally, those years were a time of tremendous transformation, which I'm sure contributed to my decision to go on and teach school to teenagers. Later, when I left the school system and started working with homeschoolers, it was logical to continue working with that age group.

I think that teenagers need things that society just isn't providing. For one, an opportunity to be involved in a meaningful way: to contribute something to society, not to just be passive recipients of education. Also, I think that teenagers actually need more, not less, leadership from adults. I don't mean control, I mean leadership. Leadership that is visionary, that helps youth to more clearly see their strengths, their options, their life's mission, that offers more and better support for them to develop skills and work toward their most important dreams.

As it stands now, there's a lot of pressure put on young people, but that pressure is not often in the interest of goals that are meaningful to their lives.

I think it's true that when most kids become teenagers, it's very important to them to have a peer group, not just a close-knit community of all ages, and not just a big loving extended family, but an actual age-peer group, big or diverse enough that within it they can find a niche where they belong. Homeschoolers who see a way to connect with such a group outside of school often aren't interested in school. But if they aren't offered, or can't see how to create for themselves, an alternative means to find their tribe then by default school naturally looks like the best place to find it. That's one of the reasons I started Not Back to School Camp.

Even though our campers come from all over the U.S. and Canada, and it's not like they're connecting with a big community they'll be able to take home with them, it still helps connect them with peers who are out of school. Lots of them travel to visit each other, and many stay in touch through the Internet, mail, phone, and such throughout the year.

Then, there's the strength of the Zeitgeist. Our culture is so strong in its narrow idea that "good kids go to school, that's just how it is." So a lot of homeschooling teenagers, if they've never been in school, start to wonder, "What is this universal experience I'm missing out on? Would I measure up if I were part of it? Am I okay?" They want to try it out.

I've recently been in conversation with a dozen or so people in their late twenties who were homeschooled. Some of them wanted to try school when they were teenagers, and their parents let them. They tried it, got to say, "Okay, this is what all the fuss is about," and after experimenting for a while, "I think I'll leave again." Now they feel great about having homeschooled. On the other hand, two of them, their parents didn't let them try school, and to this day they still wonder, with a bit of resentment, "What would it have been like?"

Of course, some formerly-homeschooled teens go to school and decide to stick with it. In the more interesting versions of this story, these kids are so grounded in their childhood experience of being able to take responsibility for their own decisions, and to follow their own curiosity wherever it leads, that they retain their full humanity even within an institution that dehumanizes so many others. They are often able to see school as simply one optional resource that contributes to their growth, rather than as the director and definer of their learning.

To support a teenager who is living and learning outside of the school system, and to help him continue to thrive that way, I think it's important for parents to actively reach out. To draw him out, listen patiently and reflectively, ask questions, help him to articulate his goals and visions, and find ways to support him in moving towards those goals and visions. For some kids, that's going to mean sending them out in the world for awhile, away from home which, of course, can be scary for parents. It doesn't have to mean that for every kid, but adolescence definitely is a transition time, a time of transformation, and parents have to be ready to do some letting go. Families that try to keep homeschooling the way they did when their kids were younger do run into resistance.

Sometimes, it helps to bring in a third party, another adult whom both the parent and the teenager respect and feel comfortable with, and let that person help draw out the teenager, help her clarify her direction in life, and help brainstorm ways for her to take concrete steps in that direction.

I think it helps for parents and other adults to recognize their own power as leaders and to be intentional about it. Not in the conventional sense of, "this is what you are going to do now," but rather, "you're older now and it's a new time in your life. I'd love to support you in setting some new intentions and articulating some goals that would make your life more the way you want it to be."

I had no idea that my first book, *The Teenage Liberation Handbook: How to Quit School and Get a Real Life and Education* (1991), would have anywhere near the impact it had. When I had finished the manuscript, but it wasn't printed yet, I remember saying to my brothers, "It would be so great if just one person reads this book and it has a big impact on them. Could you imagine if people read it and then actually got out of school?" The idea seemed incredibly far-fetched, though exciting. My brothers said, "Yeah that would be pretty cool. Won't happen, of course, because it's just too radical, but . . . yeah, nice thought."

For me, the important thing was just to write that book. I felt called to do so, regardless of the outcome. So, to be met with a strong and positive response, that was amazing! I still get a lot of response, the book continues to impact people's lives (and yes, they continue to read it and actually quit school) and I feel deeply fortunate that I was in the position to write it back in 1990.

My second book, *Real Lives*, has also been pretty impactful, though it hasn't sold nearly as well. It's a collection of essays by homeschooling teenagers who tell their own stories in depth. The book helps demystify homeschooling, and gives a rich sense of some of the different possibilities. I would definitely like more people to get their hands on that book.

Some have asked me if I would call my approach to living and learning, if I had to define it, anarchistic. Ten years ago I might have, but I wouldn't use that term now. I'm not sure what term I would use; actually, I shy away from labels. Maybe I'd say that I aspire to natural learning and living. I'm interested in supporting a natural way of learning and developing. Or I might call my ideal approach creative, connected to a larger movement of people that sees and shapes new directions, who don't think in terms of conforming to society as it's already established, but rather step back and try to think freshly about the questions, "How can I best live my own life?" and "How can I learn in such a way that I'm helping to create the society I want to live in?" Although I haven't read the book, *The Cultural Creatives* (2001), I'm pretty sure I'm at least partly stealing this idea from it.

I guess I could use the term anarchistic in the sense that what I advocate is definitely about leadership from the ground up. I'm all for individuals discovering what's right for them and following their own path, rather than following a top-down system dictating how we should live our lives and how we should learn.

I would love to see us as a society not thinking so much in terms of "education," but rather thinking more broadly in terms of "life." We tend to see things in boxes and categories, which doesn't always serve us. When people say "education," sometimes I like to say, "If you substitute the term 'life' for 'education'—every time you say 'education' or 'learning,' try saying 'life' instead—that might invite you to look at things in a different way." (I probably stole that idea too, most likely from John Holt I suppose, it all starts to bleed together in my mind at this point: what's his, what's mine, what's some other guy's).

In broader realms, too, I would love to see us think less in categories: over here we have health; over there we have learning; and over here we have work. What about a life or a neighbourhood that mixes all three together so the edges are rubbed out? I would love to see a less institutional society and a more integrated society.

I have also edited a book about the African-American dimension of homeschooling. *Freedom Challenge* (1993) hasn't sold many copies, which I'm sad about. I wish that more homeschoolers in general—not just African-Americans—would read it, because it's important for us all to be aware of ways that we can be more welcoming, and understand more of what is true for sub-groups of the homeschooling community. I'd love to see more African-Americans reading it too. In the African-American community, traditionally, there is a high value placed on education and, perhaps by default and through not being aware of other choices, that translates largely to a high value placed on schooling. So, I'd just love to see more African-Americans considering the possibilities, and then including the option of homeschooling in their dialogue about education, even if most ultimately chose to stay within the system. For whatever reason, people are way less interested in that book than in my other work. Nonetheless, I think it's important, and I very much enjoyed working with the writers; it was a fun project for me.

I taught school for three years before I wrote *The Teenage Liberation Handbook*, and although I'd had difficulty working in schools, I loved working with teenagers. I missed that. For a while I felt satisfied with the correspondence I had with my readers. But, eventually, I just really missed connecting in person. I opened a resource center here in Eugene, Oregon, mostly for teenage homeschoolers, thinking that then I would get the pleasure of working with kids face-to-face again. That project never really got off the ground, it had a few sparkly moments, but mostly it just flopped and drained my bank account. I was still hungry for that connection. At the same time, I was being invited to speak at homeschooling conferences, where I'd encounter groups of teenagers around the country, and in Canada. I'd meet some kid in Ohio who was talking about plans for a bicycle trip across several states. Then I'd be in California and talk with a girl who had just built her own bike, and I'd think, "Oh, I wish those two could meet."

My motivation to start the Not Back to School Camp was a combination of those two things: First, I wanted to personally have flesh and blood contact with homeschooling teenagers both for my own enjoyment and also to keep me from getting too abstract in my own thinking about homeschooling, and, second, I thought it would be great for them all to meet each other. Camp has been really fun, I love putting it on. It's a lot of work, sometimes a crazy amount, but it's rewarding for me and it's inspiring for the campers to meet each other.

It's very much a co-created week. We invite everyone to teach an hour-long daytime workshop on something they love, and around 60% of our campers take us up on that. During workshop blocks you can usually choose between four or five offerings that might include anything from identifying wild edible plants to math games, beginning Japanese to jewelry-making. It just depends on what people happen to be interested in. Workshops are a lot of fun, and a chance for campers to get a taste of what their peers are excited about.

We have talent shows, among other things, in the evenings. The performers range from professional musicians who have already been touring for three years by the time they are 17, to kids who maybe just took their first tap dancing lesson three weeks ago, complete beginners. Everyone is received with great appreciation and applause, and it's a very encouraging time for kids. They get affirmed. It's an extremely supportive experience and I love that about homeschoolers: they tend to be very warm. They're not spending their time in a tightly-ranked institution where they compete with each other for grades or for popularity, and maybe that's why they tend to be more relaxed socially. At any rate, it's a pleasure to see them support each other, and to watch them welcome each other on the first day of camp! New campers get mobbed with hugs when they arrive.

I'm working on a book that feels important to me, and I imagine that when I'm finished I may also be finished with the book-writing-and-editing chapter of my life. This one is kind of a parallel to the *Teenage Liberation Handbook*. It's for teenagers who are in the school system and for whatever reason, maybe their parents' beliefs, or a home situation that is worse than school, or unschooling sounds too radical or too scary, and are planning to stay there. I feel that it's important to speak to these kids too, to say, "Okay, so there you are, in school. What are the actual choices you have available, right there where you are, in the situation exactly as it is?"

I've been working on that project for a while, it comes with its own set of fascinating questions, and it will take me another year or so. After that—I don't know. I know I'll keep running Not Back to School Camp, but I may take off in a whole new direction. I've been interested in counseling and learning about psychology. Maybe I'll go to India!

Postscript

I abandoned the book, life just got too demanding in other realms. Camp continues to grow and thrive: we're now in session five weeks each year. Counseling and psychology: I didn't go down that road. Instead I put more energy into my passion for dance and am now in the process of learning to teach an ecstatic dance practice called Soul Motion. I also took up Argentine tango, and I continue to perform bellydance. The "whole new direction" turns out to be motherhood, as I recently adopted a miraculous little boy. And, yes, I went to India.

An audio version of this piece appears in podcast and can be found at:

Llewellyn, G. (2004, April 21). Interview by B. Ekwa Ekoko [Podcast]. Guerrilla Learning with Grace Llewellyn, Radio Free School. Hamilton, Ontario.

Retrieved from
http://radio4all.net/index.php/program/9050

References

Llewellyn, G. (1996). *Freedom challenge: African American homeschoolers.* Eugene, OR: Lowry House Publishers.

Llewellyn, G. (1993). *Real lives: Eleven teenagers who don't go to school tell their own stories.* Eugene, OR: Lowry House Publishers.

Llewellyn, G.(1991). *The teenage liberation handbook: How to quit school and get a real life and education.* Eugene, OR: Lowry House Publishers.

Ray, P. H., Anderson, S.R. (2001). *The cultural creatives: How 50 million people are changing the world.* New York, NY: Random House, Inc.

———————

Grace Llewellyn is the founder and director of Not Back to School Camp, a gathering held in Oregon and Vermont that draws over 250 unschooled teenagers each year. She's also the author of *The Teenage Liberation Handbook: How to Quit School and Get a Real Life and Education*, and the editor and co-author of three other books on unschooling. A former school teacher, she has been involved in the homeschooling movement in many ways since 1990—always with the goal of supporting people in engaging more deeply and intentionally with their learning. In her other life, Grace loves to dance. She is particularly smitten with Argentine tango, bellydance, and ecstatic dance. Grace lives with her son in Eugene, Oregon.

CHAPTER 17

GETTING KIDS ON THE STREETS

MATT HERN

We live in a culture that perceives kids as incapable of learning without being taught. It's an idea that is difficult to divest yourself of. It's easy to see, when you have children, that nobody would think to teach a one-year-old how to talk. One-year-olds can pick up the most complicated languages in the world of their own volition. They don't need workbooks, they don't need anybody sitting there hawking over them and telling them how to do things and pretending that they're teaching them. But somehow, five years later we expect that children need to be taught how to read the exact same language they taught themselves to speak four years earlier.

I've been around unschooling children for the last decade and they all learn how to read, one after the other, in ways that are so enigmatic, so crazy and so incomprehensible to the outside viewer. But they learn how to read.

I am opposed to the idea of teaching reading. After all, kids all want to grow up to be competent; they want to grow up to be literate, smart, capable people. Nobody wants to grow up to be stupid and ignorant. Certainly nobody wants to grow up to be illiterate.

Sometimes kids learn to read late. Typically boys, frankly, for reasons that I couldn't even begin to guess at. But kids learn to read between the ages of 4 and 15. Some kids learn early, some kids learn very late, but by the time they are in their mid-teens the early learners and the late learners are pretty much indistinguishable from one another.

At some point, they are absolutely going to want to learn how to read because there's no question that it is an important part of life. I believe that everyone wants to learn how to read and is capable of learning to read, except in very isolated cases. The key is to have a lot of reading around kids, adults reading a lot, books and magazines all over the place, trips to the library. I want kids to read for sure, but really, I want them to love to read.

I've noticed a lot of kids that I've known over the years who have been deschooled, even kids that have not done any academics, I mean essentially no classes, being able to slide right into high school or university with their age group and do just fine. It comes to a point where people say, "Jeez! I really want to get my high school graduation," or, "I really want to go to university," or, "I really want to do this, and be trained in that." It might take a little extra work, a summer course to catch up—whatever it takes—but kids will do it once they are motivated.

Once the motivation is internal rather than external, people are eminently capable. There's no point in trying to drag children through a curriculum that they have no interest in. It's not useful to force people to learn things they have no interest in because, not only will they resent it, they won't learn it either.

If you take a kid's day, and you fracture it so intensively into little one hour blocks, and demand they move from subject to subject, more or less arbitrarily, one of the things that happens (and this is really important in developing soldiers and compliant workers) is that kids lose the capacity to make decisions for themselves. Because at the sound of a bell you have to be able to go *dong* "It's math," *dong* "It's science," and not sit there wondering "Why am I doing this? I'd like to do something else." It is important to the school system that kids not even begin to ask that question. The point is to be able to respond to authority and to respond at a moment's notice—without questioning.

We expect kids to sit in a school all day long, passively respond to authority, move to the sound of a bell, and only evaluate themselves in terms of other people's expectations and mechanisms. Then, all of a sudden, they graduate from high school and are expected to be able to run their own lives!

People often ask, "Why aren't teenagers more responsible? Why can't they take care of themselves better?" Well, they've never had the opportunity to do it. I think it's reasonable to think of the possibility of little kids, from birth, really being able to make good, rational decisions about what they want to do with their time. I think it's reasonable to presume that people want to grow up to be competent, healthy human beings.

I think you have to start with the idea that people are capable of making good decisions for themselves. You have to believe that people are not born into original ignorance. The idea of education has evolved, at least within the Western mind, from the conception that people are born into original ignorance and that unless they are saved from their own stupidity they are going to be lost. I think it's an idea worth scrapping, and I'm paraphrasing from Ivan Ilich here, because people are not born inherently stupid.

People are born natural learners, and naturally interested in their world. We all know that from being around groups of kids. There's nothing worse than standing in front of a group of kids, or even one or two adults, and trying to "teach" them something that they have no interest in. It's terrible, it's dispiriting. Nobody wants to do it, it's totally painful. It doesn't go anywhere. But if you're with a group of people who are very interested in learning what you are talking about, I hesitate to use these word, but it goes like magic. People pick up things so fast it's amazing.

Compulsory schooling doesn't even succeed at the very narrow standards which it sets for itself. If you go to the No Child Left Behind website and look at the first graph they offer, there are monstrous numbers in terms of increased spending. You find that education spending in the U.S. has doubled since 1985. There's an incredible amount of money being spent on education. Last year $700 billion was spent on all levels of education, but notice on that same graph there's a straight line right across the middle of the spending that indicates reading competency. For the last 30 years, nothing has changed. Only 32% of fourth graders can read competently.

So, despite the fact that we are making kids go to school from an increasingly young age, it's not working. Not only is it not a good way to live, I don't believe it's an effective way to learn, and the numbers bear that out. After a hundred-and-sixty years or so of compulsory education, people are getting dumber, not smarter.

Some argue that there's a tendency for deschooled kids to opt for high school once they become teenagers, mostly because it's the one setting in our culture where kids can meet and do things together. If there were alternatives, kids would probably choose something else. My response is, "Sure. That's fine and good." I have no problem at all with kids going to high school if they think it over and decide it is a good, valuable route for them. I am against the reflexive-zombie route of going to high school, just because. I would much prefer that people make conscious, thoughtful choices. There's really very, very little choice for most kids, which is why I started the Purple Thistle Centre with a bunch of teenaged friends.

I noticed that a lot of the kids that had been part of my life for a long time, who had become teenagers, 14, 15, 16, and 17, were starting to drift away from Windsor House (an alternative democratic school). Windsor House has its own internal, institutional community and logic. Teenagers, I think almost by definition at a certain point, begin to look into the wider world. They want to begin to assert themselves and they begin to slowly pull themselves out of familiar surroundings. I noticed a lot who were drifting away from Windsor House weren't really finding it anywhere else.

Some of them were attending high school, some of them were getting jobs, some of them were attaching themselves to college programs. There was no kind of institution or setting for deschooling kids that I really knew about out in East Vancouver. So I sat down with seven kids, in the fall of 2000, and we started talking about what would it look like if we could start a new kind of place for youth.

We started batting around ideas. We had no money but we each started putting $20 bucks a month into a pot and just seeing what would happen. We talked about starting a business, maybe a café. At some point along the way, we ran into a $15,000 grant from a local foundation, and opened a community centre called the Purple Thistle Centre. We opened it with all kinds of ideas, but we weren't really ready. We had a clean slate: a nice space, and we live in a downtown neighbourhood where space is pretty hard to come by.

Eventually we came up with some broad subject areas, of things that people were interested in. I think they are very common things that teenagers are interested in: art, music, writing, photography, video production, music, theatre, travelling, direct action, activism and so on. We started thinking, "If we could do these things what would it look like?" We started gathering kids in groups of between 5 and 15, in each one of these areas. We set up teams and hooked up each with someone in the community, a mentor—usually an adult but not always—who had stuff to share.

We work on two bases: The first is creativity and skill development. For instance, in the writing group we explore all kinds of writing genres and styles, read to each other, perform, and practice all the time. The second part is that we are doing some kind of community project with each group so that, not only is it personal development, it's working in the community as well. For example, the art group is working on a great mural at the community centre about the history of the immigrant working experience in Vancouver.

Currently, we have an art group, a writing group, a photography group, an exchange group, a travel group, a film group, a direct-action group, and a bunch of others all working at the same time out of this little place. We schedule different times for ourselves and the kids just go for it. They go for as much as they can. We have a whole bunch of other side projects: Spanish classes, bike classes, sexual education, and health education. Whatever we can think of, we do.

Every Monday night we meet as an operating collective, where everyone is invited to make decisions about how the space is run. We have a whole bunch of food and we sit and make decisions. I try to instil a family-style atmosphere, because a lot of the kids don't have great family structures. We are trying to make it a home-away-from-home. We try to create an atmosphere of kindness and generosity in a place where people can make decisions and have their voice heard, but not in a one person-one vote atmosphere.

It's called the Purple Thistle Centre but it's an Alternative or Supplement to School (ASS). Lots of the kids are in school. We have kids who are homeless, who sleep under the SkyTrain Bridge. We have kids who are 23, 24, who are in upper level university. We try to keep everyone mixing together without any kind of ghetto-ization of ages or schooling-level. I think that, too often, poor kids get shunted off together, or university kids only spend time with other university kids and learn to think that people that aren't in post-secondary education don't have intellectual stuff to share, and that's not true.

Sure, it's taken a lot of work, but it hasn't taken a ridiculous amount, because one thing teenagers have is a lot of energy, enthusiasm, and optimism. The problem is keeping up with demand. There's an endless stream of kids coming through every day, who want to do something: "Can I do this?" "I want to do that." Some of it's crazy and some of it's not. Trying to keep up, and trying to help kids facilitate their dreams, there's just a never-ending barrage of things that kids want to do! It makes me laugh, when people say kids are lazy and just want to sit around and watch TV all the time. As the person who tries to facilitate and tries to hook kids up with other people, and tries to find money for other projects and find places, there is just no way I can keep up.

The idea of most youth centers, that you'll find in almost every city, is to try to get kids off the street and out of trouble. That's a very common phrase. What you see in youth centers is pool tables, video games, ping pong and whatever. That's all cool, but it strikes me as condescending to kids. Get out of the way, let adults do their thing and just wait until you're an adult to be part of this stuff. So we do something different: get kids on the street and highlight for them and the community that they can make a positive contribution to their community and culture.

There's a certain kind of mentality that many unschoolers and homeschoolers tend to get, an "us against the world" kind of thing. "Pull up the draw bridge and don't let anybody in. We can make it ourselves." It's an individualistic, do-it-yourself view point, but in the end, it's self-defeating, I think. The bringing up of children is central to any culture; it's a social phenomenon, a social project. I would never use the phrase, "it takes a village to raise a child," but there is some kind of truth there. Critically, it's a social question: when you talk about, "What is education?" you ask the question, "What is it that people need to know?" which is a really sideways way of talking about what the good life is.

There's no way that question can be answered in isolation: that question has to be a social question. On a prosaic level, homeschooling is tough because no parent wants to be with their child 24/7 and more than that, no kid wants to be with their parent 24/7. That may be a crass way to put it, because we all love our children and we like to think that our kids all love us, but it's true. We all have lives we want to lead, and so too do our kids have lives they want to lead away from their parents.

It's a big world out there and just because you don't go to school doesn't mean that you can't be a major part of it. In fact, it is schooling that isolates kids into age specific groups, institutionalized away from the community rather than having them out exposed to all kinds of different people, of all kinds of ages, from all kinds of cultures and predilections.

I think unschooling has to be a community event. To unschool your kid, or to allow your kid not to go to school, involves a larger social commitment. It's not just "everything stays the same but we keep our kids out of school." It's a whole lifestyle change. The idea of deschooling implies an entire cultural and social stance. Changing the way we view schools has to be about changing the way we view the world. It is absolutely essential that we talk about deschooling, or school resistance, as something that is not just available to privileged folks. Deschooling cannot be reduced to one more lifestyle option for those who already have vast privileges: It has to be possible for everyday people, or it loses any progressive, radical, or transformative impact.

Of course, the pressure to be schooled is constant and very powerful, but the bigger question is not, "Why are you keeping your kids out of school?" It's, "Why are you putting them in there?" The answer for the overwhelming majority is because they badly need the childcare! Not because they think it's a good idea, not because they think their kid is learning a whole lot. It's because they need somewhere for their kid to go while they are working. That is the raw, crass truth of schooling: it's cheap daycare. That is solid, understandable and viable logic. But really it's just straight up child warehousing service, and we should acknowledge that.

One of the great tragedies of schooling is that kids learn to hate adults and adults to despise kids. Because kids all believe that adults are out to screw them somehow, because they are used to the manipulative authority of teachers and administrators. Adults like passing on their knowledge, and there is nothing that adults like better than to have a kid around who is interested in what they do.

A lot of kids who get sent to school come from families with alternative approaches, or sympathies for alternative pedagogies. They are interested in doing something different with their kids, and a lot of families really resent the fact that they have to send their kids to school every day, but they just don't have a choice: There is nothing else for them to do. There are a tremendous number of families in every community that know the school they are going to isn't the greatest thing, but that's just the way it is.

The thing I like to do more than anything with teenagers, and I've done it for many years now, is take them traveling. I started doing this years ago, at Windsor House with my partner, taking teenagers on month-long camping trips, and we continue to do so with the Thistle. We have been through Montana; camped in Utah for 33 days; we went to Death Valley; and through California. For the last few years, we've been taking kids from the Thistle up to the Northwest Territories, right on the Arctic Centre, for a youth exchange. The idea is to get native and non-native kids together to travel, hang out, stay in each other's houses and get past simple tolerance toward a hospitality and embracing of difference.

One of the core (and explicit) intents of school is restricting the imagination of kids so that they don't believe they're capable of bigger, more adventurous projects, as they spend all their time inside a classroom abstracting. It's one of the great tragedies of schooling: The endless abstractions, constantly talking about things as if they are somewhere else, as if they don't really exist, and certainly not for the student.

Being out of school enables people to actually interact with the world in a direct and meaningful way, all the time. You're interested in deserts? Well, hell yeah! Let's go to a desert! It involves a change in personal mentality, a change in lifestyle and expectations. I think too many times parents and kids are governed by a sense of fear of "what if." "What if we're not keeping up? We should be in school." There are lots of legitimate worries, but really I want to encourage people to be as adventurous, as brave, as imaginative as possible. To think big with the kids around you, and not let your worries get the best of you. People who live in fear get no peace.

An audio version of this piece appears in podcast and can be found at:
Hern, M. (2003, September 9). Interview by B. Ekwa Ekoko [Podcast]. Matt Hern: Self Design and Alternatives to School Part 1 of 2, Radio Free School. Hamilton, Ontario.
Retrieved from http://radio4all.net/index.php/program/7735
Hern, M.(2003, September 14). Interview by B. Ekwa Ekoko [Podcast]. Matt Hern Part 2 of 2, Radio Free School. Hamilton, Ontario.
Retrieved from http://radio4all.net/index.php/program/7767

17. MATT HERN

Matt Hern is an activist, organizer, writer and academic who lives and works in East Vancouver with his partner and daughters where he co-directs the Purple Thistle Centre and founded Car-Free Vancouver Day. His books and articles have been published on all six continents, translated into ten languages and he continues to lecture globally. He holds a PhD in Urban Studies and teaches at SFU.
Hern lectures worldwide speaking about deschooling, alternative education, sustainable urbanism, safety/security/risk and participatory democracy.
http://www.mightymatthern.com/

CHAPTER 18

IMPROVING UNSCHOOLING THROUGH STREWING

AND SPIRITUALITY

SANDRA DODD

In the old days, before the Internet was so big, all the homeschoolers were in one place, on a user group. I learned a lot because we were all mixed together. One day, someone who was very sceptical of unschooling said, "How do you get all those things in front of your children?" and I said, "I just strew it around. I just strew their paths with interesting things." The concept stuck. The idea is to just have things in your house that are interesting enough to pick up and turn over and mess with. Strewing stuff around can cover a whole lot of science and history and math all by itself. If we had a little building set (I find things at thrift shops) or magnets, maps, books, or things that had been given away from the fast food drive-through, we just collected four or five sets so we could build something bigger.

There's a book in our bathroom right now about archaeology. I didn't say anything to anyone, I just put it in there. We have a little bookshelf in the bathroom. My fifteen-year-old son came out this morning and said, "Did you see in that archaeology book that they think they know why people believed in the Minotaur and the maze?" He told me a long story about an archaeologist on an island off Greece. If no one had ever mentioned that book, if it looked

199

like nobody had ever read that book, it wouldn't have hurt my feelings because I just put the things out there and periodically switch them around.

I think I got the idea from when I was studying education, in the early 70s, which was the height of the school-reform days. I was in New Mexico, which was kind of a hotbed of school reform. There was a book called *The Open Classroom* (1999), written by people in New Mexico. I went to school with professors who just took for granted that the schools would be reformed, all of the research of the 60s and 70s was going to be implemented and everything would be better. I was young and idealistic and I wanted to believe that too.

One of the things they taught, about how the open classroom worked, was that it doesn't make sense to try to drag a class of thirty kids through one activity. Just put the interesting things out and they'll discover them, and they'll show each other, and they'll ask questions. I did that for a little while when I was teaching, and it worked. I've done it with my children, and it worked. Before we had children, my husband and I were together for seven years, and we did that with each other. We were involved in a medieval studies club. We made costumes, he made armour, and we made tents together. That took geometry, but we didn't say so. It was making tents: Trying to go from historical paintings to figure out how, with triangles and rectangles, they had made a tent with one center pole. We had a lot of activity like that between ourselves. We had friends who were artists, and interested in history, interested in music, and when you have the information swirling like that you start to see that everything is connected.

Some of the things we have from when we were younger remains in our house, and the kids just pick it up. They know about the items or they will say, "How do they keep the patterns straight on those Indian-print bedspreads?" I don't know—let's go find out. We can pull up a sample of block-printed cloth from the house. It's been easy for us to just rearrange the things in our house so the kids discover something new.

I think everyone's home can be a kind of museum. We went to our neighbour's house and he pulled out photos from when he was growing up. They were places my son and I were about to go and visit. People don't think to ask. You don't pull a book off someone's shelf and say, "Oh, you know that author? It's autographed!" I think people forget. People think of museums as other buildings, far away, that belong to the state, and their house as just a house. Sometimes that word "just" gets in the way of seeing the possibilities, and how rich each thing, each place is.

We found some castle blocks. I saw them when my son was a baby but they were very expensive, from Spain. I think it's worth looking in catalogues at things that you can't afford because then, when you are at the thrift store and you see it, you know what it is. They make really nice castle models.

I don't ever say, "All right! Attention every one! I'm putting out the castle blocks!" They just appear, and then castles are made, and people talk about them, about particular castles they are trying to make, or why this sort of arrangement would work because, since they played it last, they've discovered something new, either in a game they played or a movie they watched or something they read. After it's not getting any attention, it goes back away and something else comes out.

I have a bowl of rocks, and they look different wet than dry. Sometimes, when people are sitting around talking, it's worth just getting a little bowl of water and sticking different rocks in it while you're talking. It doesn't interrupt the conversation, and they can play with it or not as they want to. We have jigsaw puzzles: When I was in England I got some at thrift stores, for the equivalent of a dollar, of the history of the kings and queens of England. We've worked them, not with the intent to learn anything, but just to work them. Everyone, adult or child, who was involved in that, discovered something they hadn't known before. As we were working them, we talked, not about kings and queens, just about whatever was going on in our lives.

I think there's an advantage to not focusing, to not saying, "We are going to work this puzzle because it's history," just work the puzzle. Some history comes, some current social stuff, some personal stories about what had been going on, some questions about things totally unrelated. If there's enough swirl of information and exchange, all kinds of things will come up. They don't need to come up in a line. If one kid knows about Roman numerals at the age of six, and the other one doesn't know until twelve, so what? The first time anyone learns about Roman numerals in the real world is when they see them and don't know what they are. They ask, and somebody tells them. It's not brain surgery. It's more interesting, when you are seeing something real, than when you're getting it because it's September 13 and you're in the fifth grade and that's what the book says you should learn.

We find it to be really fun to discover things, but it's easier to discover things when they are there to discover. Maybe strewing is a bit like hiding Easter eggs. There just might be a couple or three things out and about, like conversation pieces. It's like putting out a pretty book on a coffee table, or an arrangement of flowers; it's no more than that, only it's more likely to be a puzzle.

Although it's incidental, that's the core of my method (if you want to call it a method), to just keep our lives busy and varied that incidental learning happens all the time. If friends, my own age or younger, come over to visit, they get caught up in whatever's going on. If the adults here are being playful and curious and open, visitors are more likely to be that way too. Whereas, the same people visiting in someone else's house, where it is a little more sombre and mature or, for want of a better word, more boring, won't do that. They go there, sit and drink beer or watch the game or whatever. But they come here and we're working a puzzle or building something and they'll get into that too. It's fun. We do things that are just fun. You can hardly walk by without picking it up and messing with it.

Sometimes, someone, my husband and one of the kids, will be doing something in one room and in the next room, some other friends are over and they are playing a video game and in another room or outside, another kid and somebody else are doing something else. That also is the idea of the open classroom. Their ideal was not to be sitting at desks reading, but to sit in a soft place, in a dark place, in a private place, or wherever you wanted, to read. They tried to have interesting places where kids could get away from the other kids. There would be, for history, timelines and costumes, sort of like what children's museums try to do now, where there are things that you can try on. For math, which now are common but weren't in the 60s and 70s, math manipulative toys, for example.

When people tried to follow this model (and there were lots of people doing it), the problem was clear. When they did the experiments, the kids were there voluntarily, or it was a lab school connected to a university where the parents were grad students or professors, so their kids got to go to school at the university, kind of like glorified daycare, but it was a model school or a lab school where they did tests on the kids. Professors and grad students who were doing research in school reform were teaching those kids. The parents were into it, they thought it was great, and the kids didn't have to be there. That's what made it work. Turns out that when they tried it in regular public school settings, it didn't work. The people who looked at it said it would have worked if teachers had volunteered, and if every child there had a choice whether to be in that program or to be in a traditional classroom. The failure was in the compulsory attendance, not the method.

Almost every type of routine damage schools can do to a child, parents can do at home. Parents can make their kids hate math. They can make them never want to read a book again. They can make them want nothing more than to grow up and get away. So, with unschooling, when people ask me what I think makes it work, I say, "The kids have to have a choice." There's a learning curve that I see with unschooled kids, and that is they seem to be ahead for the first few years and then there's a period of time, just roughly from about nine or ten to about twelve, when they can seem behind. After they are twelve or thirteen, zoom! They seem to be ahead again.

It just seems that in school, there is a period when children are eleven or twelve when they've just been crammed full of math facts, and geographical facts, and science terminology, and they just seem full-to-bursting with knowledge. The kids at home might still be playing Pokemon and coloring books, you know, and they look up and the school kids are naming places and things that they don't know, they're reading textbooks, they're doing long division, they're writing in cursive, things that you can see from across the room. They think, "What are they doing? I don't know what they are doing. I can't do that!"

But then what seems to happen with the unschoolers that I have met and talked with, is sure enough, when the kids got to be thirteen or fourteen, a kind of maturity came upon them and they said, "Oh! Well, I guess if I want to learn cursive, I'll just practice it. Is this it?" And they do it! They look at something and they say, "Is this all?" And they've figured out on their own how to do math, they are multiplying double digits in their head. They might not know how to write it down on paper, but they know how to do it. They start to develop their own map of the world and history of the universe where all of the facts are starting to gel into a model of the universe. They're understanding a lot and making a lot of connections.

About that time, the kids at school get all burned out and realize that all these facts they are learning are only leading to another year of facts. It's like Rumpelstiltskin, "Oh, you turned that straw into gold? Next room. Bigger. More straw. Oh yeah, you don't get to keep the gold." They are getting very irritated by the time they're fourteen, whereas the unschoolers are saying, "This is cool. I'm glad I didn't go to school!"

Another thing that happened with my kids, and with some others I've known, is that when they get to be fourteen or fifteen, they've either got a job, a really cool volunteer position, or become involved in a hobby so that they're in a position of teaching. Whether it's karate, or horseback riding, or ice-skating, they've gotten to the point where they know enough that they are a senior student, and they are given some position of responsibility.

Whatever it is, if they are given something real (and sometimes it's specifically because they are not in school during the day), and they are given the kind of responsibility that is given to an adult, in a way it makes them an adult. They feel that shift of not being one of the kids anymore, of being one of the adults. You see a change in their posture, and their bearing, and the way adults treat them.

At the same point, the kids at school are just barely in high school, maybe, with a batch of kids who are bullying them, picking on them, they're tired of it and see no end in sight. The best they can hope for is to get good grades so that they can go to college. They are at the point of greatest dismay in public schools, while the kids their age who are unschooled are saying, "Huh! I wonder if I'm going to go to horse camp or if I should take a college class? Should I go to karate three times a week so that I can get a black belt, or go work at the gaming store?" The kids in school don't have any of those options, so at the same time that they are made small, the unschoolers have been made large.

If families can just make it through those few years, past that rough hump of, "My kid hardly reads, he doesn't have cursive, he doesn't know the times tables, and he's twelve, and he's starting to get whiskers and he doesn't know anything," while the kids in school seem all together, because that's just before a lot of the kids in school start to say, "To hell with this, this is crazy. Why am I doing this?"

A lot of the things I have learned, I've learned because someone took an interest in me as a person. So, I've done that for people my whole life. If someone mentions they are interested or curious about something that I like or that I know, I'll lend them a book, I'll bring them over and show them my stuff. That's my way of paying back those people who helped me.

The kind of learning I was doing is the kind of learning I've tried to provide now for my children, which is, "You're interested in this? I know someone who knows that," or, "I don't know that answer but I know someone who does." I try to hook them up with real people who know real things, not in any kind of formal apprentice's way. Right now, my middle son, Marty (who's almost sixteen), is making boots with a friend of ours who has been doing leather work for a few years. He's making historical boots, some for Medieval and Civil War re-enactments, but mostly Renaissance-style boots. The company has sold boots to Disneyland and to movie productions, and so Marty is doing that, and is learning what is historically-accurate for different time periods and purposes. They make boots that look old, but are made of modern materials. Marty knows what he's doing and he gets paid—not much, minimum wage—four afternoons a week. We lucked into that, because we made friends with, paid attention to, and sought out people who were creative and curious and busy.

I don't know about Canada, but the U.S. has a mythology just as sure as Rome or Greece ever did. Part of that mythology is the phrase that just comes up as though it's a truth: All men are created equal. But what does that mean? It almost gets like *Animal Farm* (1945) where they want to create the equality after the fact. It's like, "You want to do something special? That's no good. We want you to be equal." If you know more than the other kids, that's not fair. There's the big whine, the underlying whine: that's not fair. There are families who say, "That's not fair, your kids are homeschooled." The homeschoolers, the school-at-home families, go "That's not fair, your kids aren't having to do work."

I don't believe people are created equal and I don't believe life can be fair unless fair means lowest common denominator, which is, everybody suffers, nobody has any good times.

Learning for fun?

At the risk of offending some people, it comes down to sin! It's a sin to have fun. It's the Christian work ethic: "If it feels good, don't do it; if it feels good, it must be bad for you; life is pain; start to suffer." I don't think that really does people any good.

One of the studies on how people learn that was done in experimental schools in the 60s and 70s asked, "What is the optimal state of mind for learning?" Schools try to get everyone very still and very quiet. That's not optimal. People don't learn very well when they're sitting still, not moving their hands, not moving their feet, while someone's talking at them. That's the optimal condition for taking a nap. The optimal condition is also not, when you think a tiger is going to bite you, and you're running away screaming, and you get so full of adrenaline you want to puke. Somewhere between those two is the right place. Three ways to get the mental state of arousal, of alertness or curiosity, are humour, music, and fun. School can't afford to do that, because if 25 kids at the same time think something is really neat and cool, they start to make noise. School is set up to keep everyone at such a low mental wavelength that they can't really learn, but at least they're quiet.

At home, if things can be fun and interesting and cool, it's easier to learn!

I know for sure that you can't pour information into people. I know for sure you can't command someone to learn something right now and have that work; fear doesn't work. Maslow's Hierarchy of Needs is something all teachers learn, and then promptly forget. Maslow's Hierarchy of Needs says that you can't learn unless you feel safe, loved, fed, not cold, not hot, not hungry, and you don't feel afraid. Yet, there are still schools and families where kids are told, "Do this or you can't eat lunch. Do this or I'll hit you." Some threat and some deprivation: learn first, then reward. They're going to learn. They are learning a lot. They are learning to get the heck away from there as soon as they can. They're learning to sneak food under the desk; to tune out adults; and to cheat and lie.

I don't want my kids to learn those things, so I keep them happy; I keep them fed; I let them sleep when they want to sleep; I let them say, "I don't want to do that right now," when they don't want to do that right now. It makes a big difference, because the level of arousal when they are excited about something is real. They don't have to fake being excited, they really can get excited. They know that they really can say no. That level of freedom and choice is unusual in our culture, for anyone.

I have a webpage called *Spiritual Unschooling* (http://sandradodd.com/spirituality). There are articles that seemed more about how parents felt, or how parents viewed their children, than about what they did. People don't become really good at unschooling without changing the way they see themselves and the world. At the core of it, I think there's a philosophical shift that has to happen. Because if people want to overlay unschooling on the same-old, business-as-usual life, it doesn't really fit very well. You have to remodel the house a bit. What the new parts have to do with spirituality is just the idea of being aware of what your child actually is doing, not what the book says he ought to be doing: To look directly at the person you're dealing with instead of looking at him through the developmental-colored lens.

Some people would say, "Okay fine, I don't need to know anything about child development or cognition or learning theory. I don't need to know anything, then, I'll just look at my kid." You'll look at him with what? There needs to be a balance of both. I think people who are going to take responsibility for their children's learning-lives, as it were, need to know what stages people go through. Piaget's stages of cognitive development are very helpful for people who know that, but that doesn't mean they should live by that in a moment-to-moment way. There are no hours in which we are teaching and there are no hours in which the children are not learning, so it changes the fabric of your life.

Sometimes, when I've described unschooling, people have said, "It sounds like you have study units," and I said,

"No. No," because although we might go on a binge, we might have a week where everyone really cares about Monty Python or whatever, and we drag out all our samples and connections and toys, and then we get tired of it and we are done. It wasn't a unit study because no one said, "Starting next Monday we are going to do China, and on Friday we are going to be through with China."

When people plan a unit that way, not only is it artificial, you don't get that excited joy and curiosity that makes it work. But what if, (speaking as someone in Albuquerque, where hot air balloons are in the air a lot), you are studying Japan and a hot air balloon lands in the vacant lot behind your house. Are you going to shut the window because it's not about Japan? That's the danger of unit studies, you doggedly move along a path that you've set regardless of what's actually happening in the world. If someone wants to learn about Japan, what's the hurry? If they are going to move there, there are some things they really need to know now. If they are not going to move there, if it's just something they kind of have an interest in on the side, or even if it becomes their burning full interest and they decorate their house Japanese, and they collect Japanese art, still, what's the hurry? They'll be learning about it for the rest of their lives. The more they like something, the more they will never stop learning about that until the day they die. I don't think there's a hurry, and I don't think telling children, "Come on, come on, there's more about Japan that we haven't learned yet, hurry," helps them like Japan, or their mother, or to learn more—it's counter to all that.

So where the spirituality comes in, I think, is the trust that your child is an organism that wants to learn; that it's how people grow. There is physical growth that takes water, food, and rest. There's mental growth that takes input, ideas, things to think about, things to try, and things to touch. There's spiritual growth, that takes more and more understanding, an awareness that it's better to be sweet to other people than not, it's better to be generous with your neighbours than hateful, and better to pet your cat nicely, than to throw it around.

At first, it's a practical consideration but, later on, as the children are looking at the world through older eyes, they start to see that no matter if the neighbour noticed or not, it makes oneself a better person. No matter whether your cat would have done your stuff damage or not, it made you a better person. I think there's a spirituality there, of respect given to the children, being passed on.

Some people try to force their children to share, teach them to share by making them share, but I've seen that if they have enough things, and they don't feel needy, and they don't feel desperate, then they're willing to share. As they get older, they are generous with their space in the house, and their money, and their computers, and their time, and their attention. It's partly because my husband and I have been really generous with them. That has built up in them. They have plenty and they don't mind, then, when we can't give. If we are having a bad day, really flustered or something, frustrated, or cranky, they are okay because they know that when we are not that way, then they can have more attention, or time, or whatever they need.

I'm speaking in St. Louis in October, and I plan to talk about the unexpected benefits of unschooling. Most of the best things that have happened, I didn't foresee. I just can't bring myself to think that a day spent laughing and smiling and doing things that are enjoyable is bad. When I've worked jobs, the days when we went in and someone had brought in something funny or interesting or a cute snack, those were the best days, and those things are so small.

For spirituality and unschooling, the relationship a parent builds with the child, if it's going to be a really good one, a really close one, has to go by a different model, because our culture says, basically, that the parents own the children; the children will be obedient; parents can do what they want to; and when the children are eighteen they can leave, but until then, it's the parents' house, it's the parents' money, and the parents say what happens. That's an extremely adversarial relationship that really can lead to no good, except future adversarial relationships.

It's not good for people's grandchildren. That's not much investment in two or three generations down, to teach your kids that the powerless lose, that older people get their way, and richer people get their way. It helps if the parents can say, "This is your house too, what do you want to do?" Give a range of choices to offer the child. If the child is bored, you could offer three or four really cool things to do, whereas my mom, and thousands or millions of other moms would say, "If you are bored, mop the floor or go pull weeds," which is punishing a child for communicating with you.

I see my children as whole people, whose lives are unfolding now. They may have memories as vivid as mine. What I do and say now will be part of their lives after I'm dead. Do I want to be the wicked witch? Do I want to be a stupid character that they grow up and live in reaction to, and avoidance of? When I see them as whole, I see that as they grow bigger, I grow smaller in their universe.

There's another traditional put-down which is, "You're not the center of the universe." I think, "Then, what is?" Are you talking astrological universe or are you talking personal universe? I am the center of my universe. I see it out of my eyes. I remember it from my memory. When I die, my universe ends. Each of my children is the center of his or her universe. I see that as a spiritual difference in how you define your child, in relationship to yourself. I think when some people think spirituality, they think, "active once-a-week sessions, designated religious centre," but I see it as more of a philosophical stance.

Some people, when they've asked me for advice, I've advised them to pretend they only have three hundred "no's," to spend, and that they better save some. Some people use them up before the kid is three. What if your child grows up and you still have 150 "*No*" tickets left, that you can chuck in the trash? That's pretty cool.

Something I need to credit to La Leche League, to Carol Rice, and to Lori Odhner, who lives in Pennsylvania now—she's a very wise woman: when I had a four-month-old baby, Kirby, they said, "You should be his partner, not his adversary."

An audio version of this piece appears in podcast and can be found at:

Dodd, S. (2004, March 16). Interview by B. Ekwa Ekoko [Podcast]. Improving Unschooling with Sandra Dodd, Radio Free School. Hamilton, Ontario.

Retrieved from http://radio4all.net/index.php/program/11724

References

Margaret, K.T. (1999). *The open classroom: A journey through education.* Andhra Pradesh, IN: Orient Blackswan.

Orwell, G. (1945). *Animal farm.* London, U.K: Secker and Warburg.

For twenty years now, Sandra Dodd has been involved in learning more about the potential of unschooling to improve lives. With two books, weekly chats, a daily-inspiration blog and a blog, the ideas are shared in all directions. Sandra is a former English teacher whose other jobs have all involved words, ideas and learning, and whose avocation is helping other parents find ways to live more richly and peacefully with their children. Sandra maintains an online collection of writings, notes, examples, and great quotes collected from over 15 years of online discussions.

Sandra Dodd has lived in Albuquerque with Keith Dodd since the late 1970s, and they've been married for most of those years. There are offspring, who grew up unschooled. Kirby is 25 and has lived in Austin since he was 21. Marty (22) and Holly (19) still live at home.

Sandra has spoken in over 50 venues, some repeatedly, in the U.S., Canada, the U.K., France and India.

Her unschooling writings can be found at SandraDodd.com

http://sandradodd.com/

CHAPTER 19

LEARNING TOGETHER BY STARTING AN
EDUCATIONAL CO-OPERATIVE

KATHARINE HOUK

I'm Katharine Houk, author of, *Creating a Cooperative Learning Center: An Idea-Book for Homeschooling Families* (1999). I wrote the book in response to calls I've been receiving about starting learning spaces, and organizations for families learning at home and in the wider world. In the 1990s, I was co-founder of such a place in my rural area. It is still thriving, serving 70 to 80 children.

When we began homeschooling, in 1983, there were no support groups locally, and I was feeling the need to at least talk to people in my area about what I was thinking and considering doing. I gathered together a group of parents, none of whose children were school-age yet. We talked about education, parenting, and homeschooling. Some of the families did indeed move on to become homeschoolers and others did not. People came from quite a distance to attend these meetings.

After a while we began inviting people in from the community to share learning experiences with the children. These evolved into weekly workshops in my home. My children were pre-teens at the time. Sometimes parents would lead the workshops, other times children would share something they were learning, and at times leaders came from outside the group.

Then I got a call from a woman, named Alicia Molinar,

who was thinking of starting a school. She was feeling a need for an educational alternative in the wider community. I wasn't particularly interested in starting a school, but I agreed to meet with her and some other parents. The learning centre idea evolved quickly as an interim step to starting a school, and I thought, "Aha! This would be the perfect setting for the workshops that are happening in my home." That's how it came about: families wanted to learn things together.

Learning is a relational experience. My children learned so much by doing things (versus book-learning) so we tried to hook them up with people in the community who could do the things that the children were interested in doing. The learning centre added a larger, more wonderful dimension to this process, such that other children could be involved, too.

Being in this organization meant that we could come into contact with families who had skills we didn't know about. This opened up a broader realm of discovery and opportunities.

How the learning center operates has evolved over time. We structured the corporation and by-laws in such a way that it is very open-ended. The organization is run by a council, and anyone who wants to can be on the council, which is not limited to a certain size. Those on the council commit to being active participants for the year.

There are regular council meetings, at which decisions are made. For example, how are we going to let people know about what we are going to do this year; planning the schedule with input from the members; problem solving, and that sort of thing. The learning center is open two days a week. Its most recent move was from a community centre to a church, which has classroom space and a big kitchen. The church happens to be next to a gym that belongs to a village. The gym became available for the learning center's use. The property also has outdoor space, in a rural setting.

LEARNING TOGETHER BY STARTING AN
EDUCATIONAL CO-OPERATIVE

Families offer whatever they are interested in offering, as learning experiences. Sometimes children themselves offer workshops. Additionally, much happens in the wider community: going to events, museums, or taking field trips together. There is an Oxfam banquet coming up that one of the mothers planned. A wide variety of experiences are offered, because each family is expected to offer something each semester. This requirement is waived for new families; they get a free ride for their first semester.

There is a spot for young people on the council. Because of NY state laws people under 18 can't officially be board members, but youth are definitely represented on the council. They can be there to voice their opinion on whatever happens to be on the agenda. Children also sometimes lead classes or workshops.

It started out being open to the entire community. At first, we structured the week so that people could be involved after school hours, or on weekends, but we found that there was not a lot of interest from families whose children were in school. We wondered if perhaps the children had enough of structured learning experiences after being in school all week. That said, sometimes people who had children in school would take their kids out to do things at the learning center but, for the most part, the interest wasn't there. After a while, we realized that families involved in schools don't feel the same need for a learning community.

We started without any money beyond a fee each family paid to cover the semester's offerings. If your organization is not paying much rent, and you aren't buying insurance, it can be done very inexpensively. I think it was $20 per family per semester, when it started. It has gone up, because insurance has been purchased and rent has gone up. At one time, the center met in families' homes, so that meant no rent. It started out very simply. The lawyer who helped incorporate it volunteered his time, so there was no expense for that. Now it is up to $65 a semester per family. There is a scholarship-type arrangement for people for whom the cost was prohibitive.

There has been a tendency to develop workshops that build on previous ones, such as Spanish 1 and Spanish 2. This is wonderful for families who have been involved for a long time. Other offerings include debate clubs, history clubs, making things by hand, drama, crafts, and choir. There is what is called Display Day at the end of each semester, when families display work done at the center, and in their homes. It is fantastic and festive to see the displays at the end of the semester. A yearbook has been developed by a group of the children, which is a wonderful memento for families to have.

There are those who do end up going to school in the teen years. Because my children are now grown, and my involvement with the center is limited, I don't know much about the current teens. Despite this, parents asked me to come in just last month and talk to them and their teens. One girl said, "It is so strange that there are only five of us." I had to laugh, because I remember when having three teenagers at the center was very exciting. This teen said that there were ten of them last year, and they really got into doing things together, so it is a matter of perspective and expectations.

It takes perseverance, and at least two people, to get into forming a learning center. It took us months. None of us was in a big rush, so we could send out surveys to everyone we could think of instead of rushing into it. We wanted ideas and perspectives from more than two people. The surveys asked about how far potential members would be willing to travel, what learning experiences they were looking for, scheduling, and more. In the beginning, Alicia and I pulled the center together, but since then, enthusiastic parents have joined in to help. We are trying to educate our children and that means we don't have lots of extra time in our lives, so sharing the load cooperatively has worked well.

I tried to make the learning center book useful. It has been selling steadily.

People have different ideas about how homeschooling can be done. We tried to keep the center's structure flexible and fluid, so it could absorb different educational philosophies, including unschooling. I know that people have put together learning groups based on the Sudbury school model. A learning center doesn't need a particular space. Now, a lot of groups organize by posting activities, meetings, etc. on the Internet, which wasn't such an option when we started. There are benefits to having and meeting in a space regularly, where you have a consistent group of people.

Ours is very much like an extended family, which is lovely to have, with shared values and a place where children can look forward to being with their friends. I'm really glad that children are seeing diverse people and experiencing different teaching styles. I would like to stress how doable and how rewarding it is to create spaces for learning together, cooperatively. For me, it was vision of what education could become. If you feel passionate about it, just go for it.

An audio version of this piece appears in podcast and can be found at: Houk, K. (2007, October 17). Interview by B. Ekwa Ekoko [Podcast]. Creating a Co-op Learning Center, Radio Free School. Hamilton, Ontario.

Retrieved from http://radio4all.net/index.php/program/25099

19. KATHARINE HOUK

References

Houk, K. (1999). *Creating a cooperative learning center – An idea-book for homeschooling families.* New York, NY: Longview Publishing.

Katharine Houk is mother of three children, now adults, who learned at home and in the wide world. She is co-founder of TALC, The Alternative Learning Center, a New York State co-operative for home-educating families, where children have prospered for many years.

CHAPTER 20

THE EVERYDAY LIVES OF BLACK CANADIAN HOMESCHOOLERS

MONICA WELLS KISURA

My name is Monica Wells Kisura. I'm a doctoral student at the American University in Washington, DC, in the School of International Relations. I am a visiting Fulbright Scholar at the University of Toronto, Ontario Institute for Studies in Education (OISE).

I have been studying black homeschoolers in Canada for eight or nine months, and have found the research to be very exciting and intriguing, because it compares quite nicely to the research I am doing in the United States on black American homeschoolers living in the Metropolitan Washington DC/Baltimore area.

It has been a bit of a struggle to find families. I would say I got back about ten e-mail responses. I began contacting potential parents, scoured the web for all Canadian homeschool websites. Some families were in the process of looking at homeschooling and some had homeschooled their children already. Most respondents were in current homeschooling families. Out of those, I've made four interviews with the possibility for another two or three. However, Canada is a big country— some of the families are actually on the West Coast—so, the challenge has been to find the niche where people are, or where people are gathering. Unlike the families in the United States, where there is a critical mass of people, and it seems to be much easier for families to find one another, this is not the case in Canada. I find that, in Canada, the population is more dispersed and so even families in the Greater Toronto Area live twenty, thirty miles apart from one another. It's still very difficult to create a synergy or, enough energy, around homeschoolers of colour.

In particular, my research looks at black homeschoolers coming together. There's also the stop-start phenomenon, due to some of the challenges that families face financially where it's very challenging to live on one income, many of them begin homeschooling and have to stop, often for financial reasons. It's not for lack of interest or passion for homeschooling.

I have found some common themes among parents that were really quite surprising to me. I hope you do not mind that I will include some of the research I have conducted in the United States, because the vast majority of literature written on black home educators is coming from there. In terms of the motivations, the common themes, I would say there are several that continue to rise to the surface. The first I have discovered is that parents are concerned about the inequities in education. They have gone through conventional schools and many have also gone on to university, so they experienced between twelve and sixteen years of conventional schooling and know what it is like. Many of them do not want their children to have the same negative experiences, because these parents report having struggled with low self-esteem, having their intellectual abilities questioned, and, even in some cases, they developed inferiority complexes. They find that through homeschooling, their children have an opportunity to not be exposed to the subversive ideas that parents felt were race-based, since there is an unspoken expectation in schools and society as a whole that black children are problematic,

misbehaved, and not very motivated. For instance, black
students are, more often than not, diagnosed with some kind
of Attention Deficit Disorder or, called into the principal's
office for behavioural problems or acting out.

I want to mention a conversation that I had with an
American mom, who made a comparison between the black
male prison population and her son. She asserted that
probably none of these guys in prison have been
homeschooled, and yet her decision to homeschool her son is
criminalized by many. She said: "So many people think that
it's criminal, but look at the population in prison!" and I
thought, "Wow, that is an interesting way to look at
homeschooling, as being a new route or potentially an
avenue to give black male children, in particular, a
refreshing way to view themselves that could lead them
away from the culture of low expectation and stereotypical
ways of being, that are perpetuated in conventional school
settings."

Another motivation for homeschooling is cultural.
Mothers really want to pass on to their children a sense of
pride in their cultural heritage. I found this to be true with
Canadian as well as American families. This was something
that was really important to them. Neither their religious
persuasion nor their particular homeschooling philosophical
orientation seemed to influence this point; it was emphasized
all the same among these parents. Heritage was very
important to them. A third motivation was to pass along
spiritual values. Parents of Muslim, Christian, or even Afro-
centric spiritualists believed that passing along some kind of
spiritual heritage was important to them.

*Q: Where do black Canadians break down along religious
lines, in terms of their particular philosophical persuasion?*

I have found families in the United States, and I think this is reflective of the larger homeschooling population as well, that the dominant discourse and the dominant voice is coming from the Christian Right or what would be considered a conservative Christian perspective. Of the many homeschooling families whom I have interviewed in the United States, a good 75% of them, I would say, are choosing to homeschool to give their children a religious education or to provide them daily, with religious instruction.

Their spirituality was often intertwined with other values, like their holistic approach to life. They are environmentally conscious, and careful about the foods they eat. They often live a lifestyle that is counter-cultural in many respects, and it was important to them to pass along these values to their children. For example, the first mom who introduced me to the world of black homeschoolers was an unschooler. At that time, I did not have any knowledge that there were multiple ways to approach homeschooling, so I assumed that there were more people like her than not. What I have since discovered, in my research, is that there are more structured homeschoolers in the black community. Now, I am speaking specifically about the American research. I found more of a mixed bag with my Canadian group, but I also have a much smaller sample that I am working with, so it is harder to make generalizations about how black Canadians approach homeschooling. I can definitely say, given the thirty families that I have interviewed in the United States that a good 75% of them would be either structured or eclectic in their approach. The smaller percentage of families would be considered unschoolers or deschoolers.

In general, of the five people I have interviewed, almost everyone has tried unschooling at some point, either by default, like "today we are going to let you kids do whatever you want to do," or by design, that it is in the actual philosophical approach they take.

I've been very interested in the issue of identity. How do
they identify themselves, as people growing up in the world?
And then, how do they identify themselves, specifically, as
homeschoolers? The cultural piece that I started talking
about earlier is a very important piece to them. So they do,
indeed, see themselves as black or African-Canadian
homeschoolers or home educators or unschoolers; this is part
and parcel of their identity. Looking at, for example, all of
the identity movements that happened in the sixties and the
seventies, where people began to feel more comfortable in
their skin, particularly black people. There began to be a
sense of pride in what all of this meant to them. The long
lineage of that goes all the way back to the beginning of the
Twentieth Century with William Du Bois (1903) and,
founder of the Universal Negro Improvement Association in
1914, Marcus Garvey
(http://www.international.ucla.edu/africa/mgpp/sample01.as
p) and all of the early activist, Pan-African literature that
addressed the issue of articulating a positive black identity.
These are the connections I am trying to uncover, or at least
investigate, regarding the question of identity. I think post-
decolonization, post-Civil rights, it is without a doubt that
the issue around Black Pride and identity is, (with the
exception religious or spiritual identity) extremely
important.

More often than not, these parents said that they wished
there were more people like them homeschooling, more
people who looked like them, and who were also
homeschoolers so that they could come together to share
resources and provide support for one another. There is the
recognition that there are cultural differences between non-
black homeschoolers and black homeschoolers, in terms of
needs and curriculum design. One of the things that the

interviewed parents emphasized over and over was the importance of the images in the books and the literature they use for teaching. They wanted images that reflected the faces of their children.

My approach to home education is to view it from a political-economic perspective, in that I am contextualizing home education as something that is a reflection of bigger social and political changes that have occurred in the world since World War II. In particular, I am looking at the global restructuring of work, how that has allowed more flex time and free time for families, so in the event that they want to start a home business, or have a mom work part-time or a dad have flex hours so that he can also be involved. These lifestyle changes are more acceptable now.

There are two other things parents say they are getting out of homeschooling, or are wanting to gain from it. One is that they want to develop a closer relationship with their family and between family members. Homeschooling mothers say that their children are closer than they were before they started homeschooling, because oftentimes parents have pulled their children out of conventional schools, or one child has gone off to school and they have seen how the family dynamic changed, but, when the child returns home or is brought home to homeschool, they notice that the family dynamics shifts between the siblings. Almost all reported that homeschooling brought better cohesion among the siblings and the family as a whole.

The second motivation is the violence in public schools, overcrowded classrooms, and the lack of discipline among students. These reports are all over the media and everyone knows about this. Both of these are reasons that contribute to parents choosing to either never send their kids to conventional schools, or to pull their kids out. The anti-public schools answer is often the default one given too quickly by the media, and has often become the central focus at the expense of other motivating factors that are also right there just below the surface.

Part of my methodology is to conduct two interviews with parents, with each containing twenty-five questions per interview. One of the questions, in the second interview, is, "Who are some of the people who have influenced you, or what are some of the resources that you've continually gone back to or drawn upon?" The answers really depend on the philosophical orientation. Many point to the work of John Taylor Gatto and John Holt as influences. Those who have more of a Christian perspective specifically point to Christian resources, which would include, Raymond Moore, James Dobson, and some others.

Mothers are the primary providers of homeschool instruction and fathers are involved from time-to-time, but generally not on a daily basis. Fathers are involved with very specific kinds of topics, which are their areas of strength, like physical fitness, math or science.

In addition to the interviews, I also gave parents a survey to complete. One of the questions asked is, "Who is the person primarily responsible for homeschooling?" I cannot recall any of them where the mother is *not* the primary person responsible for homeschooling. The role of the father is very frankly to financially support the family so that they can undertake this endeavour. I use the mother/father dichotomy because all of the families I have interviewed thus far are heterosexual couples. I was hoping for some same-gender couples and my survey, unlike some other homeschooling surveys out there, does ask the participants to define the gender of the parents/guardians.

I think this hints at one of the broader cultural challenges that African Canadian or black Canadian homeschoolers face. That is, the perception that they are going against the grain; that they are rather odd for choosing to homeschool.

In particular, historically, whether families are Canadian or American, there has been this trust in conventional schooling, and even a reliance on conventional schooling as a means or an avenue for social mobility. So, education in the traditional sense has been viewed as something very important to these families who are now really counter-cultural in their approach to learning, which is seen as bizarre. Mothers reported to me that family members asked, "How can you possibly teach your child? You don't have a teaching certificate. You don't have any specialization." I would say it is about fifty-fifty, that most parents get some kind of resistance, fifty-percent of the time I would say it was from family, and maybe fifty-percent of the time it's from friends. Most all of them report that when their parents (the children's grandparents) who initially questioned whether or not this could possibly work, the grandparents became convinced that it was effective once they compared the achievements of the homeschooling family with their other grandchildren! They saw homeschooling really did work, and that the children were fine. In fact, many even praised the parents for doing such a great job. In other words, the extended family generally comes around and even become advocates of homeschooling.

Q: What are the conditions necessary to get more black families to even consider homeschooling to begin with, let alone move to an unschooling approach?

I strongly believe that because of the additional cultural factors at play, that to even get people to the point where they would consider homeschooling as an alternative educational option is a big step. It is a leap that people have to make and there are two things going against them that are genuine psychological obstacles. I mentioned earlier the point that there is longstanding faith in conventional

schooling as the vehicle for upward mobility, and it has been
the case for families for many generations in the United
States, due to Brown vs. Board of Education, or in the
Caribbean, due to tradition. Many of the families I have
spoken to in Canada are immigrants from the Caribbean. So,
in the Caribbean, their parents feel they left a very good and
solid educational system. They feel the same system exists in
Canada and that if conventional schooling was "good
enough for us then it is good enough for your children too!"
This is not the case, and many people of colour report a
negative experience in schools in both Canada and the
United States. In the United States, you have a very different
social context, the Civil Rights Movement, and the fact that
many people fought so hard to integrate schools, and to have
a place at the public school table. The older generation feels
a sense of betrayal, which is a strong word, but there is a
sense that to homeschool means one does not appreciate the
struggles that people who came before them went through to
give African Americans an opportunity to have a
conventional, especially public school education. We must
take into account these looming psychological barriers,
which have cultural roots and may be preventing many from
even considering home education.

The second piece when you talk specifically about
unschooling as an approach, which is self-directed learning
that allows the child's interests to move the curriculum, you
have the issue of black parents feeling like this approach
would be disregarded. Grace Llewellyn's (1996) book,
Freedom Challenge, is written by black homeschoolers
themselves. Llewellyn made the observation that black
families are already battling the social issues of supposed
racial and intellectual inferiority, so there is more of a
tendency to lean toward a structured approach. Tracy Romm
(1993) made a similar observation in his 1993 dissertation,

Home Schooling and the Transmission of Civic Culture in which he examined the lives of four white and four black homeschooling families.

One of the challenges these families are facing is getting their children to a place where they feel society will accept and acknowledge that these children have a certain level of intellectual ability and capability. Thus far, it seems to be true that most black parents are leaning towards a structured approach. Ironically, they are less inclined to use standardized tests. In fact, most of the parents that I have spoken with, whether they were structured or eclectic, did not, nor do they plan to use standardized tests or exams to measure their child's progress.

I think it is going to take another generation, frankly, for more people to become comfortable with the idea of homeschooling, first of all, and then possibly another generation beyond that before more families to move toward unschooling.

What I have discovered is that, when I ask the question, "If you could change anything about your experience as a home educator, what would that be?" Almost all of them say, "I would be more relaxed." So I do believe that there will be, and that there are signs that families are moving toward, a more relaxed approach to learning. Given that mainstream homeschoolers came to light during the sixties, seventies, and eighties, but most black homeschooling families, even those so called "old-timers" really did not get on board until the nineties, there is a ten- to twenty-year lag, so this is why I am calculating that it may be another ten to twenty years before black families really feel comfortable with home education as an alternative, and then unschooling as a viable practice.

I want to conclude with something that may be a bit radical, a thought that occurred to me fairly early in my research. After interviewing a number of homeschooling

families, and again thinking about this in the much broader
context of political-economy, I began asking what political
changes, what economic changes have occurred to open this
opportunity for people to homeschool? It dawned on me that,
since the decolonization movements in Africa and the
Caribbean, and since the Civil Rights movements in the
United States during the sixties, homeschooling is probably
the most radical statement that black people have made
regarding self-determination and resistance. I think that
home education, particularly for this segment of the
population, has the potential to be very radical, and move the
community as a whole to a different level of consciousness.

An audio version of this piece appears in podcast and can
be found at:
Wells Kisura, M. (2006, June 14). Interview by B. Ekwa
Ekoko [Podcast]. Black Homeschooling in Ontario, Radio
Free School. Hamilton, Ontario.
Retrieved from
http://radio4all.net/index.php/program/18579

References

Du Bois, W. E. B. (1903). *The souls of black folk: Essays
and sketches*. Chicago: A.C.
McClurg & Co.
Llewellyn, G. (1996). *Freedom challenge.* Eugene, OR:
Lowry House Publishers.
Romm, T. (1993). *Homeschooling and the transmission of
civic culture* (Unpublished doctoral dissertation).
Clark Atlanta University, Atlanta, GA.

20. MONICA WELLS KISURA

Dr. Monica Wells Kisura has dedicated her life to advancing educational innovation, access and equity, and to building bridges of mutual understanding across cultures. In 1987, Wells Kisura became the first Black woman to serve as Student Body Executive Vice President at Seattle Pacific University. Wells Kisura was named a 2005-2006 Canada-U.S. Fulbright Fellow, an honor reserved for a select few in Canada and the United States. As a Fulbright scholar, Wells Kisura conducted pioneering research at the Ontario Institute for Studies in Education (University of Toronto) among Black/African Canadian home educators living in Ontario, Canada. In 2005, American University's Offices of Multicultural Affairs and International Student Services granted Wells Kisura the Trailblazer Award in recognition of her "service as an inspirational example to others while striving for excellence in academic, personal, and professional growth." During that same year, Wells Kisura was invited to attend the CONNECT seminar, in Ottawa, which identifies and mentors emerging American Canadians. Dr. Wells Kisura received her B.A. in Communication from Seattle Pacific University (1988), her M.A. in International Politics from American University (2005) and her Ph.D. in International Relations from American University (2009). She currently teaches for the Literacy Council of Prince George's County.

CHAPTER 21

THE PRAXIS OF SELFDESIGN
AS A NEW PARADIGM FOR LEARNING
BRENT CAMERON

I've been working with Wondertree for twenty-one years—
not as an educator or a teacher, but more as a father. The
entire work I've been doing around learning was inspired by
my daughter, and my observations of her in the first five to
six years of her life. I was transformed by watching her learn
how to talk. My observations of the evolution of learning in
a natural way was so profound that, when she walked out of
kindergarten after two weeks, I thought, "We have got to be
able to support young people to learn in such a way so that
we do not impose the industrial-factory model of education
on our children." I started working with her, much in a
home-learning environment, and pretty soon I had ten kids,
and continued working with those ten kids for the next ten
years.

We created a high school, at one point (1993). It was a
very successful experiment in natural learning. My daughter
is 26 now.

I wrote a Masters Degree thesis, and I'm now working on
a doctorate. I'm attempting to understand, and explain, a
whole new way of thinking about learning, and a whole new
way of working with children that is fundamentally based in
respect and evolves a technology, a language-based
technology, of how we speak respectfully to kids. Out of this
emerges the question, "What is the technology of learning?"

233

It's an epistemological question, in the sense of, how do we work as human beings? How do we think? How do we remember? How do we understand?

SelfDesign works with children and adults in a respectful way, to allow their natural genius and excellence to unfold. It's a question of how should we support this natural unfolding of our human intelligence?

I don't teach. It's not a model of changing the classroom or making schooling better. Instead, SelfDesign has nothing to do with schooling, it has nothing to do with classrooms or education. I think the industrial model of schooling is a rather recent experiment that emerged out of the industrial age, and the need to have obedient workers in our culture. When I really looked at "How do I design an appropriate learning experience?" I didn't look to schools at all. I didn't try to improve them. In fact, I totally ignored them. What I did was look at human individuals—my daughter, in particular, who I was intimately able to observe, and then a group of young children, followed by a group of teenagers.

When I say I worked with them, I mean that we met every day in a learning center and the curriculum (which I define as experience) emerged from our enthusiasm and our conversations. Learning is something that we do as we live; it's something that emerges as a change in the way that we understand who we are and how we work with the world.

As a natural process, our learning emerged out of the conversations that the children and I had each day, what we were curious about, and what mattered to us. What emerged in the minds and in the interests of the kids became the work we did in learning. This went on for eight or nine years, and then we moved into a high-school program where we continued to give the youth freedom to create their curriculum out of their own curiosity. We never had a high school, actually. We just really went back to the pre-industrial model for learning, which was the village, the community and the family. The mode of learning that was really excellent, at that time, was apprenticeship, based on what we do naturally when we learn, which is to model.

As a species, our forté is learning. We are designed to model and get strategies from the people around us who are good at things. That's built formally into a mentoring-apprenticeship kind of relationship. A part of our program was opportunities for kids to model excellence.

During both Wondertree and Virtual High, the tuition and any government funding went into an account that was accessible to the children and youth who designed and funded the program with me and other mentors.

The decisions were made based on consensus. We worked together as a management team and decided who we would hire, how the money would be spent, and what we would buy as resources. We would interview about ten people, every September, and then ten new people every January. We would hire six, seven, or eight of these interviewees to do pottery with us, to do clowning, to do story writing; whatever the kids felt was exciting and important to them at that time. Wondertree and Virtual High were a kind of research and development phase of my work, where I proved the principles of natural learning in a variety of forms. As the Wright brothers proved the principles of flight, we gained insight and understanding to the process of self-designed learning and have now created a learning community as a model for the transformation of education beyond the paradigm of schooling.

This small, Wondertree program, operated consistently in Vancouver for over 25 years until 2009, when it folded into the much larger online SelfDesign program that began in 2002. Currently, in 2011, there are over 1500 learners in our online learning community working from kindergarten to Grade 12. Each individual learner is on his or her own individual program and the context for learning is lifelong, from zero to 89, plus or minus a few years.

I'm really interested in the post-industrial village, in living sustainably on the planet. I have invented a model for lifelong-learning that patterns itself on the logarithmic spiral. We are incorporating this SelfDesign LifeSpiral into our awareness of our lives, as a learning journey. I have a huge admiration for home learning and unschooling. I've come to realize that the SelfDesign Learning Community starts with every learner, and extends homelearning and unschooling beyond the paradigm of schooling, building an Internet-based network of conversations for global learning.

SelfDesign is a Learning Community, funded by the Ministry of Education in British Columbia (as a school) although it is not the experience of anyone in the community that we are a school. What it looks like from the outside and what it is on the inside are two entirely different animals. What we are doing is getting government funding and connecting people through the Internet, into a metaphor of a village on-line, where people can have all kinds of conversations. From that emerge all kinds of legitimate learning experiences. The job of SelfDesign is to track each individual's learning experience.

We are using the funding to give learning consultants to families. In the USA, each family gets $2,000. In BC, they receive 50% funding (compared to public education) from the government, so every learner who makes a LearningPlan receives a Learning Investment of over $1,000. It's become quite a large network: Last year we had a hundred, this year we have grown to five hundred learners, with a thousand parents, and fifty consultants who work with groups of ten or fifteen kids.

We started the SelfDesign program from the insights into learning we gained in running Wondertree and Virtual High. For the first two years of our pilot project, we were restricted to one hundred learners. Since September 2004, we have been growing about 25% per year, and now have about 1,500 learners, all online. Sometimes, they get together in LearningCircles or Centers.

Our program exists because children learn as a way of living. Parents of young children do a weekly observation and reflection of what the kids are learning. As a way of professionally-influencing the learning process we encourage parents, through informing and supporting the learning process initiated by the children. With parents providing weekly insights into learning, our Learning Consultants provide supportive comments. Over time, a rich and deep conversation emerges into the process of learning, and eventually most learners between the ages of 10 to 14 step in and begin doing their own observations of their own learning process. This technology of self-responsibility, self-awareness, and introspection has an empowering effect on the learners. When they first start, a lot of the parents were quite resistant to the idea of a virtual village. They said, "Look, our friends in the neighbourhood, those are the real relationships we have and this is just virtual."

I think it's really important to have the technology become transparent, and to really look at the fact that what we are doing is creating conversations and relationships and understandings between people of similar interests.

Certainly, what has happened in our village in the first two years is that people, although they live in communities, are often misunderstood in those communities, because they are different. In SelfDesign, what they've found is a wonderful kinship of like-minded home learning families who can share ideas and resources. SelfDesign feels like an actual community has emerged, and that is so rich and so exciting, even though it is online.

What's happening is that people are spending holiday

time together; driving across the country to meet their new neighbour who is five hundred kilometres away. The kids are in such rich conversations with each other that friendships have been created out of shared interests and feelings.

We live in a very authoritarian culture, where we are told what to do, in direct ways by people in authority and in subtle ways by people in the media. It's very much a controlled language style. Certainly, the model for parenting, for generations, has been mostly about authority and control. Kids don't understand a lot of things, so we think that gives us permission to tell kids what to do.

The free-school movement was a pendulum swing in a new direction. It resulted in a permissive kind of environment where we didn't tell kids at all what to do and allowed them the freedom to explore and discover. That's a very important experiment. I think what we are attempting to do is to create a new, third position: one which is not authoritarian and not permissive. This third position can be described as engagement: Engagement of equals, and real involvement with kids as equals, so the relationship that emerges is one where each person is an authority for themselves, or more clearly, the author or designer of their own life.

As an adult, I get to represent what I think and feel and what I'm observing. In the same way I want to be heard and respected for that, I create that kind of relationship with a young person. It's both an enfranchising and validating of the child's world-view as legitimate for them. It comes down to a very open-ended, conversational environment.

One of the things I discovered, when I was researching my Ph.D. thesis, was that there was a research initiative done in the United States, where they researched 15,000 families to find out how many minutes and hours of conversation they engaged in each week.

The average time for conversation was down to a few seconds, statistically. That means a few families were having conversations, while most never engage in conversation. When families don't eat together any more, I mean that's an optimal place for busy people to stop and sit down and talk, it eats into the opportunities for real conversation. In my informal surveys of parents in my parenting workshops, who are doing excellent in their lives, one of the real big factors is the role of conversation and understanding in their family situations.

Conversation is not defined as, "Have you done your homework yet?" "Take out the garbage," "It's time to go to bed"— these are not conversational pieces of language. It's just really important, I think, to start the dynamic of relationship around conversation.

If we all sat down and thought about the real aspects of conversations that we've enjoyed and that are really rich, I think we could come up with twenty qualities and principles for conversations, and then we could really ask ourselves if we, in fact, have those kinds of language relationships with our kids. I think that is the basis of a real rich parenting environment: This willingness and ability to sit down in many ways, on many occasions, and have kids share their ideas, understanding, and feelings, and to ask and answer questions. That's the beginning.

Initially, a kid's job is to play. What I experienced is that when I played with my learners, and really engaged with them, the kind of relationship emerged where work, learning and play became identical activities. That is the way of the master of living: to enjoy one's process.

As kids mature into teenagers, I think it's really important that they start participating in the work, in the results of being in a family. Before that, I think it's really important that kids play. I also think it is very important that adults play with them. I have found that the kind of relationship where you get into their world, and join them and engage with them in their reality, creates a situation where they are far more likely to come and carry on a conversation with you while you are washing the dishes, to be with you in your world.

As human beings, we are designed to model. First of all, bonding is the initial important connection, which is also described as attachment. Children tend to feel abandoned when we don't play with them, when we don't engage them. It's very difficult if we don't continue that important engagement relationship. It's very hard for them to model if they aren't still in that engaging relationship. Thus, I have certainly noticed that kids who have really bonded and connected with their parents tend to work along side their parents, as modeling is what's built into their neurological structure as a strategy for survival. Kids naturally work with adults, if the work is something that, again, can emerge out of the relationship, and out of the conversation that we have with kids.

There's some pretty amazing research coming out of cognitive neuroscience. Dr. Allan Schore (2011), for example, is able to look at unique neurological developments in the right prefrontal lobe that are directly the result of the attachment process in an appropriate bonding experience. He has also shown that this area of development is responsible for the sense of self and other, of others in an empathetic way.

There is evidence that in the language patterns, and in the thinking patterns of young people, if they don't have a bonding experience—the sense of self, the sense of other— the opportunity for empathetic kind of thinking is very difficult, perhaps even impossible, for people who haven't bonded well. One of the key components of bonding is to share the same mental state: To be in the same mental, emotional, quality of mind.

When I do my workshops around the country, I show two pictures. First, I show a picture of a father lying on the floor and the baby is lying on his chest and they are looking face-to-face, touching skin-to-skin. Their faces are a few inches apart, and they are connected, mirroring each other. The father is making the sounds that the baby is making, which is influencing the baby, and that's influencing the father. And this recursion, this around-and-around of mutual influencing, exists where the father goes to the mental state of the child who is very much in the present moment. The father has to let go of all of the busy things in his life and in his thoughts and go to the state of the child, because obviously there is no way that the child can go to the state of the father.

Then I show another picture of a baby, in one of those plastic buckets that parents carry their children around in nowadays. And it's sitting on the table and the baby is in it. The father is being a very attentive, typical father, looking after the kid. He's got a cup of coffee in one hand, the newspaper under one arm. He is talking on the telephone to someone at work and he is fully clothed, standing six feet away as he's looking at the baby, but he is obviously engaged in conversation on the phone. Although he is looking into the eyes of the baby, the baby is looking at a person who is not sharing the same mental state. There's no opportunity for recursion, the connection of one with the other. These differences are so important. Being present is essential for a parent to be able to connect with a child, because children live in the present moment. They haven't invented time until they are three or four years old. Parenting, in our parenting courses, is a lot about practicing turning off the mind, and being present and engaging the young person in their state. Very important!

I lived the first thirty years of my life as an unbonded

individual; in the core of my being, I felt abandoned. I carried a lack of sense of self and other. When I was thirty, my daughter was born, and over the next year while she was bonding with me, I bonded with her. A calm came over me, and in a sense I came home to my starting place in life. Certainly, the research shows that bonding is optimally done as an infant. Yet, as a healing process, it can take place at any time, given the right energy and circumstances it can transform the individual.

I think we learn more without being taught than by being taught, far more. I think we've got a culture right now—a paradigm, a belief system, and a group of teachers who are certainly well-paid, and well-reinforced by experts—which says that learning doesn't take place unless you are taught. From experiments like mine, and the experiences of thousands of home learning and unschooling families, and certainly from *SelfDesign: Nurturing Genius Through Natural Learning* (2006), the book that I have written, the assumption of the efficacy of teaching is clearly being challenged. As well, I think the kind of learning that takes place from being taught is a lower order of learning. This has been a 21-year experiment, where I started out not knowing any answers. I was willing to experiment and see what would happen. I am absolutely thrilled with the results, and I'm just now compiling my understanding of what actually happened in those 21 years.

I've created a circular map of the 8 different kinds of learning that I witnessed over these years, and have put the model called the SelfDesign Paragon in the *SelfDesign* book. Only one of the eight legitimate learning processes is learning that emerges out of being taught. The other 7 are modes that occur naturally in relationship, through discovery and inquiry.

One of the interesting kinds of learning that occurs is one that is the most mysterious and that seems to be a kind of learning that takes place without even having experience, let alone being taught. It almost doesn't take actual, practical experience for this learning to take place. Just to speculate, I called it "LifeQuest learning" where somebody gets, inside, a deep sense like "I want to be an astronaut," or "I want to be a concert pianist," or "I'm a ballet dancer." Whether it's a genetic pre-disposition where that information is embedded in the genes, or whether it's a reincarnation or even related to the morphogenic field work of Rupert Sheldrake (1995) where we can unconsciously access a field of information that's available around the earth—these are just a few of my speculations. We can't explain the Mozarts, the Einsteins, these huge leaps of knowledge and learning that takes place in certain individuals.

There's a lot of mystery about how we really learn and, I think, looking at the children that I've worked with, I didn't teach any of them to read. When I look, in comparison, at what's going on in public schooling—where they are teaching children how to read—they end up with almost 50% of children with reading challenges. They end up with a lot of children who can't read at a level well enough to cope in modern society.

I've worked with nearly a hundred children, now. We've never formally taught any of them to read, and yet I've yet to see a child who can't read exceptionally well, or a child with reading difficulties. They have all become readers because I didn't teach them.

Let's take an example close to home to illustrate this. My own daughter didn't start reading until she was ten. When she did start, she certainly wouldn't let me teach her. She sat down, and in a month was reading at a Grade 7 level, with almost no help from me. Because she brought the intellectual development of a ten-year-old to the process, it was easy and magic for her. By the time she was thirteen, I was at the university doing my Masters Degree, and she often came to the campus with me. She became fascinated with an English History course that was advertised, and ended up talking with the Dean of the English Department, who supported her taking the course. If I had taught her how to read, I would have taught her how I read: slowly and painfully. However, because she learned naturally and incorporated an entirely different strategy, she is now a speed-reader. This story of a ten years old girl, who was not a reader and three years later is attending a 2nd year English history course, is not a unique example, but a common story with a common theme. This is an example of a kind of learning that (if we trust kids and give them the opportunity to allow their learning to emerge from their curiosity) is consistently a huge acceleration of learning, and a demonstration of excellence. I've never known a young person to have learning difficulties in the field of their interest, in learning that emerges spontaneously from their curiosity. Ultimately, I believe that learning difficulties are an artifact of learning that is imposed and taught at inappropriate times, in inappropriate ways, largely in violation of the neurological sensibilities of children and their natural developmental stages.

As I was re-writing my book, I was looking at the chapter on children's rights. I focused on the right to have learning emerge from your curiosity as a fundamental human right. I reflect back to John Holt's work, which is always profound. He talks about the freedom of thought as a fundamental freedom, even more important than a freedom of speech. The right to think about what we want to think about, and the right to learn what we are curious about, are fundamental freedoms we don't allow children in this culture. In the big picture, Wondertree and SelfDesign are just two more Rosa Parks events in children's rights, just like the events that occur across the world in unschooling families.

THE PRAXIS OF SELFDESIGN AS A NEW PARADIGM FOR LEARNING

I started to think about my experience at school, and the kind of imprisonment I felt day after day, and year after year. I decided to go into education as a radical, to change it, and I completely failed. I left education to become a businessman when my daughter walked out of kindergarten. When I started an educational experiment in support of my daughter's natural ability to learn, I modeled it on my business experiences rather than my schooling. Over the years, I began to find myself more and more in the role of a counselor to children and families. Many of the children and families that came to our program came because they were moving away from a negative public education. Although our program is designed for self-responsible and enthusiastic learners and functional families, it was not always the case that we attracted such families. I, therefore, invested a great deal of my time helping families get back into balance and helping children heal from traumatic public- and private-school, being-taught experiences.

I evolved an idea that I first became aware of as a tenet of Neuro-Linguistic Programming, and developed it as a relational learning principle: The idea is that in any relational dynamic we never take anyone's choices away from them, or limit or confine them in any way. If you think about it for a second, taking away choices is the operative process of authority. In school, we take a lot of choices away from kids so that they sit at desks, so they sit still, so they listen, and so they all open their books at the same time.

What we are really doing is that we are taking choices away from them. Any time we take choices away from another person it becomes a kind of torture, a kind of confinement. It's limiting and destructive to what intelligence is really about, which is having more choices and increasing our choices. Schooling, just by the politics of keeping control of children, is counterproductive to what we are attempting to do: make them more intelligent and increase their ability to make choices.

I was reading some information about Stockholm syndrome, which was coined from a research study into a situation where people in Stockholm were captured by bank robbers and held captive for a considerable period of time. Psychologists who studied how these captives behaved were amazed that they grew to have affinity and sympathy for their captors. It makes sense, when you understand it as a strategy for survival: When you are in hostile environment you try to minimize the hostility of your captors. You are nice to them, but then it goes further to the emulation and modeling of their captor's beliefs. This particular group of captives actually raised money for the captors when they were on trial.

I began to appreciate similar behavioural parallels in how teenagers act. A lot of the behaviour that we see in school and that we attribute to children as laziness and avoidance of responsibilities are really symptoms of imprisonment. Stockholm syndrome explains how children feel victimized in school, yet are so intimidated that they like their teachers. The same way, children are in a double-bind when they like authoritarian and abusive parents? This phenomenon exists because we cannot really be in a meaningful and positive relationship with people in authority, and it means that our relationships are a coping mechanism, a survival strategy in an adverse environment. We've built our entire culture, and the structure of schooling, around this dynamic as if it is the norm.

The practice of imprisonment of children through compulsory education is deemed a legitimate process necessary for proper education. The idea of taking away children's rights is dismissed. It undermines all the positive aspects of good schooling, due to its deep disrespect of the psychological integrity of children.

THE PRAXIS OF SELFDESIGN AS A NEW PARADIGM FOR LEARNING

I propose that these ideas be considered in the analysis of learning disabilities—which could be just strategies for surviving in a hostile and abusive environment. I touch on these ideas in *SelfDesign* where I mention a document written by a group of teenagers at Virtual High, in 1995, called "The Declaration of Learner's Rights and Responsibilities."

Today's adult generation lives in a schooled culture, so we don't know what is normal. We were all forced to learn and think as a consequence of a compulsory school environment. The small, yet significant, population of unschoolers and home learners today are a breakthrough in understanding human learning, allowing us to reflect on the monopoly of schooling. A whole generation of young people, who are outside the paradigm of schooling, can now offer us an insight into learning beyond schooling and teaching.

My daughter and her friends, who I've known for years now, are quite a unique group of people because they are happy and self-responsible. They live life with a sense of well-being that stands out in a crowd. They love learning. They are curious about all kinds of things. My daughter thinks nothing of grabbing a 1,000-page philosophy book. At 33, she reads Steven Hawkings out of fascination, while most people her age (who were schooled) are still turned off learning. She loves learning, she enjoys her life, and takes responsibility for what she's doing and what she accomplishes.

Our relationship throughout all of her growth years was really wonderful compared to how so many teenagers and parents get into conflict. We have gotten along all these years—not perfectly, as she experienced the breakup of her parents as a teenager, which is difficult for any young person. However, I feel like the luckiest dad in the world. I

247

got to spend every day with my daughter from breakfast through to dinner. We were together on a great learning adventure. Not only did I create a dream job, a life challenge and lifework, I also got to invest every day in watching my daughter grow up.

I can see SelfDesign as a program playing the role of the child in the fairy tale, *The Emperor's New Clothes* (1837). All the experts are unwilling and unable to see the truth of the situation, and pretend that it is all working as planned. The very fact that most children and youth (statistically about 80%) do not consider that their education is meaningful sets the stage for someone to speak out that the system isn't working—that the emperor has no clothes. A few brave people have challenged the experts (who are trying to make kids wrong, the ADHD phenomena, give the kids drugs). The tendency of education and medicine is to make the kids wrong, rather than investigating the negative effect of schooling on children.

Wondertree and Virtual High worked with many children with so-called ADHD. We don't believe in diagnoses, in that we treat all children with respect, giving them opportunity for freedom and choice. This works well for so-called ADHD children, since we give them much more variety of opportunity and freedom, so if they were on drugs when they arrived, they soon weren't, usually out of their own choice: They realized they didn't need them in our environment. If they were supposed to go on drugs, they discovered they didn't need to, because of the kind of environment in Wondertree didn't trigger the kind of reactive behaviour called ADHD.

Learning *is* joyful and exciting and passionate and invigorating. Learning is an aspect of the natural flow of a well-and-happy human being. I realize there are situations in which learning can be hard and challenging, when we get stuck, or go beyond our capacity. It's important to realize that learning has two dimensions: It requires a great deal of courage, because if we are learning, we are moving off into the unknown, and we are also going to make mistakes, because we are in new and unknown territory essentially guessing and learning from trial, error, and success. It is common to say trial-and-error learning, however we are learning through error and success. Learning can be really frustrating, it requires a great deal of focus, and it can be challenging. There's a wonderful quote that I came across, that I have been using for a description of our new teen program. It comes from Zen philosophy. It's about the Masters who, when you look at them, you can't tell whether they are working or playing. There's an integration of opposites, the whole work/play difference is lost, that work is hard, play is easy. I think it's when we lose our usual distinctions, when we find enjoyment in everything including the hardness of things, so that when we can say, "I enjoy the struggle, I enjoy the difficulty," we are at a place of mastery.

Often, in SelfDesign, and self-initiated, self-motivated, and sustained learning, we end up working really hard. Harder, in fact, than if we were motivated by somebody else. Yet, it feels easier because we are in touch with our passion, and our purpose is being sustained through designing our own lives.

Several years ago, I was asked to write a chapter in a book about technology and the future of education. While I understand that there is a future, I appreciate that it's only a construct of the mind. I've never lived in the future, nor will I ever. I'm always in the present moment. The sub-title of my chapter was something like, a wonderful future emerges from a well designed and lived present.

One of the biggest disruptions to our children's integrity is that we take them out of the present moment and orient them towards the future, as if it were real. As teachers and parents, because this has happened to us, we tend to ignore how children are in the present moment. We don't ask them how they feel, or what are their desires and passions in this moment, as a guide for their learning. What children are supposed to do is get to work learning, because if they don't learn they won't be successful in the future, when they are adults. As part of the process of transforming children into adults like us, we make them future-oriented and present-ignorant. "You'll get your freedom; you'll get to run your life, when you are an adult. But now you have to learn the number of things you have to learn, and you have to ignore how you feel, your feelings and inner desires are unimportant, suppress them." We end up with a culture of adults who can't be in the present moment. They have been practicing for twelve years, how to live for the future, not for the present. They never end up getting present, sometimes for the rest of their lives, and we call this apathy.

SelfDesign is creating a new paradigm of possibility: the chance to become an adult without fully forgetting what it is to be a child, the chance to become an adult and rediscover our child worldview, and incorporate playfulness into our work, to bring the passion of the moment into the purpose and process of our living as adults. This creates a new kind of adult, an adult not so isolated, who has not only become what he or she thinks, but also who he or she really is, as an aspect of their original and integral self.

The world is changing faster and faster, everything is speeding up, there's some wonderful work that Buckminster Fuller did, showing the speed in which we have travelled on the earth, and the increase of those speeds in the last few hundred years. It doesn't matter if we are talking about speed of travel, or the speed of information transfer, or growth of information worldwide. One of the things that is happening with our computers is that they are not only going faster, but dividing time into smaller and smaller chunks. The whole world is speeding up all around us, and so many people are busier now than any other time in human history. We've got more things to do, more information to understand, and more jobs to do. The irony of the great time-saving devices is that they end up taking more time to earn the money for them, and more time to learn how to use them. In this sped-up world, where everything is going faster and faster, I have learned that the only real way to cope is to go slower and slower, and to stop altogether. I am talking about finding the still place, the quiet center at our heart.

The first chapter of *SelfDesign*, which is called chapter zero, is about this principle as a key to paradigm shifting. Our current society is still influenced by Newtonian models of thinking. Descartes' influence on modern science is fading, yet still central to this paradigm. I had the wonderful opportunity to work with a gentleman from England for many years, a philosopher and scientist, Douglas Harding, and he taught me a whole series of experiments to do so I can stop my conscious mind and into the present moment in my unconscious mind. I have learned to step back into my body, and as an embodied and present human being, to find infinity in now, to live in this busy and ever-changing world by becoming the still point, by getting clear and finding my essence as love.

As adults we end up in a situation where we are trapped in our conscious minds, trapped in our thoughts, where we actually become who and what we think. Our identities become what we think of ourselves, which is really a composite of what other people have said to us about who we are. Very seldom, as adults, do we ever stop and really experience the moment for the moment. So his experiments are marvellous. I share one of them in *SelfDesign*.

Once a person is able to be present, the next step is to

understand how to live elegantly. Our understanding obviously arises out of our languaging and our conversations. It is therefore imperative that we understand the deep psychological implications of our structures and usage of language as a tool for self-designing and self-actualization. The founder of Neuro Linguistic Programming, Dr. John Grinder, realized that well people, and people with significant problems, both speak English, yet typically engage in totally different usage and patterns (as cited in Cameron, 2006, p.23). He also realized, through his observations of two famous therapists, Virginia Satir and Milton Erickson, that human beings can be transformed by shifting language patterns (as cited in Cameron, 2006, p.7). SelfDesign focuses on languaging as a fundamental tool for self-awareness and the optimum design of one's self. We, of course, all use language to think and design our behaviours and activities, however we have largely, until recently, been unable to look at how we use language as a psychological process. Now, through introspection and self-attunement, we can observe, evaluate, and align our language with our essential and unique natures to become the authors or designers of our own lives.

For example, many years ago I was reading about how the Hopi describe the world, and that they don't have a future tense. They don't have a past tense. They only have a present tense. So, a Hopi doesn't go down to the stream to get a drink, the Hopi stay still and bring the water towards them because they stay in the present moment. They don't see themselves in a body walking through the world. They see that body as the still place, and use their feet to pull the stream and the world towards themselves. It seems absurd from within the paradigm that we live, however this is something that I've been practicing for twenty years. I had this insight when I was a young man, yet it wasn't until I met Douglas Harding that I understood the importance of this whole idea of staying still and staying present. Seeing all the movement of the world as something I'm not driven by, but I am able to observe and influence brings a new measure of meaning and freedom to living. I can work very hard and be relaxed. I can be very busy and be still. This gives me an opportunity to work with children in a unique way, because I appreciate that they naturally access this still place as the condition in which we are all born. Becoming an adult is really losing access to and forgetting even the existence of this still place. I think it is essential that we lose our still place in order to find it again and understand it in a new way.

This achievement of rediscovering the child's worldview is the fourth and final stage of maturity in the SelfDesign model of human development. Most people only move to the third stage, and remain there through their old age. SelfDesign is an epistemological work: a way of living that is about becoming aware of how we work and function as human beings, and how to optimally design ourselves in harmony with our essential human nature. SelfDesign is about becoming the author or designer of our own lives, creating an identity in harmony with others, maturing and developing through introspective and transformative learning every day of our entire lives. SelfDesign is about ignoring a paradigm of schooling that served the Industrial Age, an age that we no longer live in. SelfDesign is about stepping into our bodies and living presently and responsibly in the ecological matrix of conversations and human community in a balanced and co-inspirational way, to evolve integrity in the individual, harmony among people, and ecological balance on the earth.

SelfDesign began with a father who listened to the integrity of his five-year-old daughter to learn what she loves, and is now a growing community of colleagues, parents, and learners who share this idea that the world is a better place when we live and learn together in co-inspiration.

An audio version of this piece appears in podcast and can be found at:
Cameron, B. (2004, September 14). Interview by B. Ekwa Ekoko [Podcast]. Brent Cameron-Wondertree Natural Learning, Radio Free School. Hamilton, Ontario.
Retrieved from http://radio4all.net/index.php/program/10039
Cameron, B. (2004, September 29). Interview by B. Ekwa Ekoko [Podcast]. Brent Cameron (Part 2 of 2), Radio Free School. Hamilton, Ontario.
Retrieved from http://radio4all.net/index.php/program/10143

References

Anderson, H. C. (1983). *Hans Christian Andersen: The complete fairy tales and stories*. (E.C. Haugaard, Trans.). New York, NY: Anchor Books. (Original work published 1837)

Cameron, B. (2006). *SelfDesign: nurturing genius through natural learning.* Boulder, CO: First Sentient Publications.

Schore, A. (2011). *The science of the art of psychotherapy.* New York, NY: W. W. Norton & Company, Inc.

Sheldrake, R. (1995). *A new science of life: the hypothesis of morphic resonance.* Rochester VT: Park Street Press.

Brent Cameron—His daughter, born when he was 30 in 1977, set him on a new journey exploring the integrity of the

human spirit. As a young radical, angry at and confused by
his education, he set out to find the deeper meaning of life.
Upon meeting Bucky Fuller he heard, "society is not
changed by tearing things down but by innovation and
making something better." Inspired by his daughter's natural
ability to learn and the fact that she walked out of
kindergarten after two weeks, he began a new educational
experiment based on curiosity and enthusiasm to learn and
engage with the world. Calling this initiative Wondertree, he
discovered that children learning in freedom and consensus
can create a learning community that emerges a quality of
learning with an integrity beyond which he never would
have imagined. With a group of teenagers in Virtual High he
further discovered the power of a community of individuals
who are becoming the authors of their own lives. In 2002,
with 11 colleagues, he launched and online version of his
ongoing research called SelfDesign Learning Community.
This program has now grown to over 2000 learners working
with over 150 learning consultants spread throughout the
province of British Columbia (2011). His book, *SelfDesign:
Nurturing Genius Through Natural Learning,* has attracted
international attention to this new paradigm work, learning
beyond the paradigm of schooling. His Master's thesis
focused on Wondertree and his Ph.D. thesis focused on
researching the long-term, life-cycle effects on graduates in
their 30s who have been incorporating the praxis of self-
designing into their own learning for years. Brent Cameron
is a model maker and a map maker. He wants to share
SelfDesign and the SelfDesign LifeSpiral with the world to
help make it a better place for us all to live in harmony and
self-awareness.

CHAPTER 22

HOME EDUCATION IN QUEBEC

CHRISTINE BRABANT

Pioneers tend to say that home education in Quebec is a movement younger than in other countries and provinces, but in all fairness, the Ministry of Education has only relatively recently started to collect data.

So while the other provinces have been collecting for a while, there is not much data for Quebec. Authorities and the parents are still learning how to work with one another. The law states that home education is allowed as long as an equivalent educational experience is being offered for the children at home.

I believe that there is something distinct about the Quebec Culture—its history of education, its institutions, its political context—which give us a slightly different kind of home education movement.

My MA thesis showed that the motivations of those who home educate in Quebec are similar to the motivations in the rest of the country, and in the U.S.: some religious trends, some pedagogical trends, some New Age, and some for whom transportation would be a problem because they live in rural areas.

Where motivations were different was in the order of the seven factors. In the United States and Canada, religious factors seem to always come first or second; in Quebec it came sixth. As for every study on homeschooling, mine had limits in terms of statistical representation, but still represented a good cross-section within the Quebec homeschooling community.

The first factor revealed that people home educate to live a family project. Living in tighter family relationships, and learning together. The idea of being really excited to see the children learn, to have the parents go on field trips and discover together, the flexibility, and this idea of the family being a very, very important unit for the education of children. I haven't seen this as conceptually strong in any other studies before.

At this point, where I'm starting my PhD, I'm exploring this idea. The family idea was dominant in the results of the study, but I don't know if it's mainly an idea of keeping the family intact and together that Quebeckers expressed, or the idea of the importance of the family as a better setting for education, for instruction, and the process of learning. I see a slight difference between the two.

In Europe, the idea of the family as an intermediate or strong factor in education is appearing. Christian Beck (2010), a researcher in Norway, has elaborated on the proposition that between the state and the children there is community and family that have to be strong factors in the education of the people. I think there is something new here: For the last two or three centuries, children have been seen in relation to the state for their education. One generation would not educate the next anymore—children would be educated through the state. Now, the idea of family and community seems like something emergent. This track of reflection brought me to do a little bit of research on the topic of citizenship education in the context of home education. Two things brought me in this direction.

First, there is the literature. The critiques about socialization are still there, but not so much on individual development. Rather, the criticism is on the impacts on society, meaning that if families and groups home educate, children might not get immersed in the national culture, not get educated about how to participate in democracy, or learn the sharing of ideas; and the country might suffer from it. It is that kind of critique that is present in the recent literature, and I was wondering how we could address that as educationalists trying to sort this out. It comes down to moral or ethical issues.

The second is that at the same time there is this new subject in the school curricula of most western countries called "citizenship education." UNESCO recommended it be included because societies are more and more pluralistic: pluralism of values, religions, of beliefs, and multiculturalism. It seems that society is also more and more fragmented. The report said that schools should not only be giving instruction, but also teach children how to live together, how to deal with differences and debate.

While my thesis supervisor is doing research on citizenship education with high school teachers, to help them understand what it means in high schools to offer citizenship education; I came up with the idea that doing such research with home educators would offer some answers on the critiques that I read. It could also help the schoolteachers with the questions, "How does a child become a citizen?" and "How can educators begin to think of the society they are in, and that the children will be in?" I find it interesting to question the social project that we have in mind when we home educate.

I think, even schoolteachers are not so clear about what a citizen is. In the curriculum, it says that schoolteachers should help the children develop a "civic consciousness," but what is that? These questions are really adult questions. We are in a bit of a hurry to offer that to children, but we adults are really puzzled by this multicultural society. We see tensions and conflicts about minority rights everyday in the papers.

I think home educators as a group have very strong ideas about society and education. They are very strong citizens themselves, because they have strong enough ideas about education to put them into action and accept life on the margin of society because of it. That takes strength. It is really interesting to hear their voices.

Personally, I think schools do their best. I've been a schoolteacher, and my husband is one. Parents do their best, too. I'm a home-schooling parent. We're all adults doing the best we can for the children for whom we are responsible. I am really less at ease when you want to impose your ideas on your neighbour's children, and I feel that is what schools do sometimes. From the moment you have a different vision of society, or what is education, it needs to be expressed. If the neighbour doesn't agree, you could have a discussion, a debate, but you can't impose your vision on his children.

From my point of view, it would be really interesting to carry out a collaborative study with home educators, so that they could express their own ethical preoccupations. I don't think home educators do what they do without any social or ethical concerns towards their children.

The Convention on Children's Rights, and other normative instruments like the Canadian laws and the Charter of Rights and Freedoms, are regularly put forward to either encourage or discourage home education. These tend to be in conflict, and are not precise. What I realize, with the help of my co-supervisor (a philosopher of law in Belgium) and in workshops on Human Rights at a Trudeau Foundation's conference, is that these large legal instruments are not that helpful when it comes to emergent or experimental practices, like home education. There comes a point where you need to learn to work on ethics, ideas, and innovations from the bottom up, not from laws down.

The real players, and their contextual networks, will inform the law with their own system of values, limits, and strengths. Home educators have opinions. Rather than trying to regulate them, we could see how they regulate themselves. That's one founding principle of my ethical framework: working from the bottom up.

Some may see homeschooling as a threat to public education. At a congress of private schools recently, the opening speaker said: "We have to work really hard to make private and public education good because, you know, there are a growing number of home educating families now." They are aware of this movement and they see home education as a challenge for keeping children in school, private or public. There is the idea that home education is weakening, dismantling the system, and sometimes that can be taken as a compliment, but sometimes it is expressed with reproach: that home educators are failing their duties to participate in mainstream education.

As home educators, it is good to ask yourself what you think of the issue, to observe how we participate in society. For now, I see parenting as the first and greatest citizen act. No parenting, no children, no society. Doing it well is a great commitment. I think that a committed mother is one of the most important citizens. Whether you home educate or send your children to school, you can still be a good or bad parent, or a good or bad citizen. That engagement, that commitment to educating your own children is already a great participation in society.

When it comes to committing to help other children, I agree too. But to register your children in school so they share what you have to offer as a family, with other children who have less, would be fine if my family didn't lose something in the process. That makes me a little uncomfortable. I feel for children who are less privileged, I am willing to offer my money, my time, my love, and energy. I see that kind of participation as a duty, but I am not willing to compromise my child's development for another child. I think that's demanding too much from a child and a parent, and it doesn't serve society, in the end.

I have been asked if schools could be returned to the community—not government regulated—if that could be a compromise or a solution. That is a hard question, since there is the movement of privatization such as charter schools, private schools, and alternative schools. I've heard that this trend is growing in other provinces, and the United States. Even here in Quebec, there is a decentralization of power in the school system; every school has more leeway to define their own educational projects.

There is a greater will to encourage parents to participate in the school projects and leadership. It seems like a general assumption that it would be better if both community and parents had more of a say in school. A major preoccupation of schoolteachers and directors is to create stronger bonds between the school and the family. It is not easy because of the history of schools in this matter. They have pushed parents and the community away so schools could be perceived as these high and respected places of knowledge, a professional place for education. The movement is now going the reverse. Maybe, in some time, there will be more of a balance in the contribution of professionals and families for the education of children.

An audio version of this piece appears in podcast and can be found at:

Brabant, C. (2006, July 16). Interview by B. Ekwa Ekoko [Podcast].Home in Quebec, Radio Free School. Hamilton, Ontario.

Retrieved from http://www.radio4all.net/index.php/program/19359

References

Beck, C. (2010). Home education: The social motivation. *International Electronic Journal of Elementary Education, 3*(1), 71-81.

Starting out as a performer and arts educator, Christine Brabant now works as a post doctoral researcher with team leaders Jacques Lenoble and Marc Maesschalck of the Centre for Philosophy of Law, Catholic University of Louvain. Focused on "family learning" (home-education) in Quebec, her research fits into their work of applied "reflexive governance" in various areas including work, health and education.

After working with home-educators for her doctoral research, Brabant has launched a postdoctoral research project with school administrators who engage with home-educating parents and their children. Her research aims to contribute to the harmonious interaction between home-educating parents and Quebec school boards, from the perspective of reflexive governance of education.

It also aims at describing the process of democratic learning of institutional players in response to a new social movement. Brabant's master thesis draws a first-hand portrait of the demographics and the motivations of Quebec home-educating families.

Having, as a dance and music teacher, and as the mother of two, crossed paths with the public and private education system in various ways as well as having experienced home-education with her children, Brabant founded a home-education group in the Eastern Townships. She also supervises the training of future elementary and pre-school teachers for the University of Sherbrooke.

CHAPTER 23

LEARNING FROM WITHIN AND FROM ALL THAT IS
AROUND US
SEEMA AHLUWALIA AND CARL BONESHIRT

Seema: I am a Punjabi-Canadian settler, born in India and raised in Saskatchewan. Carl, Mahto, and I divide our time between Coast Salish territories on the west coast of Canada, and the traditional territories of the Sicangu Lakota Nation (now a part of South Dakota).

Carl: I am a member of the Sicangu Lakota Nation, born and raised in the homelands of my people. I am a survivor of many attempts by the U.S. government to eradicate my nation, steal our lands, and destroy our way of life. Despite being forced to attend residential school, I continue to speak Lakota and practice my people's way of life. These lifeways belong to our children; it is their birthright and should never be denied to them.

Seema: We have been asked to share some of our thoughts about why we homeschool our son, Mahto, who is nine years old at the time of these reflections. "Homeschooling" is not a label we embrace as a reflection of how we are raising our son, but we recognize it is the most common way most people would label our approach to education. Others refer to us as homeschoolers, homelearners, even unschoolers.

Everybody has different ways of learning and labelling their life experiences, I guess. Our commitment is to ensure that our son can live and learn in environments where he feels at ease, happy, creative, and engaged. We are also committed to a pattern of life that allows our son to learn the traditional and cultural knowledge carried by his parents, and extended family, and community circle.

For me, it seems strange to even think of institutionalizing my child from a young age. We believe that he belongs at home with us in his early years so that he can experience and learn the beliefs, values, and rhythms of his family and cultures. There are so many things that I would be denying him if I sent him to school, like the freedom to be himself, and the freedom to experience and learn for himself what his natural rhythms are in relation to all living things around him. On the other hand, there are so many aspects of mass schooling that I have found to be very negative and even harmful.

My experiences of discipline, teasing, and bullying in school are not unique, and I continue to hear horror stories every day from friends and family who share with me what is happening to their own children in schools today. Racism was a constant throughout my educational experience, embedded in the curriculum, and the attitudes and actions of many teachers and students. I don't force my son to experience his life in artificial learning environments. Learning happens through observing and listening, and we do little to interrupt these natural processes, wherever they may occur. Any child raised in Canada deserves to understand our colonial past and present, so they can be knowledgeable about the consequences for their future. As my son shares his father's Lakota heritage, we want him to know his people's history that has been passed down through his grandmothers and grandfathers, not the Eurocentric, racialized fantasy that children are being indoctrinated into in schools today. I will not willingly participate in the destruction of Native children's cultural identities.

Carl: Racism and colonization are two processes that continue to affect Native peoples in a negative way, and this is why I feel we need to homeschool our son. At the age of four, I was forced into boarding school. One does not learn anything when being forced to, when something is imposed upon one. For me, this is one of my main reasons I don't want my son to attend school from an early age. I don't want him to have to experience the same things I have experienced. I want people to know what happened to children at boarding school, what happened to me, and why it is not safe for Lakota children to attend schools today. I was not properly clothed, nor was I adequately housed. The things that were done to me should not have to happen to any child.

I homeschool my son because he should not have to face the discrimination and racism against Native children that is a part of schools. Our Native children are learning to cope with this in a very hard way. They see non-Native kids progressing when they are not, and they know that non-Native kids are getting more opportunities, and see themselves falling behind. When they have issues, there is no one to help them cope with what they are dealing with. When they fight discrimination they are not listened to, they are often blamed, and even sent to jail.

Seema: Lakota women in my husband's community have taught me about the phenomenon they refer to as the "school-to-prison pipeline," where Native children are judged harshly and punished for the same acts that are ignored or downplayed when carried out by non-Native children. Non-native Canadians have the power to ignore all this if they wish, too, indeed my experience has been that most Canadians are unaware of the way schooling has been used as a weapon to destroy Native nations.

Sometimes there is a superficial understanding, but often people dismiss these concerns as past problems. If these issues are discussed at more than a superficial level, many non-Native people turn away and even shun those who try to discuss them. Even in the homeschooling community, we have found there are parents who resent us mentioning these concerns. Meanwhile, I can never ignore the fact that Native children in my province are removed from their homes at ten times the rate of non-Native children. It boggles my mind to think of how many Native families are destroyed every day by governmental agencies, whose policies have genocidal consequences. In British Columbia, every single Native language that is left faces the threat of extinction. Colonization continues, and educational institutions continue to often be dangerous places for Native kids.

Carl: Our son has more opportunities to learn at home. When he was younger he learned through the web of life around him: the plants and animals, the natural elements, and all living things. We observe the things that he likes to do—the people and animals he is drawn to, the activities that engage him—and we support him in any way we can. When he got a little older, he started to enjoy classes at community centers and other places. He goes all over the city to learn, and classes help him because he gets more time and opportunity to learn about things that are not taught in a classroom setting. Bow-making and archery, for example, have been a love of his since near the beginning of his life. Through his love of bows and arrows, which he made for himself from two years old, he learned patience, perseverance, self-reliance, and a way to express his artistry and creativity.

Instead of subjecting him to an arbitrary schedule that every child is supposed to follow, we prefer to let him make sense of his own natural rhythm in his own sacred time. It helps him develop a sense of himself and encourages self-awareness. For example, he likes to play basketball throughout the day and it helps him develop self-discipline. It helps motivate the mind, while strengthening the heart and one's physical form. Because he's not expected to sit down all day long, he can exercise whenever he wants. Schools don't give students enough physical education, which causes a lack of motivation in their minds and a general laziness.

I like that he has opportunities that school kids don't have. For example, he gets to learn from older people, and people in the community. In today's system, they don't let older people talk to kids because they are scared they might mislead them. There seems to be no trust in the classroom setting. School kids don't really get to interact with people beyond the classroom, or the schoolyard, very much. In my people's way, we teach our kids how to live beyond the classroom setting.

Homeschooled kids can learn from everything around them, and develop an awareness of how they feel and how they want to respond to different people and different questions. That is something children tend to be denied in school, because if the child expresses how he feels he may be told, "No it's not that way, it's this way." Kids are graded, and degraded, because of their answers to certain questions. Amongst homelearning families, I have not witnessed bullying, something that is so common in schools and which creates so much stress for young kids, as I know it did for me. Another thing that bothered me in school was the favoritism that was demonstrated over and over again. In the classroom, teachers would favour certain children over others, and give them advantage over others. This would create a hierarchy and create bad feelings among those who felt harmed by this. Some kids are made to feel "smart" and others "dumb" but, sometimes, the "smart" ones were not really that smart; they were just given undue advantage. Outside of school, I had an opportunity to learn in more natural ways: by watching my elders, exercising my curiosity, and following my dreams. I am glad my son can learn a lot of the things we used to, in the ways we used to, like making bows and arrows.

There is a lot to being a home learner, as it helps one to stay on track with what it is one wants or needs to learn. In the classroom, student concerns are not addressed, especially the concerns of Native kids. Homelearners get to go on field trips to learn in natural settings. They get to spend a lot of time learning how things work behind the scenes, under the lid, and behind the curtain. They can exercise their curiosity without limit or shame, interacting with humans of all ages, and with many non-human friends and relations, too.

Today, the kids who go to school tend to forget how to listen, so they can't hear what is being expressed to them. Homeschooling is a good idea because it gives the child a better understanding of what to learn and what not to learn. That's individual freedom and this freedom is fundamental to a Lakota way of life.

Seema: I grew up in Canada, and I was formally educated from kindergarten through grade twelve, and beyond. My parents maintained our cultural traditions within the home and spiritual instruction, oral history, and meditation were part of my daily life. Despite this, the pressure from outside the home to assimilate into dominant Eurocentric culture was overwhelming.

I feel that the most important thing I can do is to love my son unconditionally, and keep him safe without interfering with his sacred path, the one that is meant for him and him alone, the one he will pursue with passion and vigor. My husband and I have found many similarities in our cultures. As a Sikh, I am committed to respect and freedom for every individual. My people are known for their commitment to spiritual freedom, not just for ourselves. We respect all cultural ways and faiths, and many Sikhs have given their lives to defend others against colonial aggression and attacks. Similarly, I have found the Lakota to be fiercely protective of an individual's way of life. This respect really shows in the way Lakota people teach their children, at least amongst those who have been able to be exposed to traditional patterns of parenting. Non-Native people must remember that most Native people today have been denied the basic human right of growing up with their language, culture, and family because of colonial institutions like the residential school system (which was developed by our government to destroy Native cultures— to "kill the Indian and save the child" as our government was fond of saying). Lakota people, who still practice their language and culture, value experience itself as an important teacher. In embracing this perspective, I respect that children can let their experience guide them, and parents can facilitate the learning and help their children draw out the lessons that the experience has brought them. Also, my husband has taught my son and me that, contrary to the Western belief "you can never go back," the Lakota believe a sacred sense of time does not arbitrarily dissect experience into past, present, and future. Knowledge and learning are more fluid than that, and experiences of the past can return to guide us in the future. Sometimes, we can pass through an experience without learning the lessons that were meant for us at that time. Years later, we can re-visit that same experience and harvest new insights and understandings. There is an expression my husband uses, that I carry in my daily walk: Listen and you will hear, observe and you will see. This expression has

helped me reflect on my experience of formal education, and
I have come to the most humbling realization that schooling
deteriorated my ability to see and hear.

When I compare myself to some five- and six-year-old
grandchildren from my husband's community, I have to
admit that my listening and observational skills are weak in
comparison. I have been so conditioned to rely on the
observations of others, through instructions, directions, and
admonitions, that I often overlook what is right before my
eyes! I have grandchildren who regularly get a chuckle,
when we travel on the back roads of my husband's rez.
Grandma (me) can't seem to function without road signs, so
my grandchildren are reminding me that I can easily turn to
naturally-occurring landmarks (rocks, trees, bends in the
river) to measure and record the environment around me.
Meanwhile, the grandkids give me directions three or four
times before I remember the way! Other ideas I reject are
that knowledge develops in some sort of linear way, and that
written knowledge supersedes the oral tradition.
Furthermore, a keen sense of observation means that
children can learn indirectly and through the experiences of
others. I have learned from my Lakota relatives that each
individual can experience the same situation in very different
ways, and that the Western preoccupation with being at the
center of every situation is neither necessary, nor desirable
for everyone. For example, many summers ago, my
husband's family was making preparations for their most-
sacred ceremony, in which I felt most privileged to be
included. Many ceremonies took place, and I remember
feeling sorry for a nephew who, rather than coming inside of
the ceremonial space with the rest of the people, chose
instead to do the work of necessary preparations outside,
both in advance and during the ceremony. One day I told
him how proud I was of him for all his sacrifices and that I

felt sorry that he was missing out on the ceremony by remaining outside. With a bemused grin, he reminded me that he was a part of the ceremony, as were all the people who could not make it there. Nor did he think he was missing out on anything, in fact, he was doing exactly what he wanted to be doing. He loved the opportunity to get strenuous and healthful exercise. He preferred tasks that allowed him solitude and time for quiet reflection. He further advised me that, during the month of preparations, he had learned more about his culture than most young men his age had an opportunity to do. He had his own reasons for choosing his path of service, and reminded me that he was sitting just outside of the ceremony listening to everything that transpired. He told me, "The day I choose to go in, I will know a lot of the songs and, when my uncle calls for a specific song, I will be able to sing it. Auntie, I haven't been away from the ceremony. I've been there the whole time, serving the way that I wanted to serve."

This was a really valuable lesson for me taught to me by an amazing young man, who found his own path to knowledge and healing, not through schooling and books, but through ceremony and service to his community. This nephew is a good teacher and role model, and I am grateful for him and his positive influence on our son.

Experiences like this have taught me that I must allow my son to experience a way of life which is natural to this continent, as much as possible through experiencing his Lakota people's ways. I could never deny him that. These ways are based on knowledge honed on a deep observation and passed on through many generations. I have come to see that the Lakota have what I consider a very scientific way of life, which marries observation and reason. I don't want to deny my son the opportunity to develop this kind of intelligence that he could never develop from sitting in a classroom and reading books.

LEARNING FROM WITHIN AND FROM ALL THAT IS AROUND US

If I were to institutionalize my son, he would not be free to observe the rhythms of nature as they occur, to learn about the medicines and nourishment offered by the plant nations, or to observe their natural cycles in order to reveal to human nations how to best utilize their gifts. For example, some medicines need to be picked or processed at certain times of the year, whether it is a school day or not. The traditional knowledge carried by my husband, and others like him, reflect scientific practices, cosmologies, and epistemologies that take time and patience to grasp, translate, transmit and internalize. This way of life is not supported by, nor does it support, capitalist patterns of schooling which emphasize the pre-eminence of urban, consumer society.

Carl: There is a big difference between religion and a way of life. A way of life is spiritual; it is not based on dogma or indoctrination.

Seema: Eight or seven hours of schooling and restricting one's movement within a specific geographical area reflect capitalist requirements. That doesn't fit the natural way of life that we long for in our family. The seasons don't unfold like that, the day doesn't unfold like that, our hearts and minds don't open like that. We have worked to adjust our living conditions in a way that allows our son to experience the world in ways that we feel will help him.

We are very lucky I have a middle class job that supports our whole family. My husband has agreed to split his time between South Dakota and Canada's west coast, so there is always a parent at home with our son. Like many kids today, our son has a rich cultural heritage that reflects more than one cultural tradition. Rather than trying to mix them up, we try to help him understand the unique traits of each of his cultures, we are not trying to make him Lakabi or Punjota.

This certainly has its challenges. There is a large Sikh community where we live, so it is easy to expose our son to his Punjabi Sikh roots. On Canada's west coast, there are a surprising number of people who claim to be adept at conducting Lakota ceremony and imparting Lakota lifeways. Sadly, most of this is a reflection of cultural appropriation and New Age spiritual tourism. Thus, another layer of education is required for Native kids growing up in cities, where it is easier to be exposed to fake Native culture than it is to have access to Elders who speak their languages and know their cultural lifeways. Despite the challenges, which in themselves are wonderful learning experiences, we give thanks for every good day we are given and for the amazing privilege of learning alongside our precious son. The hard times do not dampen our desire to continue in this way, indeed, I would have to say that keeping our son out of school continues to be a real focus for us. We are both willing to make whatever sacrifices we can to keep him out of school.

Carl: My wife and I have a deep respect and love for all children. Children should be raised in a good way. One should never strike a child, nor should a child be humiliated or bullied in any way. When children become agitated they don't need to be reprimanded or blamed, they just need help calming down. When children behave in a disrespectful manner, there are many ways to teach them how to show respect without resorting to controlling tactics.

Schools don't really function in a way that can help children calm down, in their own way and their own time, when they become agitated or upset. Children who find it hard to constantly behave, according to the demands of school, are often shamed and labeled as disruptive which further harms a child. Those who refuse to assimilate are treated with suspicion and scorn.

LEARNING FROM WITHIN AND FROM ALL THAT IS AROUND US

Seema: I have observed what my husband talks about, with regard to the Lakota traditional belief that children should be treated with respect and gentleness. Rebukes and that kind of discipline don't really come through. One similarity I have observed in both Sikh and Lakota cultures is non-interference, sometimes interpreted as non-violence. We don't like to interfere in our children's sacred learning path. We have faith that the wisdom of their choices will be revealed as time goes by.

When children are engaging in a course of action, they are pretty much allowed to see where it unfolds, as long as they are safe. When they start interfering with somebody else's freedom, when they start bothering other children, or being harsh or not being generous, or straying from the courageous path of truth, there is a way of trying to help children understand that without making them feel bad, without trying to make them feel small. In our cultural traditions, there are teachings that mitigate against stereotyping children. One should not make pronouncements, like this is a good kid, this is a bad kid.

Carl: A child often misbehaves while being forced to do something or say something that does not suit them. In my people's way, we recognize that the good can be the bad and the bad can be the good. In my people's way, there is no wrong and there is no right, it's all a learning experience. My "red road" lies somewhere between the artificially-constructed poles of good and bad.

Seema: Neither my husband nor I are Christian, so we are both acutely aware of the deep indoctrination into Christian values, beliefs, and rhythms of life that continue to define schooling in Canada and the United States. Carl and I both have the experience of being taught by teachers who

275

tried to impose Christian values on us, including the idea of original sin. But we don't see our children as being born "fallen" or anything like that. Children of all nations, human and otherwise, are a gift to this planet and they are teachers in themselves.

Balance is something that we emphasize and strive for in our family. In Hindu scripture, there is a saying, *vishva prana meri atman hai* (all living things are a part of my soul). In Carl's language, they say *mitakuye oyasin* (we are all related). This is not only a sacred belief we both carry, it is also a basic teaching we meditate on and do our best to practice. We do not fight our circumstances, we learn from them as we try to make a better world for ourselves and others. In the context of ongoing relations, we accept that there is a purpose: why we came into each other's lives, and why different people have been brought into our lives, because we are all connected by the spirit that is all life! Each and every person should be treated with respect, not because of how they're treating you, just intrinsically, so that basic respect for one another is really a foundation that I find everything grows out of.

Both our languages are laden with terms of respect for all our relations, human, and otherwise. In Lakota, the way it is spoken is so respectful and gentle and, in Punjabi, terms of respect are added when speaking a person's name.

Also, it seems that the Lakota language cannot be spoken without a lot of laughter! Humour is a really important teacher in both Lakota and Punjabi culture. When I think of how many Indigenous nations today are continuing to try to survive extermination at the hands of colonizing forces, particularly those nations whose lands have been usurped and absorbed into new settler-based societies, I get a deeper understanding of the necessity of laughter for survival.

I firmly believe that Lakota people can teach humanity a way of life that can serve us all. They have all these incredible ways of teaching that many men and women over generations have given their lives to maintain, and that these ways persist is a testament to their strength and resilience. For myself, I feel nothing but gratitude to the Lakota people, especially my husband's family and community, for accepting me into their lives, and for continuing to teach me one of the natural ways of life of this continent. I am so happy for my son that he has access to such knowledge and lifeways.

I've learned from my Lakota relatives that generosity, courage, truth, and respect should not be viewed as values to aspire to but as practices to be enacted daily. For this reason, in our home, everybody and anybody is welcome. Doesn't matter how much money you earn, or whether you yourself have a house to live in. Everyone is welcome, everyone is a relative. We want Mahto to feel that way about everyone around him as well. This reflects what I have learned as a Punjabi Sikh, but it is not reflected in the attitudes and behaviours that children tend to be indoctrinated in at school. When I was growing up, we didn't use the terms Mr. and Mrs. They almost sound insulting in a cultural tradition where anyone around my parents' age was referred to as aunty or uncle, and kids older than us were referred to as brother and sister.

Mahto is being raised in the same way. He doesn't hesitate to call the woman he meets in the park "aunty" or referring to a man panhandling on the street as "uncle." He's easy with that and the concept that everything is related is natural for him, because this is the way he has been taught to orient himself to the world around him. He used to be teased by school children because of this, but by the age of six, he already was so self-assured that, rather than bowing to peer pressure, he simply took the time to explain to them why he referred to others in familial terms. It seems to work for him, and for the people he meets in his daily life. It seems there are a lot of lonely people in our society who appreciate even a small moment of connection with anyone. I notice that people really like it.

Carl: Something I'd like to express is that, in my people's way, we remember and respect our dreams as teachers. We look to our dreams for guidance and understanding, for within our dreams lies a certain answer we may be overlooking in our daily life.

Seema: It seems that many cultures have understood this, yet in industrial capitalist societies, dreams are ridiculed and sensationalized, even programmed by the hyper-stimulation of mass-media content and structure. Perhaps there is a purpose in preventing people from dreaming, but I know for certain that my sacred sense of time is continually disrupted and dissected by the Julian calendar, and by the expectation that my life should follow a pattern dictated by the needs of the workplace. As I mentioned before, the artificial divisions of past, present, and future, and the segmentation of our lives into days, hours, minutes and seconds forces people into schedules and cycles that are not always conducive to dreaming, or to having the time to reflect and learn from our dreams. The hurry-scurry of our lives today makes a lot of people think of sleep as an inconvenience, so our connection to our dreams, and our respect for the knowledge and guidance that comes from dreams, is diminished. Forcing kids to get up and go to school, even when they are in the middle of dreaming, is a clear reflection that there is no respect for dreaming in the curriculum for Canadian school children.

Our son is largely on a schedule of his own choosing, including what time he goes to sleep and what time he rises. As a mother, I believe it is my responsibility to ensure that

he gets all the sleep he needs and, given the prevalence and
constancy of artificial light in our society, he also needs to
be able to maximize the gift of darkness which is so
important to support the development needs of his mind and
body. In his early days, he had no need for appointments,
alarm clocks, or backpacks. As his path in the world
continues to evolve, he has taken on more activities that
require him to schedule some of his time in co-operation
with others, for example, he takes classes in archery,
fencing, painting, animation, and circus arts, and classes are
scheduled at specific times. He has found teachers who he
prefers, and they tend to be people who practice what they
teach. Since these activities are of his own choosing, he
never complains about meeting the schedule, even when he
had to get up for horse-riding lessons at 6:00 am!

Carl: In my people's way, we recognize that life itself is
a learning experience. We see teachers in everyone and
everything. Sometimes the lessons are direct and sometimes
they are inside out. For this reason, we should remain open
to all that cross our path. We teach our son to not be
judgmental, to see that everyone has their own way of life,
and it is not for us to force our way on others.

Sometimes people ask if we would ever let our son go to
school. Yes, I would let him, but he will have to come to his
own understanding of it before he makes that giant step. It's
a matter of knowing.

Seema: We are deeply concerned about ideas that
continue to haunt the Canadian curriculum for school
children, such as the Eurocentric focus, and the cognitive
imperialism that demands that everyone assimilate to the
norms and goals of mass consumer societies, but the
question is no longer a hypothetical one. Mahto has started

to express an interest in attending school. In case it is more than just a passing fancy, I have been sharing information with him about what school may be like, including the need to start early in the day, remain largely inactive during the day, give one person (the teacher) an inordinate amount of attention, tolerate mean and disrespectful behaviour of others, and let others choose the activities that will fill your day. He is deliberating about whether these factors are worth the trouble. His attitude is that if he decides to try it, he can always exit the situation if it does not agree with him. He is mature beyond what my assumptions about nine-year-olds led me to believe in the past. I think he is strong enough in himself to get something out of school, if that is what he wants, although I must admit I face this decision with some trepidation.

At the same time that I have reservations, I also know that my son has many friends who enjoy school and I also know people who enjoyed the schooling experience. I don't want to close my heart and mind to the possibility because, if my son decides he wants to go to school, I have to maintain my commitment to support him and make it the best possible experience it can be for him. I admit it is a challenge for me to suspend my disbelief, but I am not so self-absorbed that I think that my son's experiences will mirror my own. I am glad Mahto knows that schooling is an option, not a requirement.

Carl: I would have to say that I continue to be concerned about what happens in the classroom, the facts that are excluded, and the stereotypes about Native peoples that continue to be perpetuated in schools. I feel sorry for Canadian school kids because, even though their country has been formed on the basis of land theft and cultural destruction, they don't really know anything about where they come from or who they are. Schools continue to deny children the right to learn about Native peoples' perspectives on their histories, and this is a great shame, and an injustice, to Native and non-Native children alike. How will they move forward in a good way, when the past that has been invented for them is nothing but a fantasy?

Seema: One of the most important things for us as a family is a ceremonial way of life that is our center. At this time, school schedules do not honour or support the cycles of nature and the corresponding ceremonies that come up at different times throughout the year. Throughout the year, Mahto often attends events with his father or with both of us, such as ceremonies, food and medicine collecting times, and traditional social gatherings that punctuate our calendar. As Mahto gets older and older, and able to travel without his mom near his side, I think he might be moving around with his father even more. At this time, I can't really see how mass schooling will fit into that.

There is no need to do more than take it one day at a time. Life will unfold as it does, and we will be ready, willing, and grateful! If schooling ever becomes part of the picture of our daily life, we will get something positive out of it for our family.

Ceremonial teachings are fundamental to Mahto's learning and growing experiences. It is through Lakota and Sikh ceremonies that Mahto has come to a strong sense of himself and his place in this world of realities. Ceremony is a strong teacher and guide and cannot be replaced by any book or any individual person, no matter how many degrees or life experiences they are armed with. The ceremonies provide the scientific basis of living a just and ethical life of balance and respect. To devote oneself to the knowledge and practice of ceremony is to work in generosity, health, and community. Through the ceremonies, ancient stories and generations of traditional knowledge are perpetuated, guarded, and passed down carefully and skilfully by those who carry the language and have been trained over many years, within a certain bloodline. Generations of practical and applied knowledge, as well as philosophical and cosmological thought, are demonstrated, reiterated, and practiced. Knowledge development is nurtured and assessed through experience, guidance, and sacrifice. I can't imagine denying my son the opportunity to develop such knowledge. I and my husband have committed our lives to ensuring this kind of knowledge can continue to be nurtured and passed on, not just for our son, but for all Native children who have been denied their birthright, their language and lifeways.

Carl: Native nations face genocide every day, and our children reap little benefit from the structure and curriculum of schools. Many Native children have their self-identities attacked every day in Canadian and American society.

We have to help native kids appreciate and respect their cultures because they face mental, spiritual, and ideological genocide every day. The children need to know that there is still a nation that is still together, that people still practice their way of life and die for it, too. It is really hard for Native kids in the city to connect with their cultures, but it is hard for all city kids to feel and connect with the natural world. Native kids in urban centers don't feel a link, because many were taken from the reservation and adopted into white families. Today they are imposing a way of life on our children that was never meant for them. Despite the myth of the vanishing Indian, there are many Indians who do know their roots, and many Indian ways are not lost.

In residential schools, they tried to commit spiritual genocide on us, and when that didn't work, they turned to mental, physical, sexual abuse. But this abuse of our people has also had the effect of deteriorating the thoughts, feelings,

and emotions of the dominant race. That is why Canadian
society feels cold and violent for Indian people. We just
want foreigners to understand that we are human beings, and
want to live the way that was meant for us. The denial of
genocide against Indian peoples is part of what children are
indoctrinated into in schools. But if there is no genocide,
then why do Indian people have to live with dehumanization
every day, in so many ways? I do not believe that school can
replace what my son can learn through nature and through
ceremony. Through ceremonial ways we can help the young
people dream back their individual, and their nation's, way
of life. Through the ceremonial ways, we will bring our
young people back into their own reality. Ceremonial ways
bring peace and justice, and are there *hecel oyate ki ni pi kte*,
so that the people may live.

An audio version of this piece appears in podcast and can
be found at:
Seema, A., Boneshirt, C. (2006, September 13).
Interview by B. Ekwa Ekoko [Podcast]. Traditional
Learning: Aboriginal Home-schoolers, Radio Free School.
Hamilton, Ontario. Retrieved from
http://radio4all.net/index.php/program/19766

———————

Seema Ahluwalia is a Canadian settler of Punjabi
Ancestry and works as a university teacher. Carl Boneshirt,
Sr. is a traditional teacher and ceremonialist, and is from the
territories of the Sicangu Lakota Oyate (Rosebud Sioux
Reservation in South Dakota). They live with their son,
Mahto, in Coast Salish territories. Together, their lifework
reflects a commitment to decolonization of thought and

action, and to building bridges of understanding and co-existence between Indigenous Peoples and Settlers who now live within Indigenous territories.

PART III

THEY'VE GROWN UP

CHAPTER 24

LIFE IS A FIELD TRIP AND YOU DON'T NEED A
PERMISSION SLIP
DALE STEPHENS

In fifth grade, I told my parents I wasn't learning anything in school. Fifth grade came and went, and I learned little from test-focused lessons, while teachers struggled to control wild students. I wasn't able to participate in art, music, or science because our school district had decided to focus on standardized test scores. One day I matter-of-factly announced that something had to be done about my education, and that it wouldn't involve public school.

My parents were taken aback. My mom had been a public school teacher and was quite invested in the system, to her even going to private school seemed like a leap. They considered sending me to the local Waldorf School, but to pay the tuition my mom would have had to return to work, 20 miles in the opposite direction. When it became clear that private school wasn't an option, I suggested homeschooling. You may wonder where I found the authority to suggest such a thing to my parents. It felt natural to do so, largely because my parents always treated me as an equal.

At first, my parents weren't thrilled with my suggestion, because the only homeschoolers we knew were ones who were doing so for religious reasons, and that didn't fly with my agnostic parents. Then, I spotted an ad in our local newspaper for a not-back-to-school night hosted by local unschoolers. Somehow, I convinced my mom to take me.

That night we found a vibrant community of local unschoolers who were hacking their education. The group of about twenty unschoolers between the ages of 12 and 18, were leveraging the resources of the world around them to create a coherent educational program. While their peers sat in class, they found internships, took college classes, learned collaboratively, studied independently, and found mentors.

I have to thank my parents for believing that I could direct my own education, with their help and support. After a recent talk at a conference, a woman came up to me and said, "I learned only one thing from your speech: your parents rock!" Had my parents not trusted that I was fully capable of being my own person, I would never have developed the skills, aptitude, and mindset that prepared me to thrive in the global entrepreneurial economy.

Our unschooling curriculum combined classes in groups, courses online, individual study, and classes at community college. Over time, our approach to unschooling evolved, and I developed my learning style. Initially, because my mom was a public school teacher, she felt committed to book learning. However, our philosophy changed: I did not sit at the kitchen table all day doing ditties, nor did I learn in a laissez-faire style. Our method was somewhere in between. Often, I assumed the role of teacher and planned many of my courses. My parents and I agreed that, with unschooling, my primary goal was to learn for learning's sake, not just to pass a test.

Collaborative classes were my favourite part of unschooling. From sixth until eighth grade, twenty unschoolers and their parents gathered every week for a history co-op. Each week, a different student or parent would facilitate the class and provide thematic snacks. In this way, everyone shared responsibility and investment in the course. Similarly, a collaborative literature course developed that shared similar principles, but on a smaller scale. For the literature course, three mother-child units met once a week for five years for "lit class" to discuss the theme of the year, which ranged from science fiction to myth.

Outside the strictures of the classroom, I engaged in real-world learning opportunities beyond the scope of school. As soon as I wasn't shackled to a desk, I become involved with a campaign to build a new library in my hometown. Our old library was in a leaky building, built in the 1940s. As you might imagine, books and water don't mix well. During rain storms, my mom and I would get frantic calls from the librarian asking us to come downtown and help cover the stacks with tarps. After two failed ballot measures, we finally succeeded in securing funding to build a joint-use city/county/school library. At twelve, I secured a position on the steering committee along with the Mayor, Superintendent, and County Supervisors. I learned to be self-confident, to voice my opinion, and to dedicate myself to a cause. After seven years of volunteering, the new community library opened in November 2009.

Even with this vibrant community, I thought I'd miss out on socialization if I didn't go to college, because my peers were going, my parents went, and that's what society expected. That's not to say I didn't have a social group as an unschooler—I very much did. However, my social life was split between my unschooler friends and everyone else. As I mentioned earlier, I learned and went to cooperative classes with about twenty unschoolers my age. But I didn't associate with them much outside of class. I was always the odd duck out. My academic friends were not my best buddies outside the classroom.

Because of this, I spent ages searching for a college with the type of community that I desired: A community where my academic and social connections would be one and the

same. I visited 28 colleges in search of a place where I
would fit into both realms. I thought a college in Arkansas
would meet that requirement. I was wrong.

At college, there were smart students with bright ideas,
but they were writing research papers, not changing the
world. I wanted to change the world, because I understood
how my actions built the future.

Before college, I lived and worked in San Francisco for
eight months at Zinch, a hot education-technology start-up
that matches students and colleges. It took going to college
to make me realize that the environment I was after—where
my academic and social groups were one—existed in San
Francisco. In Silicon Valley, young entrepreneurs eager to
change the world surrounded me. I'd found my people.

The founder of the start-up where I worked tried to
convince me not to go to college. I dismissed that idea,
arguing, "I might as well give it a try and if I don't enjoy it
I'll come back." I only lasted eight months in Arkansas
before I came skipping back to Silicon Valley.

When I did come skipping to enter the big, bad real
world I didn't flounder, for I'd been directing my own
education all along. The initiative I'd developed seeking out
mentors, the passion I'd uncovered from pursing my
interests, the communication skills I'd honed from years of
networking, the hustle I'd perfected from constantly
challenging authority, all applied to life as well as my
education.

I still get funny looks from people when they ask where I
went to high school and I say I didn't. They ask, "What
about prom?" I retort that I didn't miss out on much. What I
got instead of prom was far more useful; namely, the ability
to do things differently.

Conformity is not the quickest path to success. Proving
that you can do the same thing in a non-traditional fashion is

more impressive than sharpening your number-two pencil. After years of being harassed about not going to high school, I stopped caring about what other people thought of me. I'm not saying that you should ignore the opinions of others. To the contrary, it is vitally important to understand what others think of you but, it is even more vitally-important to be confident in yourself.

Now, as the leader of UnCollege, the global social movement I lead challenging the notion that college = success, I'm putting the same skills into practice, by challenging authority in new ways and ignoring those who vandalize my Wikipedia page, disrespect my age, and call my ideas dangerous. Ultimately, I take pride in acting in ways that disprove all those naysayers.

I act with authority, by standing up and pointing out that the university has no clothes. In just five months, UnCollege has gained thousands of members from seventeen countries. The team has grown from one to six people, and I've spoken at conferences in many countries. For my work with UnCollege, I received the Thiel Fellowship, a program sponsored by Peter Thiel, cofounder of PayPal and the first investor in Facebook. Thiel gave the top 24 entrepreneurs who were under twenty years of age, from around the world, $100,000 each to build the future. Penguin will be publishing my first book, *Hacking Your Education*, in early 2013.

Stephens, D. J. (2013). *Hacking your education: Ditch the lectures, save tens of thousand, and learn more than your peers ever will.* New York, NY: Perogee Trade, Penguin.

At 19, Dale Stephens leads UnCollege, the global social movement changing the notion that college is the only path to success. In May 2011 Dale was selected out of hundreds individuals around the world as a Thiel Fellow. The Thiel Fellowship recognizes the top entrepreneurs from around the world under the age of twenty. He is a sought-after education expert appearing on major news networks including CNN, ABC, NPR, CBS, and Fox.

CHAPTER 25

PIONEER UNSCHOOLER

KATE CAYLEY

I was home schooled throughout my life, until I went to university. I'm part of a small theatre company called Stranger Theatre, which I co-founded after leaving university in 2001. I work with the company as a director, co-creator, and writer. I'm also the artistic co-director of a theatre festival, called the Cooking Fire Festival, which is a festival of new outdoor work performed in city parks in Toronto. I am a writer, and a playwright-in-residence at the Tarragon Theatre in Toronto, where my first full-length play, *After Akhmatova* was produced in the spring of 2011. My first novel, a book for young adults called *The Hangman in the Mirror* (2011) was recently published by Annick Press. Homeschooling was lunatic fringe when I was a child. I was born in 1978, so this was the eighties and early nineties. It's been really interesting to see it become, I won't say mainstream, but more acceptable. When I went to the university and began the application process, I had to explain the entire concept. By the time I graduated, it became a little bit more normal, not that it was common, but at least it had a reference point. Since then, the university I attended has accepted a number of homeschoolers.

I had pretty interesting parents, and lived in a large city. Toronto didn't have an enormous homeschooled population, but it definitely had some—it always had some. I think my experience was very different than someone growing up in a more rural, or small town setting. I don't think I felt isolated. I felt it was trickier when I was high-school-age, because most of the people I knew who'd been homeschooling decided to go to high school, and I didn't want to go that route. I had some close school friends, and they experienced the world very differently from me.

I did not feel pressure to go to school. I think my reasons for not going were partly fear of the unknown, but also wanting to see it through to the end. I had had myself registered as a dropout when I was 16, because I was so tired of school boards, so when I applied to university this was a problem. I had no school records, I was registered as a dropout, and most universities that I approached said I would need to take a make up year. I thought, "No, I'm educated and I'm capable of starting university in a first year program." It was quite an uphill slog, trying to get myself into university when I was 18. [There are easy ways to get into university without a high school diploma. For example, see Ricci (2008) (http://jual.nipissingu.ca/PDF/v211.pdf)]

I didn't feel like an oddball, but I was an oddball—deeply an oddball. It didn't bother me much. It bothered me when I was 13 or 14, but 13 or 14 is generally when people are miserable, so there's nothing unique about that. Other than that, it really didn't trouble me. Of course, I went though periods of being extremely focused on my peer group as a teenager. Growing up, I definitely had more contact and close relationships with adults. Not just my parents, but friends of my parents and people they knew. I think that was a gift. One of the things that is strange about the school structure is that you're kept rigidly within your peer group, which seems like a sad loss. It's more interesting to have contact between generations that isn't institutional (student/teacher) or familial.

Being homeschooled straight through to university also meant, of course, that I was at times lonesome. I think, ultimately, it was still interesting to have the experience of real solitude. At times, I found homeschooling difficult because I'm very social, but I had moments in university where I thought I was going a little bit nuts because I was suddenly living in a context where you were social all the time. Even though I loved it, I really missed the contemplative aspect of being alone.

I think that not being at school gave me other opportunities. A big one was that I became pretty independent about trying to discover the city at a young age. My reference point was not the school, so I went on my bike and visited museums, arts galleries, libraries, and theatres. It was pretty clear, since I was about thirteen, that theatre was my path. I was able to work more, so I saved money. When I was eighteen, I went and traveled around Europe by myself before going to university. In general, I was able to develop a very specific intellectual life around my reading. Sometimes, that came with a sacrifice of other things, my school math, for instance, is really not up to scratch but my reading always was. Of course, there are many schoolers who also lack confidence in their ability to do school math. Looking back, as an adult, I started to feel that the really definitive difference between being in school and not being in school was not being bored. Everybody I knew seemed to think of certain sections of their childhood and adolescence, as a long period of intense boredom, and that wasn't true for me. Not to say that I was never bored, but just that I could pursue my path. When I got to university, I started reading Plato's *The Symposium* (1973), who says that knowledge is only possible through love: through the particular thing that you pursue freely, from love. Not being in school gave me the opportunity to realize that learning derives from love, rather than obligation.

University was fine, I loved it. It was a small school, a liberal arts college in Halifax that had been very welcoming to me, even though I had no school records. As for the work, I think I found it very exciting. It was a school where, in the first year, very few people were from Halifax. People come to that school from outside, so everybody was in the same boat. Most were away from home for the first time, so I wasn't odd in comparison to others. I had very interesting professors and small classes. I don't know how I would have felt in a situation where all my classes had 200 people in them.

It was exciting, because I had grown up without competition, and suddenly I was in a context where I became competitive. It was interesting to be competitive in that way for four years, and I did quite well. I had a very good time, though by the time I graduated I was ready to be out of school. I don't know if that had to do with homeschooling, but I felt that it had been a wonderful experience but I didn't want to be in that context again.

There are so many different approaches to homeschooling; I was unschooling. Obviously, growing up, it was all over the map, very chaotic. It's been interesting now to see the changes in outlook between then and now. I often feel, now, that I meet more homeschoolers who work on a more structured model. Sometimes I think it's good, and sometimes I feel it's too regimented, not allowing the possibilities of actually getting out of the entire model.

I think I was ten when I met Ivan Illich. He's been a profound, profound influence on me. As an adolescent, and also when I got older, particularly in the last few years since his death, I felt the influence even more strongly. He was a champion of the attempt—often flawed because concrete actual things are flawed, only the theory is ever perfect—to de-institutionalize yourself. To understand that the school, the hospital, whatever institution you are grappling with, is not the only avenue through which a life can be lived. I feel like that has been his particular gift to the way that I'm fumblingly trying to live my life. I feel this even more than when I was a child. The idea that you can't live your life without experts, or expertise, or gaining expertise, or somehow being always in the context of an institution, is so profound.

It was lovely to have met him as a child, because when I was that young I was not really conscious of someone as anything other than a friend. You can become conscious of them as a mentor, as a great man, after you're conscious of them as someone who's a presence in your life.

At Stranger Theatre, I do the writing and directing, though it's a very collective process in rehearsal: We might change it a lot, in fact we often do change it a lot, and a lot of it is using text from other sources, or developing text or structure in rehearsal. Maybe you start with a literary text, or you start with a folktale, or you start with an odd historical episode. Currently, we're working on a piece about a servant girl, in 18th century Montreal, who was sentenced to hang for stealing a pair of gloves, and who saved her own life by persuading the man in the next cell to become the hangman and marry her; it's based on a true story.

We've always worked with either a historical story, or a short story, and then a script is developed from collaborative work in rehearsal with the performers, who are also the co-creators. We use some text from the original text if we have one, plus text from anything, everything, like poetry, and news reports, and I add writing to that. It's not as experimental as it sounds.

When we started, I wanted it to be political. We've shied away from that a little bit, in that we're telling political stories in a roundabout way, through historical stories where the mode of expression is very tongue-in-cheek. This is partly from being pretty weary of a lot of political theatre, because it's very-heavy handed, and sometimes not very good. We've been all over the map, which I think is good. In some ways, we've been around for a long time, and in other ways we're also really young, so we're just kind of finding our way.

With my own unschooling, I was sometimes alone in the house. I was homeschooling straight through, from the age of five to eighteen, and so the dynamic of that changed massively. I always marvelled at people who managed to homeschool their kids in an extremely rural area, because I think it was a really good thing that I could go out and see the city. I had periods where I was lonesome, and I think that might be inevitable and not a terrible thing, but I also found that when it was time to make friends, I made them quite easily.

When I was younger, my mother was involved in getting together a homeschooler's gym, where we met on Thursdays. People brought food and everyone would run around. There was a group of women, particularly my mother, who really, really wanted to see that happen, so it became a really strong social group. It wasn't huge, but it was huge enough that you had your scene, and you had a gang, and you could go out and run around and get yourself lost. For us, the emphasis was on getting together, eating food, and having the kids run around, with the parents being able to sit around the table and ignore us for four or five hours and talk to each other. The focus was on unsupervised play, and on just having a community to get together and be together, it was chaotic and interesting.

I think that the only thing that I really felt, that I really realized as an adult, was that homeschooling and unschooling can only work from a constantly evolving, working knowledge of what is possible and good. I'm thinking of "good" with a capital-G here. Not as a political good, not as something that's doctrinaire or "better," because everything contains its own flaws. But it's a remarkable way to be educated by osmosis, in the possibility that you can live your life, at least partially, out of the context of an institution.

An audio version of this piece appears in podcast and can be found at: Cayley, K. (2005, December 14). Interview by B. Ekwa Ekoko [Podcast]. Kate Cayley: Grown without school. Radio Free School. Hamilton, Ontario.

Retrieved from http://radio4all.net/index.php/program/15538

References

Cayley, K. (2012). *After Akhmatova*. Toronto: PGC.

Cayley, K. (2011). *The hangman in the mirror.* Toronto, ON Annick Press.

Plato. (1973). *The symposium.* (W. Hamilton, Trans.). Middlesex England: Penguins Books Ltd.

Ricci. C. (2008). Open universities: You do not need a high school diploma to get into university. *Journal of Unschooling and Alternative Learning.* Retrieved January 25, 2008, from http://www.nipissingu.ca/jual/PDF/v211.pdf. (2)3, (16 pages)

Kate Cayley is a playwright, poet and fiction writer. Her first collection of poetry, When *This World Comes to an End*, was recently published by Brick Books and was named one of the season's best collections by *The Globe and Mail*. She is a playwright in residence at Tarragon Theatre. She is the artistic director of Stranger Theatre, and has co-created, directed and written eight plays with the company. She has also written a young adult novel, *The Hangman in the*

Mirror (Annick Press), which won the Geoffrey Bilson Award for Historical Fiction. Her poems and short stories have appeared in literary magazines across the country, and her first collection of short fiction, *How You Were Born,* will be published next fall. She lives in Toronto with her partner and their two children.

CHAPTER 26

GROWING UP WEIRD

KATE FRIDKIS

I'm not going to lie; the transition from unschooling to college was very difficult for me. I think that had to do with the particular school that I went to—a really big state school and, later, a smaller graduate school. They were really different experiences, and I thought, "Oh man! I should have done this one first!"

A lot of the things that were tricky for me were the obvious. Like, I thought it was so ridiculous to be sitting in a classroom; I'd never really spent time sitting in a classroom before. I looked around and everybody was facing forward, and a lot of people were falling asleep. The professor was at the front, at the board, trying desperately to keep everybody's attention. It seemed like such a silly format to me. It was a little bit rough, but I adjusted, and I did enjoy being able to meet a lot of professors, and to be exposed to a lot of subjects to which I had no previous exposure.

I have a problem with the idea of a balanced curriculum. I've never liked the notion that well-rounded education is the ideal education, because I think that when people pursue that model of educational success they end up with a lot of people who maybe know a little about a lot of subjects, but who aren't experts at anything, and who also haven't learned how to pursue their interests.

The idea of balance, maybe in its ideal form is awesome, but when it's applied broadly it prevents people from learning what they love to do. When you learn to love learning, and do things that interest you, whatever it is that interests you ends up connecting you to a whole huge network of other stuff, other subjects, in really surprising ways. Maybe you end up being more balanced than people expect, in exciting ways, but it's never through pursuing well-roundedness.

The truth is that you learn something new in absolutely every environment. It's not like there is an environment that you can go to where you get access to all the important information. You learn everywhere! The idea that I love, and always find true about unschooling, is that you are always learning, because you are living. Of course, when I went to college, I learned from interesting people who I wouldn't have otherwise met, but to be perfectly honest I would have learned somewhere else, too.

As an unschooler, I felt like an adult. By being around adults, and being in the community rather than in school, I had a lot of contact with grownups who didn't expect to end up being my friend because here I am, a kid. It is kind of expected that kids are going to be with other kids, and adults with other adults. Everyone is going to be slotted into their particular age bracket, and that is where they are going to stay—which is kind of a strange idea really, because it is so useful for children to learn from people who are older.

My experience as an unschooler consisted of being around adults who told me, "You seem so grown up!" It wasn't that I was grown up, it was just that I was interacting with them as I would with a friend. Through these relationships, I was able to talk about things that were relevant to adults. I was able to have a lot of educational and relational experiences that other children didn't have access to. There is a lack of fear of adults, in unschooled kids; they are not afraid of speaking with adults, and are not wary of adults. The schooled peers I met in college, who were still

301

afraid of interacting with adults when they were twenty, surprised me.

Another thing about unschoolers being grown up is that they just have a lot of responsibility, which is something people don't expect from kids in school. I have to qualify that, and add that kids in school have tons of responsibility. Not the same kind of responsibility, not the kind where you get to decide what you do with your time, and what you learn, and what you pursue. For them, it's the kind that I shrink from, like having to do hours of homework, or getting straight-A's in every subject. That sounds so stressful to me, I can't imagine how anybody does it.

For a long time, I felt I needed to defend my life to the world. I felt I needed to explain that I was valid, that I was smart and successful, because they kind of assumed otherwise. A couple of years ago, I felt tired of trying to defend my existence in these very solemn terms. I thought, "You know what? Everyone is weird; everybody is different. And it's so much more effective to relate to people as people, because we are all human." My particular weirdnesses, and my particular weird experiences, they are really valuable and great. Just like I think other peoples' particular weird experience are valid and great. I just don't want to defend myself. I also want to be able to laugh at myself.

I was once asked whether we really need schooling. No one had asked me that question: I feel like people should ask, it's a great question. I blog sometimes for Lisa Nielsen, who hosts the Innovative Educator and works with New York City schools, introducing technological innovations into the classroom, and building a network of interconnectivity between schools. Her goal is getting everyone online, expanding education beyond the walls of the school and across state lines. I think that is the direction school is heading, just like it is the direction that everything is heading. It doesn't mean that everything is going to change overnight. But if it really did change overnight, and schools stop being school, I think it would be the logical result of what is happening anyway.

I think the way our consciousness works, our interaction works now as a nation and globally as well, is much less concrete, much more in the realm of ideas. That is what the Internet has done: connected us with people. We are friends with people who we have never met. We are exposed to their ideas and information, and it is free. There isn't so much of a hierarchy of information as there used to be, when you had to go to find people who possessed a certain body of information, and they had to be the ones to impart it.

It sounds radical, but in terms of knowledge and learning, I don't think it is incredibly radical to say that schools are not as necessary as they used to be. The way that they are necessary will continue to be valid until society changes dramatically in other, economic, ways. People need their kids to be in school because they are working, so it's hard to imagine a world without school, before imagining a world in which jobs have been dramatically restructured.

Although, as Beatrice Ekwa Ekoko observes in our interview there's a movement of unjobbing (personal communication April 19, 2010) the equivalent of unschooling: People becoming more self-sufficient and the whole nature of work changing with the Internet and technology, and more people working from home. If we could plunge into this new world where there wasn't school, and jobs had been completely rerouted, I think that we would see a lot more people starting their own companies. Things would be intertwined in a new way, but only new in the sense that it was widespread because, again, we are already seeing that things are moving in that direction.

Now, with the economy as it is, we are seeing tons of new job innovation, and the entrepreneurial base is growing enormously. People are forced to do something different, and think creatively, and that is fundamentally what unschooling is.

An audio version of this piece appears in podcast and can be found at: Fridkis, K (2010, December, 28). Interview by B. Ekwa Ekoko [Podcast]. Unschooler Kate Mende-Fridkis: Embracing the weird. Radio Free School. Hamilton, Ontario. Retrieved from
http://radio4all.net/index.php/program/48260

Kate Fridkis works as a lay clergy member at a synagogue and writes a blog called *Eat the Damn Cake*, which is syndicated on *The Huffington Post* and *Psychology Today*. She also writes a column for *Home Education Magazine*. Her work has appeared in *Cosmopolitan, Slate, Salon,* and others. A new mother, Kate has recently published her first book, *Growing Eden* (2013)—a memoir about being pregnant in New York City and making the kind of choices that sometimes result in growing up, or at least growing.

CHAPTER 27

I LOVE MY LIFE

ELI GERZON

Success

Success and schooling are two things closely linked in many people's minds. In my case, both my parents left in the middle of college and have started their own successful businesses. As a result, I never really thought I needed college for success.

Regardless, I think there are many different ways of defining success. I guess the most conventional definition would be to make lots of money and get lots of recognition. My definition of success certainly includes making enough money, but that's only a part of it.

For me, real success is providing for whatever family I have, and doing all I can to share my true gifts with the world, and making some sort of meaningful contribution. In some ways, that's more pressure than conventional definitions of success. In other ways, it's a very simple, humble, and humbling thing: You figure out what you can do, you put your whole heart and all your smarts into it, and you accept whatever big or small part you end up playing.

The way to find those true gifts is by following your bliss: your joy will naturally lead to what you're meant to do, what you truly want to do. But by naturally, I don't mean easily! It can require facing some real challenges. Still, I've found that after (or even while) facing those challenges, I find real meaning and happiness.

I've done two things in my life that have brought me both money and the type of satisfaction and meaning I'm talking about. Since 2002, I've run my own natural landscaping business that I've used to make a living and finance my solo travels around the world, to over a dozen countries.

Inspired by all the learning and growing I did during those travels, I started Worldschool Travel Tours, in 2008. It's small group travel, especially for homeschooling and unschooling teens and young adults to gain awareness of the world and experience personal growth. I've led three Worldschool Travel Tours: First to Mexico, in 2008; then Japan, in 2009; and Japan again, in summer 2010.

Landscaping gives me a great, simple, daily satisfaction. With Worldschool Travel Tours, I get a deep and meaningful satisfaction when I see or hear about how much a young person has grown and changed from experiencing a whole new part of the world.

Schooling Background

I went to a Waldorf/Steiner school for first and second grade (ages 6-8) and then public school until ninth grade (ages 8-15). At fifteen, I chose to leave school and did homeschooling/unschooling for the other three years of high school.

Why I chose to leave is something I've written and spoken a lot about. I had been frustrated for years with the lack of concentration on real learning, and school was crushing my soul, to be honest. I was starting to discover a lot about the historical and present actions of the U.S. There are a lot of atrocities my country has committed, and continues to commit, using our tax dollars. My main source for history was James Loewen's book *Lies My Teacher Told*

Me (1995). My main source for understanding present day and recent U.S. injustice, imperialism, and lies, was Noam Chomsky—from his speeches and articles.

I figured, "I could be discovering the truth about the world, instead I'm reading lies in our history books and wasting time doing busy work and studying things I might not need to study or could learn more easily outside of school."

The cons of my unschooling lifestyle have been that I've often had no idea what I was going to do with my life. Of course, unfortunately, this is something that many young people, schooled or not, face. That's been very challenging for me. I have been tempted to go to high school or college for the relief of being normal, and having a set track to follow for awhile.

I've taken several college classes. I really enjoyed them, learned a lot, and, yes, got pretty good grades, but I know I couldn't stomach going full time.

The main positive aspect of this lifestyle is that I have created a life of which I'm happy and proud. I certainly had the opportunity to do some healing work, I know was very important for me to do, during my teen years. I've also done a lot of exploring of the planet, and the world of ideas. I doubt I could have done as much, if I was in high school or college full time. In the end, because I didn't follow the usual track, I've had the opportunity to find my own path that works for me. It's not set, it continues to change, but I'm happy with the direction I'm going.

View of the World

I love the world I live in, and at the same time I want to see it change in many ways! Everywhere I've traveled around the world, I've found an unbelievable amount of richness and beauty in the natural world, and in people and the art that they create.

As far as what I'd like to see change, I believe that we need to stop causing our own self-destruction and figure out ways that work for us to live together in small or large groups. I spend a lot of my time trying to figure out how we'll do that!

Climate change, or climate chaos as I think is a more accurate label, could very well cause our planet to become a very difficult place for us to survive, as individuals, as nations, as civilizations, and even as a species. Clearly, there are deeper issues at work. It's easy to see we're destroying our planet, especially with modern science, and yet some of us deny it and we continue to contribute to the destruction as individuals, groups, and inactive bystanders.

It's clear that the U.S., with the most powerful military in human history, wages unjust wars, and supports others in waging unjust wars and oppressing people. Yet, we continue to bomb and invade new countries.

It's clear that wealth is unjustly distributed all over the world, including in the U.S., the wealthiest nation in human history. Yet, the gap in wealth continues to widen.

I write this a day after marching in Boston in one of the many marches in cities across the world, on October 15th, 2011. We were protesting many of these injustices (climate change was not addressed). The Arab Spring has spread across northern Africa and the Middle East. And now, the Occupy Wall Street movement is spreading to cities across the U.S., and the world. Even mainstream media, like the *New York Times* and *Fox News*, have started to speak favourably about the Occupy Wall Street movement. I think there is hope.

Still, even if there is great success with movements like these, even if dictatorships are toppled, occupying armies run out, some sort of wealth-equality established, and people have freedom, we're still left with the question of how to actually live together.

The bottom line for me is that we, as human beings, have a great capacity for good and also a great capacity for wrongdoing. This capacity for good is something upon which unschoolers and people who trust in freedom often concentrate. But freedom can give people the freedom to oppress, exploit, and control others. Freedom can give people the freedom to do cruel, wrong, evil, bad things, on small scales, and on large scales.

How do we address this? How do we allow people to be free while preventing them from hurting or impinging upon the freedom of others?

I've often thought of having no rules, but now I think that can only work on very small scales, among people with very common interests, within particular, limited parameters. But when the groups get bigger or the parameters are widened to the greater outside world, rules and leaders are needed.

I'd really like to concentrate on the wonderful things about unschooling. I have been paying a lot of attention, and feeling amazed and hopeful about the Arab Spring and Occupy Wall Street movements. But my mind has largely been on the negative things of which we're capable, and how to address them in a way that is effective, respectful, and even loving.

It's quite a big topic! I think one important thing is flexibility and adaptability. Different approaches work for different situations and different people at different times. We need to be adaptive to the situation, to the world, as we encounter it. This is part of what I call "worldschooling." The other important point, from my view, is really looking honestly at each situation. Being honest when something is an issue. Sometimes, just letting an issue be is the best approach. Sometimes, action is needed, and it's important to address the issue as best we can, while accepting we may or will make some mistakes.

When we make mistakes, we need to look at them as honestly as possible to help us do better next time. If we learn from our mistakes, we can do things better in the future. Even more importantly we can pass along the wisdom we've gained, while, again, knowing others may have to be flexible and adapt to their own situations.

Advice to Young People

Regarding unschooling, for those young people who want to convince their parents of the value of leaving high school or college and exploring and learning from the world itself, I'd say: "Be persistent!"

Parents want to know that their children are going to be alright. Show you've done your research, that you really care, and you are really insistent about living without school. Beyond the information itself, when parents see your dedication they can see how you might apply it to other areas of life.

I have known high schoolers whose parents were reluctant to let their child leave school, or unschool, but the parents really came around. It's just as often that the young people themselves want to go to college/university. I know many parents who have urged their children to skip or wait on going to college but the young person goes.

I think those young people are often looking to college for an adventure, a challenge, meaning, and even a passage into adulthood. My advice: travel! It's a cheaper, more meaningful, and more real endeavour. Even the parties are better.

Of course, there are many other ways to find adventure, challenge, and meaning. I think it's about following your personal bliss that leads you to the experiences and lessons that are just what you need. Still, sometimes it can feel like you'll never find your own path, and maybe you will decide to go to school or college and that will become part of your path.

I decided to continue putting my trust in myself, my communities, and the world, without the institution of college. For me, it's paid off well: I have found a path that works for me and I have the flexibility to change it when I want or need to. Things can still be really challenging when I feel lost, but ultimately I love my life.

Added in February 7, 2013:

I discovered 350MA in early November, 2012, and went to the 350 New England convergence later that month. That changed my life. Here were hundreds of people, from around the Northeast, getting together to take on the most important issue humans have ever faced. They were well-organized, emphasized the need for attainable goals, and looked honestly at the severity and urgency of the issue. There were a few high-school-age young adults, many college students, lots of white haired folks, and everyone in between. They were serious about the issue and also had camaraderie and knew how to have fun.

For me, unschooling has always been about the freedom to learn the truth about the world and do good things that create big, real, meaningful changes. I know that's the vision many other people have for unschooling, but I don't see that happening. Unschooling is about freedom. People do a lot of different things with freedom. Not enough people seem to be placing emphasis on actually taking real steps to change the world, rather than talk about it.

I've been someone who has talked about changing the world a lot. I'm finally involved with actually trying to change the world with 350 Massachusetts right now for two reasons: First, I know the work they're doing is absolutely needed, right now, and, second, I feel like they can actually accomplish their goals.

Whatever gifts I have can be put to good use in the organization. That causes me to really love my life. It's strange to derive so much happiness from working on something as terrible as global warming.

Maybe I'll get disillusioned with 350MA or 350.org at some point. The only hope I see for the future is some sort of grassroots, people-powered movement. The government and established environmental organizations have clearly not done enough to steer away from the path of destruction that we're on. In ten days, I'm going to the Forward on Climate Rally in Washington, D.C., my first time going down to D.C. for a protest. I think it will be an historical turning point. I think it has to be.

In the end, all we can do is our best. The future will bring what it brings, but I finally feel like I am doing my best, maybe for the first time in my life. That feels better than anything, and I'm truly thankful for all that brought me to this point, including unschooling and my travel tours.

References

Loewen, J. (1995). *Lies my teacher told me: Everything your American history textbook got wrong.* New York, NY: Simon and Schuster.

Eli Gerzon is in his late twenties and is from Boston, Massachusetts. He went to school until the age of 15 when he decided to leave school and educate himself, inspired by the unschooling philosophy and dissatisfaction with his school experience. Since the age of 18, Eli has traveled extensively around the world on his own and lead travel tours around Mexico, Japan, and the U.S. for the last few years. He runs his own landscaping business during the spring, summer, and fall and usually travels during the winter. Eli has visited or lived in Western Europe, East Asia, Southeast Asia, Central America, and the Middle East.

CHAPTER 28

I'M EDUCATED

CANDRA KENNEDY

Currently, I work at two different places teaching individuals with visual impairment. I am in the process of putting the finishing touches on a script I have been writing, that I'm going to produce for a fringe festival here in Philadelphia, in September. I'm working on getting my cast together, and doing readings for that, and touching up the final draft of the script. I'm in the middle of recording an album of songs I wrote a couple of years ago. I have a part-time job. I have produced videos, in response to *Good Morning America's* (2010) coverage of unschooling. I decided to make those because one of my friends, who also was unschooled, (I met her through a camp called Not Back to School Camp, when we were both teenagers), had shared the video clip with me. She made a video response to it first. After she showed it to me, she encouraged me to make a response as well. Initially, I was just planning on leaving a comment on the message board, but then I thought that maybe a video might be a way to reach more people, and express myself in a different way. *The Good Morning America* piece, I felt, was very one sided, a pretty unbalanced presentation of unschooling. I thought it would be good, especially since they only showed kids who were in the process of unschooling, right now. I thought it was important that people see someone who had already been there, done that, and who is in the next phase of her life, and how unschooling shaped who I am today. I

314

don't think the *Good Morning America* video showed that family in an unbiased light. Some of the things they showed the family doing came across as really negative. Unschooling was part of my life too, but it didn't affect me in a negative way, the outcome was eventually positive.

Given how the *Good Morning America* video was edited, how they focused on just this one family, I think the negative representation was intentional. It's been a long time since I've seen that video, but I do remember there being one point where the kid tried to start to answer one of the questions the interviewer asked, and they cut off the kid's answer.

The question we need to consider is: Why would they portray a negative representation? Why would people feel threatened by unschooling? There are a couple of reasons. Some people feel that people who think unschooling works are insulting people who went to school; It is like saying that, "You went to public school, so obviously you didn't get a good education. You're not educated." Some people honestly feel unschooling is attacking them, by claiming to be more successful than public schooling.

Also it is something different, something people don't know about. It's a hot topic for parents who have children, who worry that unschooling is damaging to kids, because they don't understand it. They think that it's sheltering children.

A lot of people have this other negative connotation of homeschooling, that it's only for really fundamentalist Christians who want to brainwash their children. Many fear that people are doing it to prevent their children from learning other things. That may be the case for some homeschoolers, especially where I grew up in the Bible Belt of Kentucky. The only other homeschoolers, except two of my friends, were being homeschooled because their parents didn't want them to learn about evolution. That kind of homeschooling gets more press than unschooling. People start thinking about it as limiting educational experience, rather than one that's trying to get rid of limitations.

Another myth is that unschooling is just for the wealthy. That's really funny to me, because my parents are not wealthy. I mean we were middle class, very middle class. My two friends, who were also being homeschooled in my area, were also middle class; their parents are by no means wealthy. I think it's really funny that people think that. We grew up on a farm raising sheep—it was not a glamorous existence.

My mother is a very intelligent person. I'm really in awe of her, and I've become more so as I get older and watch her and how she lives her life. She is incredible. I feel very lazy compared to her. She says she grew up very conservative, very Catholic. My grandmother told my mother that she thought my mother was crazy for going to college and wanting to become something that was not a teacher. In my grandmother's eyes, that's all a woman does: She goes off to school and becomes a teacher, or she gets married. My mom had this total rebellion from that: She stopped being a Catholic, and she became a Democrat—she is very liberal—and then this unschooling thing. I really don't know how it even got implemented in her brain. I think she read John Holt and John Taylor Gatto books and started thinking about it.

I know she was frustrated with her own schooling experience, because she got really good test scores, was a straight-A student, and felt like she didn't learn anything. She felt she got out of school and had no practical, real-life knowledge, and couldn't even remember a lot of stuff she learned in school, because she felt that she learned it just for a test. She felt her intelligence was squandered by spending so many hours in school. She decided, "I'm going to try this. I'm going to try this experiment with my kids and see what happens if I don't send them to school, and see if it's any better for them than it was for me going to school."

She is busy doing her own stuff a lot of the time. She's got a million projects right now. There's a contingent of Somalians living in a town very close to her, so her newest project is helping them get integrated into the community. They've had a lot of problems getting a mosque for themselves, so my mom has been doing all this activism work. The hospitals don't understand how to deal with a lot of the physical issues that the Somalians have, so she's over doing seminars at hospitals, teaching them cultural compassion. She's created an organization that she totally came up with on her own. She's amazing.

She wasn't doing a lot of that as I was growing up, she was really focused on us. She was devoted to taking us to different activities and being involved with them. We rode horses, and had a group of kids in the area who rode horses. She was a leader of that group, and it took a lot of organization. Once I moved out, and my brother got older, she's got free time and she's devoted it to activism, working with the Obama campaign, doing this stuff with the Somalians in Mayfield and so on.

As for my brother, Calen, he's in science and technology, a computer guy. Lots of time you hear people say that unschooled kids will go for the arts and don't usually go for science because they don't have the background, and that seems so silly to me. Some people go for the arts because that's what they like to do, and some people go for science because that's what they like to do. It's got nothing to do whether or not you go to school. There are plenty of kids in school who want to do theatre, or other arts. My brother hates the arts and humanities. He can't sing a note, and he is not really interested in anything like that. He's always been really science-minded. My mother was dismayed that he was such the typical boy, loving cars and engineering, and I was like the typical girl who wanted to dance, be on stage, and

317

sing. My mother remarked, "Come on guys, don't you want to do some theatre Calen? Don't you want to do some math Candra?" But, my brother loves engineering. He would build little robots all the time at home, and spent a lot of time on the computer as a kid, which worried my parents for a little while. "He needs to maybe do something else. He's spending all his time on the computer." Eventually, my dad came home from work and was talking about how they were having problems with their network. My brother who was thirteen or fourteen at the time, said, "I'll fix it." My dad asked, "How do you know how to do that?" My brother said, "I know." My dad said, "Sure, if you think so."

He went in and started working on the network. He started volunteering there, working with their IT guy. Eventually he knew more than the IT guy. He's worked with computers ever since. He started his own company, and is working with Dell. He's doing something with hospitals, where he's helping them enter in all of the medical records digitally, which is a huge thing going on with all hospitals right now.

He did not go to university. Now, he's told me, he needs to get his Windows Certification, which you don't need a college degree for. With that, you're really employable, in the computer world. I don't think he has his GED, but he hasn't needed one for any of the jobs he's done.

Getting into university was not a problem for me at all. I got into the first one I applied to; the university that I already decided on. I was offered a big scholarship, and it was perfect distance, about five hours away from home: not super-close, but not super-far away either. They had a really good theatre program, and I liked the town.

I got the scholarship because they have a Governor School for the Arts. You audition to get into it, in different disciplines like theatre, dance, creative writing, and singing. They accept fifteen people every year, or something like that. It's a summer program where they pay your room and board and you do intensive summer classes, seven days a week, in your discipline. You can only try out when you're a sophomore or a junior in high school, or around that age. I got in when I was a sophomore. There is a special fair for anyone who's been to Governors School, where people could come and audition for a bunch of colleges at once. I got to go do that college fair through the Governors School, and a bunch of schools offered me scholarships. I ended up going to Stevens. I wasn't actually accepted at that point, so I had to talk to admissions. I told her that I'm not actually in high school, so, what do you guys need from me? She said I should send them my transcript, which I didn't have at that point. She also said I might need my GED, but they were not sure.

I came up with a transcript. My mom helped me piece together what I'd done through the years, and put it in a form to look official. I described how I did math by doing taxes every year, and measured a barn to determine how many hay bales went in there, and used this list of textbooks. We sent that in, and I did my GED while I was waiting for my acceptance. They accepted me before I actually wrote my GED, so I did get it. On top of that, they accepted me into the Honours program at the school, which I was sort of shocked by. "How can you accept me into an Honours program when I don't have any grades, this is so weird."

Some have suggested that it was because I had talent, and that's probably what they really needed from me. Getting in was really easy. It was a small private college, so that might have had something to do with the ease of getting in. I don't really know, since I didn't try to go to any big universities.

Everything about my unschooling life was so wonderful. I loved having the freedom to really pursue what I was interested in. Having been in a school setting, I think being cut off by the bell is such an awful thing. If you are really interested in learning something, reading something, or you're having a great discussion, it's awful to have to cut that off at the hour mark: we're not talking about that anymore, so go off and do this other thing. I loved, as a kid growing up, just being able to devote an entire week to a book, if I wanted to. I remember getting Kant and just reading it for a week straight. I didn't do anything else. I just sat there and read this book non-stop. It was wonderful. I was able to just completely immerse myself in the writing, and not have to stop and do something else for a while.

The ability to learn so many different things was really great. If I was in school, there was no way I would have done all the activities that I did. I was taking dance twice a week, teaching dance twice a week, and taking violin twice a week. I was in two different orchestras two days a week, and my acting troupe one day a week, rehearsals for shows I was in, my horseback riding, and I started a young writers club. I was so busy, there was no way I would have been able to do all that stuff if I had been in school. I would have had to focus on just violin, or just dance, or just theatre.

In a sense, I was living a really rich life. It's almost like I was not waiting to live when I grow up, or to think, "Someday I can do these things." I was just doing them. It's so funny that people think kids have to wait. No, you don't have to wait. You can act like an adult would, just follow your passions. Do what you love doing and learn. It's not like learning stops for anybody when you get out of school. I hope not, I'm still learning all the time. I think it's silly that people think you have to put off living until you are an adult.

I went to school one day. It wasn't because I wanted to. I was over at a friend's, or meeting a friend, I don't remember. I went with my friend to one class, for some reason. Maybe she invited me, and I thought, "I'm going to check it out and see what's going on here." She was the same age as me. I remember going in and they gave us a sheet of paper with a colour-by-numbers, but it wasn't colour-by-numbers. If it was a verb, you coloured it red, and if it was a noun, you coloured it green. You were supposed to be learning verbs, nouns, adjectives, and stuff like that, in making this picture, and they spent half an hour on it. I thought, "This is awful. I would hate being told to do this every day. Oh this is awful." I was very glad I was not in that situation. I never wanted to go to school. I think, when I was little, I told my mom I wanted to ride the bus. She said, "If you ride the bus you have to go to school." "No, I don't want to do that, I just want to ride a bus."

I hope the mainstream schooling system can learn from unschoolers. I feel that some of it's moving in the opposite direction, with this really big focus on standardized testing being the measure of people's intelligence, or how well the school is doing. That's kind of the opposite trend for me, because I think standardized test scores are completely pointless, in most cases.

There's a lot that public school could take from unschooling, and I think it is possible for it to change if people are willing to let it change. People are getting a little bit disenchanted with the way the public school system is working. I'm not sure if people think the unschooling model is something to put in schools, people are leery of trusting kids to learn, which is really sad.

I feel they are so entrenched in these old ideas of learning and education, with new technology there are a lot of professions that have to catch up. For instance, the medical profession is digitizing all their records. People still don't really know what to do with all this technology we have. That's exciting and pretty awesome, all these opportunities that nobody knows how to deal with yet. I saw a video of a guy, it wasn't supposed to be about unschooling, it was supposed to be about the powers of computers, but it really spoke to me on an unschooling level. Sugata Mitra (2007) put a computer in a wall in India, and the kids would just teach themselves. It was amazing. They learned so much, all on their own, because they are curious. It's so funny that people think that kids don't want to learn.

One of the nice things I think, that came out of me doing the video for *Good Morning America* (2010), was that I had a couple of kids contact me and ask for help. They said, "Help me, I want to get out of school so bad and my parents just don't believe me. What can I do?" I had some good email exchanges with them, which was really nice. A lot of them had really good ideas. One girl said, "I wrote out this whole curriculum for my whole year, of what I'll do if I'm not in school." What parent couldn't look at that, and not see how motivated this girl is; she'd laid out an entire year's curriculum for herself that's well-rounded, interesting and that she could get a lot out of. I thought that was a great idea on her part. It shows that she was organized and dedicated. I think that's a big thing.

If you want to get out of school, not just focusing on how bad school is for you, but on all the positive things that will happen if you are out of school, and all you will accomplish if you are not in a formal institutionalized setting.

An audio version of this piece appears in podcast and can be found at: Kennedy, C. (2011, March 23). Interview by B. Ekwa Ekoko [Podcast]. Candra Kennedy: Grown unschooler. Radio Free School. Hamilton, Ontario.

Retrieved from http://radio4all.net/index.php/program/50383

References

Extreme parenting: Radical unschooling [Television episode]. (2010, April 19). In Good morning America. New York, New York/USA: ABC News.

Kennedy, C. [Goatprincess84]. (2010, April 25). Response to segment on unschooling by an unschooler [video file]. Retrieved from http://www.youtube.com/watch?v=kp-6VgpcQ-8

Mitra, S. (2007, February). Sugata Mitra shows how kids teach themselves [video file]. Retrieved from http://www.ted.com/talks/sugata_mitra_the_child_dri ven_education.html

---

Candra Kennedy is a puppeteer, playwright, director, producer, standardized patient and orientation & mobility specialist located in Philadelphia PA. She currently works as an O&M specialist and standardized patient while pursing her passion for theatre. Her recent play (self-directed and produced) Water Bears in Space was called "Utterly, transcendently bizarre" and "a blast" by the *Philadelphia City Paper* and *Inquirer*, and garnered rave reviews from the over 400 audience members that attended. In her spare time, Kennedy works on her Español at a local Spanish school, her trapeze skills at a local circus school, and has traveled to eight countries. She credits her lifelong curiosity, self-motivated work ethic and desire to learn in great part to her upbringing outside of the public school system.

http://stumblegoat.tumblr.com/

CHAPTER 29

REDEFINING SUCCESS

JESSICA CLAIRE BARKER

Through my blog, I have discovered that "success" is quite a touchy subject. In this day and age, it is very hard, even as an unschooler, to break through, or get around, what mainstream society preaches as "success."

The standard, at its core, seems to be college = wealth = success (whether this is actually true or not is beside the point, for the purposes of this argument many believe it to be the case). College means you get a high-paying job (whether or not you actually like it is irrelevant); wealth means you make tons of money at this high-paying job, therefore having the financial capacity to live a good life with a lot of things, instead of the opposite, a horrible life with not a lot of things. As an unschooler, this confused me, which led to my redefining of "success."

Every time I set foot in a different place, whether it's across the street or across the country, I see the most gorgeous landscapes and the interesting quirks that land has. I meet new people who, for lack of a better word, are amazing. There's the avid cuckoo clock-collecting poet, the old man with the family-run bakery serving the most delicious Danishes, the homeless guy who helps me find the bus station in exchange for someone who'll listen to his story.

That's why I like to say, "Success is what you make it,"

even though it's rather clichéd. The thing is, every person in the world is different. Those I have seen thrive in life are those who haven't conformed to doing life "the way you should," and, instead, have simply been themselves. Life turns out quite swell for them. It's understandably difficult, though: We can say we don't care what other people think, but that is a rather taxing undertaking when those people are proclaiming we'll starve or freeze to death if we don't follow this sure-fire path.

I was an unschooled homeschooler, if that makes sense. My parents wanted me to at least do the basics of math, reading, and writing. They only really had to "make" me do math, since I would read and write till the cows came home. I had a lot of freedom to pursue my own interests: I got kits and books through curriculum companies, took ballet and drama classes, read books from the library, and watched television. Those were my forms of learning intake. Output was often in writing, playing, painting, performing, and talking with great enthusiasm.

The best things about being unschooled were the freedom of time and the freedom of pursuit. I have a feeling that, had I ever been put in a nine-to-three school environment, I would have died in so many ways. I would have had no time to imagine and create, and no motivation or energy to pursue anything beyond what was being forced down my throat for the majority of my day.

I am extremely self-directed, and, frankly, I like to do what I want to do, when I want to do it. Of course, it's not reasonable to apply that to everything in life, but when it came to learning in my grade school years, my curiosity and love for learning were able to flourish and grow because of the freedom I had.

When I was nine, I spent a few months finding out everything I possibly could about snakes. My mom did supportive things: She arranged a trip to the science museum and suggested I write fact pages and draw pictures and, of course, that reinforced my learning. All of that led to me working with snakes last year at a wildlife center, for three months, which was pure joy for me.

The downsides of unschooling are, to me, very few and hard to acknowledge (I'm not biased at all, can you tell?). I can admit that it is not for everyone. Many people prefer, or require, a lot more structure, assignments and deadlines from an authority, or any number of elements more common in a school situation. There's nothing wrong with people that prefer classrooms—they aren't stupid or unmotivated or anything, they are just wired differently, and I respect that, even as I can't fully understand it.

The same goes for college and beyond. The key is to do what you truly and honestly want to do, however you feel is best. That could be going to college and becoming a CEO, by-passing college and starting up a small gym downtown, or anything in between or otherwise. Being successful is you doing what you want to be doing, in my opinion. Of course, you want to stay alive while doing this, but I will get to that in a minute.

For instance, I'm not a professional concert pianist. I just started taking piano lessons a couple years ago, but I consider myself a successful piano student because I am learning exactly what I want to learn, and I am at the exact point I want and need to be in my lessons right now. The same goes with everything in my life. To me, success is accomplishing exactly what I want and need to accomplish at this specific time in my life.

Now, onto pecuniary matters: Right now I work as a prep cook and dishwasher at a local Italian restaurant. This may not be one of my giant main goals, such as working with wolves or publishing children's fiction, but I have had a curiosity about the restaurant industry since I was very young, and I find myself soaking up every minute of my time there, learning from both what I am doing and what I am observing of the operation as a whole. As a plus, I am earning money that I am saving for my next travel adventure: Taos, New Mexico, with a blank slate, anyone?

I am almost 21-years-old. This is a wonderful, ideal time to be learning and discovering. A question I get asked frequently is, "Will you ever figure out what you want to do in life?" I like to spend my time doing many things at once. I like to change it up often. My primary interests are animals, wildlife, nature, farming, alternative education, writing, and music. Frankly, I have no desire to settle on one career path for forty-plus years of my life. This doesn't make everyone I talk to very happy.

Besides my job at the restaurant, I am working on a set of small articles about what living and working in different areas of the U.S.A. has taught me, doing an autodidactic poetry study, maintaining gardens around town (also bringing in money), writing a set of juvenile mystery novels, and attempting to maintain my *Life Without College* blog (http://lifewithoutcollege.wordpress.com), among other things. I just returned to North Carolina, from farming for four months in Louisiana, which was one heck of an adventure.

In November, I am helping lead the Unschool Adventures Writing Retreat in Durango, Colorado. I attended the retreat two years ago as a student, and had since been dreaming of leading the next retreat if the owner of Unschool Adventures, Blake Boles, ever decided to repeat the trip in any way, shape, or form. Now it's finally happening!

These things are bringing me great satisfaction, and, again I feel successful in life as I am right now. That doesn't mean I don't take the future into consideration. To the contrary, I have many plans to further learn in my areas of passion, whether it means directly making money with those things, or making money in other ways so I may continue to pursue my passions in my spare time with the money generated.

A way I would like to see the world changed is for there to be more acceptance, and not just tolerance. Travel has really taught me that each person can only see things from one perspective: their own. We think we grow out of the egocentric stage once we reach our teens, however, it really just evolves. We become more aware, but as humans we cannot help thinking about ourselves, our rights, our needs, our beliefs, 24/7. In this, incidentally, we are all alike. Unfortunately, it makes a lot of people rather unhappy when I say a gay liberal and a straight conservative are both human and equally worthy of both love and respect, but again, we are all thinking and doing what we feel is right. Honestly, that is the biggest lesson I have learned from my two years of traveling, and being unschooled in general: there are so many cultures, so many groups of people doing different things than what other people are doing. That is just it: we are all humans, doing things in life. He's an atheist, I'm a Christian, she's going to college, I'm not, he's ordering hummus, I'm ordering grape leaves. That's the message I'd like to send to the world: This life is a luncheon, so let's enjoy the food, enjoy each other, and in the end, thank everyone and think back at how great, even how successful, that luncheon was.

Jessica Barker is 23-years-old, an autodidact with a great love for traveling anywhere and learning anything. Her website is *College Rebellion.* Jessica also writes for *The Unschooler Experiment* and offers mentorship through *Zero Tuition College.* When she is not writing, she spends her time in the garden, playing with animals, and chef-ing at a local restaurant in Burnsville, North Carolina.

CHAPTER 30

UNSCHOOLING EXPERIENCE

PETER KOWALKE

I am in touch with a great number of grown homeschoolers, and, lately, I have been talking to a number who now have their own kids. I just talked with one a few days ago, Lynda Young, in Florida. As I talk to these homeschoolers, I've been trying to sleuth out, "Are you doing anything different? Are you doing anything wildly crazy?"

In some regards, I'm disappointed because there is not a lot of wild and crazy going on. It's not dramatically different than what their parents did, and what people who aren't grown homeschoolers are doing. The one difference that I am noticing, so far, is that a lot of the grown homeschoolers I've talked with are calmer. They are not as stressed about the process. They are okay with their children reading late. They're okay with their children not knowing geography, or their children following their interests, and maybe it looking a little scary at points.

One thing Lynda Young did say, in our conversation, that is interesting is that there sometimes is a little alienation, in the sense that she is around all these other parents who are sending their kids to school and doing "normal" things while she is not. She has a family bed, and one of her children is nursing for a really long time, and she is unschooling, and there's this litany of unusual, alternative parenting habits. If you look at the family, it seems all great, but the priorities and values are a little different.

What is interesting is that I am seeing grown unschoolers chart their own course as parents, which is what they always have done. There is a lot more thinking about it individually. Sometimes the solutions they come to are a little bit different than the mainstream. That is something a lot of unschoolers are facing. This is not necessarily bad, and sometimes it is a competitive advantage—sometimes you want to stand out, especially in this economy. So being different has its advantages. But if you just want to blend in and be like every one else, maybe homeschooling is not so good for being average and normal and doing things like everybody else does.

One of the things I've found with a lot of grown homeschoolers is that at some point they do try to assimilate, to almost downplay the homeschooling. I've got to say, the last few years I've tried that, I've been a mainstream magazine editor. I haven't been tracking the movement's numbers very closely. I may not be the best person to talk about the nuances of the movement right now, but what I have noticed, anecdotally, and what I witnessed prior to that, is that everybody knows a homeschooler. We are well passed the "what is that?" stage we used to be in.

At this point, I have a sort of pessimism. The people who said that the movement was going to get bigger and bigger have been wrong. It has topped out, to some degree. It's a lot of work to homeschool. It takes a certain level of dedication, and not everybody is willing to put in the time, so I think it's always something that is going to be a minority activity. You're always going to have only a subset of the population homeschooling. I think the numbers get blown up so much because you have a lot of school-at-home, correspondence schools, and the like. You have a lot of homeschooling that really looks a lot more like institutional schooling, than what homeschooling traditional has meant.

I think you have to ask yourself "Why? Why are people

doing it?" I see a lot of homeschooling, but it's a version of school in many cases. What I have not seen is a big increase in self-directed learning. I have not noticed any trend with more people doing that. You might think that there would be, given the way that our workforce is evolving, but it doesn't feel like it's exploding.

I am not the biggest fan of the college system and the way that we institutionalize education. It always seemed a little strange to me, that you don't go to school, you homeschool, and then when you get to college age you go back to institutionalized education. Philosophically, the reasons I homeschooled were because I didn't see institutional education being a good idea. That critique still holds, so I don't see colleges preparing us particularly well.

I went to college, it was a long and drawn out process because I didn't want to be there, but I felt that I needed that degree and the certification. One thing that the education system does, which is so pernicious, is that it ties certification to education; certification is tied to one form of learning. There is a certain logic for certification, because not every employer can take the time to figure out someone's qualifications, but the sad part is that we should be able to learn what we need any way we can, not just through institutional education. There should be a way to certify what we know, irrespective of how we learned it.

Sensing a business opportunity, however, the education apparatus really has restricted how we can learn. You pretty much have to do college! Even the alternative colleges like Hampshire and Reed are really variants on the traditional college models, so it really forces you to do it as a way to get the necessary certification. That's a real shame.

Of course, there are grown homeschoolers who criticize the system, and some of them try to not go to college, and others actually do not go. My read on the usual outcome, and it does vary wildly, is that it certainly is not easy to skip college. A lot of homeschoolers will do college because, as much as we dislike it, we don't want to fight again and again that battle we are tired of fighting. There are a number that have gone without college, and I am always excited to hear that. A lot of the folks I talk to who don't go, you do see later on at some point a fair number of them struggle, or question their decision not to go. They don't often say, "I should have gone to college," but a lot of times, between the lines, I'm hearing these grown homeschoolers say, "This is hard. It is not as easy as it sounded. At first I thought I could do the unschooling thing and not go to college, it will be great, but this is tough."

The problem is that it is so much a part of our culture. It is not that they are not learning or that they cannot do it. We are not set up as a society to recognize people who unschool college. It is an uphill battle to make a larger amount of money without college, unless you're an entrepreneur. The most successful grown homeschoolers I have seen who skipped college are those who live lightly, and are much closer to being back-to-the-landers. It's a real challenge to skip our society's certification process. I'd like to think that we can get past that, but I don't know. I am somewhat pessimistic about changing the whole direction of society. I'd be content just to carve out a little corner for myself, at this point, I think.

Some days I feel successful, and other days I don't. The days that I don't feel successful are the days when I am making direct comparisons with my peers, using their metrics. It really does come down to the fact that I am in a society, and every society has its values, what they consider success. As much as you want to define it the way that you think it makes sense, the dominant view of success is put upon you.

I define success in terms of how many loving relationships I have, how many good strong connections I have with people. I define success in terms of what I accomplish, and if I do it in a moral way. I define success in terms of, "Am I healthy?" I was just out to dinner with a good friend, and she is working herself to the bone. She gets four hours of sleep, she's constantly unhealthy, and her hair is falling out. She is an extreme case. She is "successful," but it's not just how much money you make. I am still opposed to materialism. Like a lot of grown homeschoolers, I don't define success based on how many material goods I have.

At the same time, it is tough to always live inside your definition of success. People are looking at you and thinking that you are not successful. Sometimes I'll get glances from people who question my success, and if I were playing by their metrics, I probably would fail. I'd like to have a pat answer, but there is no easy answer. If you walk a somewhat individual path, that's kind of the price you have to pay.

I believe that home educated kids question a lot, and I am glad I was homeschooled. I still plan to do that with my kids when I have the opportunity. But, yeah, I do think that grown homeschoolers, especially unschoolers, do have more time to think about things and to challenge. I think that the challenging comes from the fact that we grew up not in school, and that homeschooling is a pretty big challenge to the system. If you can question schooling, you start to ask, "What else can I question?"

That is part of why I like hanging out with homeschoolers. They are doing a lot of fun, interesting things. There is some kooky behaviour sometimes, certainly some failures along the line, but pound-for-pound there is a lot of trying things, experimentation, and open-mindedness, that is a beautiful thing.

One of the things I have noticed in my own life is that you get tired of challenging all the time, of being a walking challenge. For me, I am gravitating toward that Gandhi saying, "Be the change you want to see in the world." Instead of trying to change the world, I am moving toward being a quiet example of change; it is less about having to convert the world. I have been noticing myself and other grown homeschoolers doing that. It is not because we are feeling any less passion about our beliefs, it's just that we're tired of fighting all the time! If you want to do it, that is great, we think we are doing something good here. I caused so many people to question schooling, I have no problem letting someone else cause that spark at this point.

Basically, there are two parts to my blog, *The Unschooler Experiment* (http://www.unschooler.com). The first reason *unschooler.com* exists is to connect with other grown homeschoolers, because they are doing cool things. There is the societal pressure to do things the way the dominant culture does it, and that can wear you down. So to hang out with, and connect with, people who are thinking in similar ways is refreshing. Most minority groups know and do this.

The other half of the reason for the blog is just to give back. There are a lot of questions that parents and others have asked over the years. That would be the more static part of the project. If you want to know if it works, and are curious about it, here you go. For those of you who are actually doing it, let's have some fun.

I was in the New York Public Library today. It was not for class. It was not because there was a boss telling me so, not because I need a skill. I was in the library studying Malaysia entirely on my own, and I was one of the only people doing that. It left an impression on me: Where is everyone? There's just me and a couple old guys in their 80s. It really reaffirmed to me the love of learning thing that we talk about, that this love really is still here. Even when sometimes it gets hidden away with all that is going on, there really is a love of learning in me. That comes from unschooling. I still am passionate about learning things, and I still am willing to question. Those are two of the lasting influences of homeschooling for me.

An audio version of this piece appears in podcast and can be found at: Kowalke, P. (2010, August, 24). Interview by B. Ekwa Ekoko [Podcast]. What are they doing now? Radio Free School. Hamilton, Ontario.
Retrieved from http://radio4all.net/index.php/program/45156

———————

Peter Kowalke is 32-year-old grown homeschooler, journalist and editor of *Unschooler.com*, a site about unschooling and what it means to be the change you want to see in the world. He's producer of the documentary about the lasting influence of home education, *Grown Without Schooling*, and currently is working on a book about his other passion, deep relationships, tentatively entitled, *The Other Half: How to Love and Be Loved More Deeply Than You Thought Possible.* He's a former columnist for *Home Education Magazine, Life Learning Magazine,* and *Home Educator's Family Times*, and he's worked for homeschooling umbrella school, Clonlara, and India homeschooling advocates, Shikshantar Andolan. http://www.unschooler.com

CHAPTER 31

I'M UNSCHOOLED AND YES, I CAN WRITE

IDZIE DESMARAIS

To me, the idea of success is pretty simple: It means nothing more or less than being happy. I find it pretty hard to comprehend how more people cannot see this. You can have a "good" job, a house with a white picket fence, or any other marker of what's often considered to be successful, but if you're not happy or not making changes in your life that add to your happiness, then it doesn't sound very successful to me. Now, some might consider happiness, as the only marker of success, to be a selfish goal, but I believe the things that make most humans happy include doing good, being kind, making the world a better place, and fighting for what you believe in. It seems to me that the less happy someone is with their life, the less likely they are to do these things.

As for what jobs or types of work would make me happy? Well, I don't want to be working for any large institutions or corporations, that's for sure. What do I want to do? Well, that's a harder thing to answer, because I'm honestly not sure. I know that I love to cook and create with food, so maybe a cook or caterer. I know that I really like being able to help people with health-related stuff, in a natural way, so maybe I'd enjoy being an herbal medicine consultant. I also know that writing, and sharing my knowledge on freedom-based education is extremely important to me and is something I definitely want to be a part of my life, so if I could make money writing about education, I'd love to do that, too.

Not only is education something I want to always be a part of my life, but also something I'm currently really involved in. As always, I'm writing about freedom-based education, both on my blog (*I'm Unschooled. Yes, I Can Write*) (http://yes-i-can-write.blogspot.ca), and in articles to be published in other places. I'm speaking about unschooling at a couple of different places this fall. I've done a couple of interviews on the subject recently, and have several more interviews coming up in the next few months. I'm involved in various freedom-based education projects in Montreal. I'm also working on a zine about unschooling, which will hopefully be completed by the time I head to the first unschooling conference this fall. Moving away from things education-related, I've been meeting more and more radical people locally, finding community close to home, to add to the North America-wide community I've found in the last several years. Because many of the people I consider to be part of my community live far away, my life is punctuated by both visitors and travel.

I think the world is a really messed up place right now. Or, more accurately, I think human civilization, our current society is deeply destructive, oppressive, violent, and just all-around not good news. The actual world? Forests and people being passionate about important things, and beaches, and poetry, and music, and stars, well, I like all that a whole lot.

I cannot possibly explain all my political views in just a paragraph or two. I suppose I should try. I don't want the state, or government to control things. I want decentralization, autonomous, truly sustainable communities. Absolute respect for the earth. But really, all this sounds so flat. I truly believe that humans not only must live in a radically different way, if life on Earth is to survive, but also that we will be much happier living in a radically different way; one based on respect for all living things, joy in the world and each other, collectively making decisions, playing and learning and being. Suffice it to say, I dream of a very different way of living and being than what we currently live.

There are so many great things, as a result of growing without school. I believe a large function of school is to instil in children the values of the dominant culture, so by skipping school I think kids have more room to develop their own values. Unschooling gives the freedom to grow and develop authentically, without all the pressure to conform, to compromise ideals, and to settle for less. I also think that unschooling is really conducive to people being able to truly get to know themselves.

By not going to school, I was able to grow and find myself in an environment that was far more supportive than what I believe I would have encountered had I gone to school, and I feel that that gave me the space to develop confidence. That my shy, people-pleasing, sensitive self would probably not have developed in a less safe environment. I honestly think I would have been one of these people who leave school with serious emotional scars. I see *lots* of advantages to being out of school.

I see most of the downsides of not attending school as being more the fault of society, rather than of unschooling. For example, there's the constant questioning from extended family, friends, and strangers. Lots of people seem to think they have the right to demand explanations for why you're not in school. Many more people just want to ask questions, usually the same few questions that everyone asks, and the constant questioning and judgment can be very draining, and hard to deal with. While some unschoolers choose to take tests like the SAT or get their GED, for those who don't, not having paperwork can make life a bit more difficult.

Something I've personally found really difficult is feelings of isolation, since the way I live, and have lived for many years, as well as the ways in which I look at the world, are just so different from those of the dominant culture. That's not just unschooling. I believe any non-mainstream choice or view sets people apart a bit. As the unschooled, green, anarchist, feminist, total hippie I am, perhaps it's unfair to blame it on unschooling. I have definitely found communities I feel a part of, especially unschooling communities. However, that's a fairly recent development because growing up, ours was the only unschooling family I knew.

Idzie Desmarais is a (grown) unschooler, feminist, green anarchist, (confusedly) queer, pagan(ish) person who makes her home in the Montreal area. She spends her time reading fantasy novels, writing, cooking up lots of tasty food in the kitchen, and dreaming of the homesteading intentional community she wants to help found someday. Idzie also authors the popular blog *I'm Unschooled. Yes, I Can Write*.

CHAPTER 32

THE SUBTLE BUT RADICAL FRAME SHIFT OF BEING A CONTRIBUTOR VERSUS BEING SUCCESSFUL

SEAN RITCHEY

I was enrolled in a Montessori preschool when I was a wee thing, and that really wasn't working for me, so my mom started doing a lot of research about education and ultimately decided to pull me out to homeschool/unschool me. That worked so well that neither of my younger siblings ever went to school. I think, overall, for the entire family it has been enormously successful.

I was unschooled for my entire kindergarten to Grade 12, and then went to community college full-time for two years, near the tail end of when I would have been in high school. That's the extent of my college. I've chosen to do entrepreneurial, self-directed things, instead of continuing on with college.

I was the oldest in my family, so the pioneer. I'm 24, so I was growing up predominantly in the 90s, when unschooling was past being a fringe movement but still not nearly as grounded a movement as I think it is today.

I grew up in Woodstock, New York, just two hours north of Manhattan. As I came into my teen years, my parent's (and my) approach to unschooling pretty naturally evolved into a very self-directed learning model, where I was the lead architect in my educational pursuits, and there was, of course, the significant support I had, from both my parents and other mentors in my life.

Moving from there into my adult life, the transition was quite fluid and felt quite natural. I have a very self-directed, very self-created, entrepreneurial lifestyle.

In my adult life, I have founded one for-profit company, and one non-profit. The for-profit venture was a green home design and build firm. We designed and built extremely energy-efficient buildings. I founded that company when I was 19, with a man in his early 60s, so there were multigenerational contributions in the ownership structure. We had a lot of fun for a 3 year run, and then had a rather traumatic fall right when the markets crashed, a couple of years ago. We had about four employees we had to layoff. At that point, I chose to take a step back, to take a breather, by no longer having employees. We wrapped up our last project, and with two projects in contract, and two more that we were working on designs for, all four cancelled within a six-week period.

I stepped aside from that, and the following year co-founded a non-profit with a lovely young woman, named Sophie Theriault, who is also an unschooler. Through that non-profit we did some interesting work around alternative education. We created some programming, including a week-long retreat for young adult social entrepreneurs and activists, who were working on powerful change in their own communities. The retreat was designed to help them examine how to design their projects as holistically as possible. The other thing we did together was create a journalism project, called the Learnalism Project, named by combining learning and journalism into one word.

For Learnalism, we examined projects around the east and west coasts that were taking a holistic approach to sustainability. The idea was to celebrate some of the success stories of how humans were creating deeply-harmonious interactions with their landscapes and with each other.

The Learnalism Project is still going. It's a very part-time thing for Sophie and me, and we still have quite a bit of material that we gathered during our three-month trip where we were doing a lot of exploration, that has not been produced and published yet. The project was designed to shed light on (and be a point of inspiration from) the success stories. What was interesting about the process was that I had left with a lowered sense of hope about the world than I had going into it. It was a very shaking experience, and I'm generally an extraordinarily optimistic person.

I thought a lot about why I had this lowered sense of hope. I've concluded that I've been aware, for as long as I can remember, that I'm a part of this generation that faces some enormous challenges, socially and environmentally. In a lot of ways, there's an enormous weight on my generation to deal with a collection of looming catastrophes. In visiting these projects, that were doing these powerful things, I feel like I was left feeling like a drop of "yes" in an ocean of "no." I was looking around the world and seeing the things that we saw during our travels, and interacting with these projects, while simultaneously there was the enormous oil spill in the Gulf of Mexico. I was reading these pieces at night, online, about the potential that if that oil spill was not capped, and not dealt with, there is a potential that it might kill all the world's oceans.

As an eco-citizen, the role our ocean's play in our global ecosystem would have more or less meant killing most of life on the planet, so looking at those kind of things, while visiting these groups of twenty people who were carving beautiful little manifestations of human life into their landscapes, it felt like a lot of "no" and a little bit of "yes."

There are people of all ages, but in particular young people, all over the world who are showing up to this conversation and to this task in a really powerful way, and in a really different way. There's also an enormous amount of apathy in our culture. I think what allows me to fall asleep at night is understanding the 80:20 principle. It's a proven mathematical equation that applies to social systems and natural systems, which is that 80% of the result, in almost any system, comes from 20% of the participants. This is true in natural systems, like peas, for example: 80% of the peas are produced by 20% of the pea pods. Remembering that it's not going to take everyone showing up, but a certain number showing up to the conversation and actually stepping up and doing what it takes. When I look around the world I think, "Oh my god, how are we ever going to do this?" I go back to the 80:20 principle, as a grounding place. We need to be working, but I don't have to lose hope.

We need to examine deeply how we are in it together, as a foundation for what we are trying to create in the world, and I think what comes from that is the realization that we need to be building rather than resisting, modeling rather than fighting, and that we need to be slowing it down, and doing the deep internal work that is the foundation of all of our external work.

I have the great privilege of knowing and working with people who are approaching it that way, and some of the best work I see happening in the world is happening from that place. Of course, there still are lots of people working in older, more traditional, hierarchical models.

I think of myself as an entrepreneur, as a project architect, and an activist. It's something I find that I'm quite good at: Designing vehicles and platforms for people to work on things in a way that is creating a different model than has existed before. What gets me going the most is when I'm working on building and creating those kinds of vehicles and platforms. I'd also define myself as a very curious and passionate human, and someone who is really grounded in really simple pieces of gratitude: that I'm alive, that I have my breath that flows in and out of my body every day. I also can be a pain in the ass sometimes, I can be egotistical, and am a flawed and imperfect human who strives everyday toward growth. I appreciate the people around me being patient and giving me feedback.

Being unschooled is a critical part of who I am. The amount of experience I got to have as a teen and young adult, being able to ask questions like, "What do I care about?" "What am I passionate about?" and then, not only asking those questions, but getting to take it to the next step, which is, "How am I going to design a way to pursue that?" and "How am I going to design a vehicle to pursue that?" That's what I mean by the natural evolution into process design and organizational design. What I do now is just the same thing, albeit on a bigger scale, that involves more people.

It spawns from the culture I grew up in, and the privileges that I grew up with, both in terms of mentors and growing up as an upper-middle-class white man, in a culture that deeply supports that type of individual.

After unschooling, I don't think you're going to be very good at just doing meaningless stuff, just for the sake of bringing home a crappy paycheque, or doing what everyone else is doing because it's the thing to do.

I've been quite active, growing up in the national unschooling movement, and I think that there is a direct relationship between security and freedom: the more security you have the less freedom you have, and the more freedom you have the less security you have. I think a maximum security prison is one of the most secure places you can possibly be in, and yet you have probably the least freedom there. Generally, our culture tends to put more emphasis on security than on freedom.

In my life, I've had the experience (dozens of times) of

coming upon a threshold that requires me to leap into an unknown, and it's scary. But, time and time again, I've been so relieved and overjoyed when I've taken that risk, taken that leap, even when it's been catastrophic, and even when it has resulted in failure. Failure has been one of my greatest teachers, and so recognizing that once I had gone through that shift of realizing failure wasn't a bad thing, that failure, if dealt with appropriately, if learned from appropriately, was one of the most valuable experiences of my life. That takes an enormous amount of courage, so that's why I'm so moved by unschoolers.

The other work I'm involved in is on the board of directors of a really awesome organization called the Common Fire Foundation. The work we do is supporting people who are building intentional communities.

I find I'm the happiest when I'm pushing myself, and pushing the envelope of the world around me, to try and be creative. I had this shift, about two years ago, where I stopped thinking about my life in terms of success, and started thinking about it in terms of contribution. It's been a simple shift of approach and mindset, but it's been internally revolutionary in how I'm thinking about and going about my life and making my choices.

If I had to summarize how I've approached my life, for people who are not necessarily feeling attracted to entrepreneurship, it's that I've made career decisions with education and contribution at the forefront. When making a choice whether or not to take an internship, or to take a job, or to start collaborating with someone, or to start a business, think about what is a learning opportunity. How is this going to be expanding my experience of the world? I then think, also, about how is this engagement with the world going to be a contribution? The combination of these two questions has driven many, many of my decisions.

My number one recommendation to people would be to amass a brilliant support team. When I say that, I mean your mentors, friends, collaborators, the people who you have around you, the people you work with, the people you learn from. They're so critical in supporting you, and shaping you into who you become on a day-to-day basis. I would recommend people being their boldest, approaching those people who they admire, who they want to learn from, asking them to be their teachers, and asking them to be collaborators.

There's a story I heard once, about a great architect who, on his death bed, said, "My one regret in dying is that nobody ever came and knocked on my door and said "teach me," because now I'm dying and my brilliance goes with me." I remember that, whenever I'm feeling intimidated and nervous about approaching someone. I have been rewarded, so many times, just by taking that leap and approaching someone, asking for their support or guidance or leadership. A lot of them are excited about the idea.

My personal e-mail, which is the best way to get in touch with me, is yourstruly@seanritchey.com. For people reading this, I would love to hear from you, if you have questions or if it would be supportive to you to talk to me. What I just said about approaching people: If there's any part of you that would be inclined to get in touch with me, please do so. I would be more than happy to talk and be as supportive as I can be.

An audio version of this piece appears in podcast and can be found at: Ritchey, S. (2011, April, 05). Interview by B. Ekwa Ekoko [Podcast]. Sean Ritchey: Grown Unschooler. Radio Free School. Hamilton, Ontario.

THE SUBTLE BUT RADICAL FRAME SHIFT OF BEING
A CONTRIBUTOR VERSUS BEING SUCCESSFUL

Sean is a hybrid of entrepreneurial project architect and "okay, now let's make it happen!" creator. His ventures have includes co-founding a green building company, and a non-profit which created educational programs for social entrepreneurs (and other humans working to make contributions to the world). Sean also works as an entrepreneurial advisor on other start-up, in both the for-profit and non-profit sectors. In addition to designing and leading his own projects, Sean serves on the Board of Directors of The Common Fire Foundation, which helps create intentional communities, ranging from cooperative houses to neighborhood-scale projects (www.CommonFire.org).

You can learn more about Sean, and see what he's up to on his website, www.SeanRitchey.com

CHAPTER 33

MORE TIME IS MORE FREEDOM

BRENNA MCBROOM

To me, the question of success is inextricably linked with the question of how I choose to spend my most valuable and limited resource: my time. In my mind, a successful person is one who utilizes her time to its fullest potential, relentlessly pursuing those things about which she is most passionate and which bring her contentment and satisfaction (with the caveat that those things being pursued must not have a damaging or detrimental effect upon humanity).

I spent a year at a small liberal arts college when I turned eighteen, and my reason for going was as uncomplicated and misguided as, "Because this is what I'm supposed to do." (This, ironically, after six years of radical unschooling. Socio-cultural messages are pervasive). When I chose to leave after a year, it was largely because of the realization that my time is finite, and I couldn't sacrifice four years of it in pursuit of a degree I might not ever use.

An unschooling mom, whom I greatly respect, is in the habit of saying, "Do what you love and the money will follow." I started throwing pots on the pottery wheel about two years ago, keeping that piece of advice in mind. I did it because I loved it, and because it fed and satisfied me, and the money started to slowly follow. After several years of hard work, I'm completely self-employed as a ceramic artist.

I would say that the primary positive result of

unschooling is that my time is my own, to spend or squander as I wish. It does not belong to a teacher or an institution. Because of this freedom, I've been able to pursue the things I'm passionate about to their fullest potential, without any hindrance. I've had the chance to learn what I'm passionate about through direct, hands-on, life experience. I've also been able to learn in the way I choose. For example, I'm an extremely visual creature, auditory processing is not my forté, by any means. If I had gone to traditional school, I would have struggled while listening to lectures, but as an unschooler I could simply learn things by reading about them. I can't think of a more important lesson, to be honest, than learning how to learn, and learning what you love.

It seems to me, that many in the unschooling community are hesitant to criticize themselves, which is understandable. However, I think that in order for our movement to remain a viable and vital one, we must undergo a nearly-constant process of self-evaluation and self-criticism as a means for growth. Because of this, I'll cite a real and omnipresent "con" that I'm struggling with in regards to unschooling.

I feel that a lot of new unschooling parents are very hesitant to do anything that resembles "controlling" their children, so they fail to stop their children when they are behaving in ways that are disruptive or damaging to others, or damaging to the property of others. Unschooling conferences frequently feature the worst displays of such behaviour, a damaging trend when you consider that such events are a primary way we represent ourselves to the outside world.

To me, this problem is only one symptom of a larger disease, namely, that many unschooling parents passively accept the principles of unschooling as gospel, rather than actively examining them.

I love the world I live in. Were I to change it, I think I would alter attitudes and beliefs rather than attempting to change governments or institutions, because, in the end, it is the things we believe and the values we hold highest that shape our world. I would change the belief that qualification and ability are inextricably linked. For example, in the eyes of many, the twenty-four-year old Master of Fine Arts graduate possesses more ability to instruct ceramics students than the self-taught ceramicist who has been operating a functional studio for thirty years, merely because of qualifications. I'm not saying that qualification and ability never come hand-in-hand—merely that they don't have to.

For those who are not sure if school, or higher education, is the right place at this time, I would say: trust yourself! If you have a nagging feeling that institutionalized schooling isn't right for you at this point in your life, listen to it. College can be a great tool to get you where you want to go, but it's just that: a tool. It's important to keep it in its proper perspective, as a means to an end, rather than an end in itself.

If you're struggling with the college question, a good litmus test is to ask yourself the following questions: I'm planning to go to college to what end? What am I trying to achieve? If your answer is something like, "Because I want to be a veterinarian," or "Because it's an efficient way for me to learn everything that I want to know about classical philosophy," then you're probably on the right track. If, on the other hand, your answers are something like, "Because otherwise I'll end up working in a fast food joint," or "Because I don't know what I want to do with my life," then I would suggest you do a bit more soul searching.

I learned, through personal experience, that there are much better places to find yourself than college: write a book, save the rainforest, teach English as a second language, revitalize your community, build a house, or live somewhere you don't speak the language.

Furthermore, never believe those who tell you that not

going to college resigns you to a lifetime of flipping burgers. Those who perpetuate this myth are usually none other than the school faculty and administrators, who are completely dependent upon your continued support of higher education for their continued employment. The vast majority of people I know who have chosen to forgo college are doing amazing things like writing grants, traveling the world, working on farms, or doing web design.

Finally, keep in mind that not going to college *now* is not the same as not going to college. I believe many people would benefit a great deal from taking a few years to experience, and experiment with, various occupations and lifestyles before they make the decision to attend (or not attend) a university.

Brenna McBroom is a long-time unschooler from Asheville, North Carolina. She currently works as a potter making functional and decorative crystalline glazed ceramics. When not at the pottery wheel, glazing table, or kiln, Brenna loves traveling, swimming, attempting to speak Spanish, and attending craft shows. Brenna is also passionate about the value of artistic self-education at the college level, and she loves to talk about pursuing an education as an artist without obtaining a degree. She has taken part in two self-designed pottery apprenticeships: one in Cambridge, Massachusetts and one in Corvallis, Oregon. She runs a small business selling pottery online, and you can see her Etsy site here: brennadeeceramics.etsy.com.

CHAPTER 34

MOTIVATION, METHOD, AND MASTERY: HOW I LEARNED MUSIC WITHOUT BEING TAUGHT
ANDREW GILPIN

On November 1, 2005, I was interviewed by Beatrice Ekoko for Radio Free School, at McMaster University in Hamilton, Ontario. Also present were: Fred Jacobowitz, my partner in the musical duo Ebony & Ivory; Carol Gilpin, my mother; and Beatrice's children Evelyna and Bronwyn. The following article is based on material from this interview.

Andrew: I'm a musician and composer, and what is now called an unschooler, but used to be called a homeschooler. I was completely self-taught at piano, which meant no lessons or teachers. This approach was the total opposite of that of Fred, who is a double graduate of Juilliard. I have no official musical training, no piece of paper saying that I can play the piano or that I can compose music, so as far as anyone else is concerned, I guess the proof is in what I do.

Perhaps I shouldn't say I had no lessons at all, I did have a very short one. When I was a young child, I heard my parents playing the piano, and I wanted to be able to play it too. My father, having studied music from public school through university, thought first of using a piano method called Teaching Little Fingers to Play. The only thing I can remember from that method was a piece called "Baseball Days," which bore absolutely no resemblance to the music I had heard my parents playing. I wasn't interested in continuing, so I left the piano for a few months and came back to it in my own way.

Carol: Actually, after that first lesson, he quit for about six months—just wouldn't do anything at the piano, so we thought he'd never go back to it. Then my husband, who's also a musician, brought home a book of ragtime by Scott Joplin, and played some. Andrew really, really loved it and wanted to play it. My husband took pieces of staff paper, wrote the notes on them, and taped them to the piano keys, so then Andrew could relate what was taped to the piano keys to what was on the staff in the printed music. That's all he used. He would go through the chords one-by-one (and I remember this very clearly) he would bang over and over, until he got it right—and he'd know when it was right—then he'd move on to the next one. It took about six months, and he was able to play one Joplin rag, very slowly, not very musically, but he was able to get the notes.

Andrew: From then on, playing the piano was part of my daily routine. I gradually worked my way through many thousands of piano works, teaching myself the language of music. If I had a question, my parents were always there to provide an answer, but mostly I persevered on my own. I still cannot explain with any certainty how I learned music, but I think perhaps that's a good thing. I firmly believe that, if as much painstaking effort and study were directed at teaching children to walk as have been used in other endeavours, many of us would be crippled for life. If learning is allowed to happen, it just happens, and it happens in the most efficient way possible.

Since I didn't go to school, I had the time to pursue my interests, which included music, reading, computers, crafts, and many other things. The word "bored" never entered my vocabulary, because there was always something new to learn. When you don't have a curriculum, or someone dividing up the day into segments and filling each one with a different subject, then you can sit at the piano and play for three hours or five minutes, whatever you need. I always thought of "playing" the piano, not "practicing." After all, if you make a meal, are you "practicing" or are you simply cooking?

Carol: "Practice" is a word we never used, any more than we would use it about doing anything else. Actually, it's kind of odd, because my husband and I have five university degrees between us, so we were schooled in the conventional way. But when we had Andrew, first of all, we did natural childbirth, and breastfeeding, and we followed that way of child-rearing, and educating our own child just seemed to come out of that.

Andrew: I was able to explore much of the classical piano repertoire, and eventually found composers whose works became my favourites. For a long time, Franz Liszt has been my favourite, because his music is so difficult but so beautiful at the same time. He found things that could be done on the piano that hadn't been done before, different sounds, and different techniques. As I moved into more popular music, I came across Claude Bolling and his wonderful Flute Suites, Chick Corea with his Spanish-tinged jazz, and many other composers and genres.

As I made the transition from playing for myself at home to playing in public with other musicians, I used to worry that I would be questioned on my credentials, asked where I studied and with whom. Some musicians did want to know my background, and those often recommended an institution that I could attend for further study. If I had followed up on all these suggestions I'd still be in school!

What I realized, as I got older, is that as long as I was
able to play the music, that was all that mattered. After all,
it's very difficult, when attending a concert of professional
musicians, to pick out those who attended Juilliard and those
who didn't! A school is just a school, and you only get out of
it what you bring to it. If you don't love music and your
instrument enough to work at it without someone looking
over your shoulder giving you direction, no teacher will be
able to change that.

My parents both took piano lessons when they were
young, and they worked their way up in the conventional
Canadian way, through the Royal Conservatory of Music's
graded exam system. While there's nothing wrong with the
musical path they've chosen, in fact, there are many
wonderful pieces to be found in the Conservatory's
repertoire books. But by building a grading system around
the music, they've essentially turned it into school. Each
year, you choose several pieces to work on, and at the end of
the year, just as in school, you are assessed on your
performance. When you finish Grade 10, or you get your
certification as an Associate of the Royal Conservatory of
Music (A.R.C.T.), then you've achieved something. Well,
you've achieved a certain number of pieces a year, and
you've achieved certain marks in exams. Even assuming you
are truly interested and continue through all the grades,
you're still only playing a few pieces per year. If you haven't
gone off on your own and explored more music, or had some
other resources, then you haven't been exposed to very
much.

After a number of years playing the piano, I developed
an interest in composing. I started off with instrumental
pieces, because instruments were more familiar to me than
voices, and for a long time I didn't like "music with words."

355

34. ANDREW GILPIN

In 1989, my parents and I started a community choir which exposed me to choral music for the first time. I had certainly heard choirs in concert before, but I wasn't familiar with the repertoire at all. Eventually, though, I began arranging music for choir, and finally composing choral works as well.

It's important to follow what feels right to you, not what someone else tells you is right. That's the whole unschooling philosophy. You might like certain music, you might not like other music, and if someone stands there and tells you, "This is good, and this isn't good," all they're doing is giving you their opinion, which is no more or less valid than your own. From speaking to many musicians who were conventionally educated, and from observing their attitudes and opinions, I learned that they had encountered many arbitrary judgments during their schooling. The attitude was, "This is good music, and this isn't good music."

At Juilliard, they might say, "Jazz—there is no jazz, it is not good music, it isn't even music, the only music is classical," because it's a very serious school. If you went to Berklee College, in Boston, they'd say, "Those stuffy classical guys over at Juilliard—jazz is where it's at." If you went to Indiana University, they might have a little bit of both. The point is, those are all someone else's opinions.

I remember a story I heard from a bass player. He was young and studying the string bass, using a particular book which told him you could only play up to a certain note, and that was as high as you could go on the string bass. Then, when he was out of school and playing with other musicians, he noticed that some bass players played quite a lot higher than that. My mother was there at the time, and I remember she said, "They must have read a different book," and we all laughed. If he had simply been learning on his own, he wouldn't have known that you weren't "supposed" to play that high, and he likely would have explored the full range of his instrument.

MOTIVATION, METHOD AND MASTERY. HOW I LEARNED MUSIC WITHOUT BEING TAUGHT

Carol: I think, as parents, we have to trust our children more than we're led to believe we should. And, I think we have to trust our own instincts more, too, as opposed to the experts. They're always ready to tell us what to do, and the meaning of what our children do, but once you get to be an older mother, you realize that the experts change, their opinions change, times change, and ideas change, but what really doesn't change is that relationship between parent and child, it's a very intimate relationship, and I think you have to trust it.

I remember when Andrew was a year old. He was just starting to walk, he climbed up on a couch, and he took about six steps all by himself. At that point, I was really surprised, I reached my hand out to him and I said, "Andrew, do you want Mummy to help you?" He got this really closed look on his face. I felt as if I had insulted him, because what I realized is that when your child needs your help, he'll ask for it. It's really important to remember that, and just be there as a support, as a protector, as a resource, but you shouldn't impose.

Fred: I'm astonished, but at the same time I have to remember that many of the greatest minds in history were essentially self-taught in what they did. So it's not that surprising that, here and there, there'll be people who just do it on their own. I'm rather amazed, because someone can get to that level without a teacher, teaching physical techniques of how to hold the hands, how for best effect to get a certain sound or colour, and obviously Andrew figured that out on his own. When you think about it, more people used to do it, there were a lot of people who were self-made and self-taught. And, you know, they just went out and got books and read and did it. It's just rather unusual nowadays.

34. ANDREW GILPIN

I attended the Juilliard School, and that was not a good experience at all for me. I was there to study with my teacher, which was good, but just about everything else that happened at Juilliard, except for meeting my wife, was really forgettable. I could easily have got a much better education at many other conservatories. Your experience at Juilliard depends on how well-connected you are, how politically savvy you are, and what instrument you play. Violinists and pianists are very high on the musical totem pole; I was nothing more than a lowly wind player.

Andrew: I've often found, with other musicians I've played with over the years, most of whom have studied music through university, that they wonder what they spent their time doing at school, if it's possible to do it another way, and that may be a disturbing thought. I mean, Fred is an amazing musician. I don't know what part of that you would say he owes to Juilliard, and what part of that is his own, that would be for him to decide. But I think people who have had a lot of schooling in music tend to find my story a little threatening.

I don't know why I chose music as my main interest. I was exposed to many things when I was young, but music was what called to me most strongly. There are other things I enjoy, but nothing else feels like music. Above all, though, the reason I was able to become the musician I am today is because my parents gave me the time and the resources to follow my own path. School would have interfered severely with that, and I know that being "taught" would have crippled my own learning.

An audio version of this piece appears in podcast and can be found at:

Gilpin, A. (2005, November 30). Interview by B. Ekwa Ekoko [Podcast]. Unschooled Music, Radio Free School.

MOTIVATION, METHOD AND MASTERY. HOW I
LEARNED MUSIC WITHOUT BEING TAUGHT
Hamilton, Ontario.
    Retrieved from
http://radio4all.net/index.php/program/15303

Andrew Gilpin was born in Edmonton, Alberta, Canada
in 1974. Gilpin's performing career began at the age of 15,
accompanying a family-run choral group. Andrew's interest
in jazz led him to form the Andrew Gilpin Trio. The Trio's
first CD release, And All That Jazz, led to performances in
Canada and the United States, as well as appearances on
television and radio. In 1999, Andrew co-founded Ebony &
Ivory, an instrumental duo/quartet which performs across
North America. Andrew's most recent recording is
Christmas Ragtime.

—End—

ABOUT THE EDITORS

Beatrice Ekwa Ekoko is a free-lance writer and blogger. She blogs extensively at Natural Born Learners (radiofreeschool.blogspot.com) and has founded Personalized Education Hamilton to facilitate self-determined learning in her community. She works for a not-for-profit environmental organization as a project manager and coordinator. She lives in Hamilton, Ontario with her husband and three children.
Visit her website to see other writing at bekoko.ca.

Carlo Ricci is a professor of education and currently teaches in the Graduate Program at the Schulich School of Education, Nipissing University. He edits and founded the *Journal of Unschooling and Alternative Learning*. He has written and edited a number of books including *The Willed Curriculum, Unschooling, and Self-Direction: What Do Love, Trust, Respect, Care, and Compassion Have to Do With Learning*; and *Turning points: 35 Visionaries in Education Tell Their Own Stories (AERO, 2010)* with Jerry Mintz; and *The Legacy of John Holt: A Man Who Genuinely Understood, Trusted, and Respected Children* (HoltGWS, 2013) with Patrick Farenga. He has also written numerous articles on unschooling and self-determined learning. He lives in Toronto, Ontario with his wife and two children.

Made in the USA
Lexington, KY
15 February 2014